Relocating to New York City and Surrounding Areas

Relocating to
NEW YORK CITY
and Surrounding Areas

Everything You Need to Know Before You Move

and After You Get There!

ELLEN SHAPIRO

PRIMA PUBLISHING
3000 Lava Ridge Court • Roseville, California 95661
(800) 632-8676 • www.primalifestyles.com

The RELOCATING series is a trademark of Prima Communications Inc. PRIMA PUBLISHING and colophon are trademarks of Prima Communications Inc., registered with the United States Patent and Trademark Office.

Section 2 © 2000 by Monstermoving.com

All products mentioned are trademarks of their respective companies.

Every effort has been made to make this book complete and accurate as of the date of publication. In a time of rapid change, however, it is difficult to ensure that all information is entirely up-to-date. Although the publisher and author cannot be liable for any inaccuracies or omissions in this book, they are always grateful for corrections and suggestions for improvement.

Library of Congress Cataloging-in-Publication Data
Shapiro, Ellen.
    Relocating to New York City and surrounding areas : everything you need to know before you move and after you get there! / Ellen Shapiro.
        p. cm.
    Includes index.
    ISBN 0-7615-2567-X
    1. New York Region—Guidebooks. 2. Moving, Household—New York Region—Handbooks, manuals, etc. I. Title.
F128.18 S426 2000
917.47'10444—dc21
00-042097

00 01 02 03 04 05 HH 10 9 8 7 6 5 4 3 2 1
Printed in the United States of America

HOW TO ORDER:
Single copies may be ordered from Prima Publishing, 3000 Lava Ridge Court, Roseville, CA 95661; telephone (800) 632-8676, ext. 4444. Quantity discounts are also available. On your letterhead, include information concerning the intended use of the books and the number of books you wish to purchase.

Visit us online at www.primalifestyles.com

To my beloved husband, Steven Shaw,
for all of the love and support (and editorial tasks),
through all the long days and nights,
I couldn't have done it without you.
And to Heidi Lynne, Buster, and Ed Shapiro,
just for being you.

CONTENTS

ACKNOWLEDGMENTS

New Yorkers can be the most generous people in the world, and I was the grateful beneficiary of that generosity when I researched and wrote this book. I'd like to thank all the people who were so giving of their time, expertise, and support:

Educational consultants Elayne Landis and Jane Hewes, the Parents League, the Public Education Association, the New York City Board of Education (especially Michelle Walker), and many local school district organizations for their assistance with the education chapter. The dozens of people at the volunteer organizations, job placement agencies, and professional organizations who dropped what they were doing to share their wisdom and advice. Irene Keating and Jacqueline Stein at Douglas Elliman for their housing expertise. Dr. Stephen Lynn for his invaluable advice on medical topics. Professor Richard Sugarman for his religion expertise and moral support. Everyone, friends and strangers, who contributed useful advice for the Moving Tips (especially Fatima and Tafima, who also made me smile). My neighbors, Ken and Jane Matthews, for assistance on a variety of issues, especially the ins and outs of real estate law. The owners of the Barnes & Noble bookstore on East 86th Street, for allowing me to use their establishment as a public library. The team at Prima, David Richardson for nurturing the project and being ever supportive, Andrew Vallas for wielding his mighty pen and turning my manuscript into this gorgeous volume, and Ben Dominitz for rooting for the underdog. My mother-in-law, Penny Shaw, perhaps the foremost expert on the greatest number of topics relating to New York City, and my parents, Jack and Sue, and brothers, Michael and Jon, and all my friends for not reporting me missing to the authorities when I sunk into writer's hibernation for so many months. To Heidi Lynne, just for being you. And most of all, thanks to my husband, and unofficial editorial assistant, Steven Shaw.

INTRODUCTION

If you want to become a real New Yorker, there's only one require-ment: You have to believe that New York City is, has been, and always will be the greatest city on Earth. The center of the universe. The Big Apple. Every native New Yorker absorbs this knowledge in the womb, and every successful transplant acquires it on arrival. That's what gives the City its strength.

Whatever your dream, you can realize it in the Big Apple. There's nothing the City doesn't offer—if you want it badly enough. For those willing to clear the hurdles and beat the odds, New York City is the last true bastion of the American Dream (just look at Madonna). In this town, opportunity is limited only by imagination.

New York is that rarest of things: a real city. People work, live, and play in the same physical space, bringing the City alive at all hours of the day and night. There are no cloistered neighborhoods or gated communities. Supermodels strut the streets like common folk, and big stars take their kids to the neighborhood playgrounds just like you, me, and the nanny up the block. Many of the most successful residents came to New York with nothing more than empty pockets and over-flowing ambition. Look what the City did for them.

Opportunity is knocking. Now it's time to answer the door.

The Greatest Show on Earth

In four centuries, there has never been a better time than now to live in New York. Tourism is at an all-time high, and crime rates are the lowest they've been in more than three decades. Unemployment is shrinking; industry is booming; construction is growing (up, of course); and every nook and cranny of the City is blossoming on account of it all.

- A newly revitalized Grand Central Station has exceeded the expectations of even the most optimistic New Yorkers: It has become one of the premier dining and shopping destinations in the world. Combined with other recently completed projects—

like the World Financial Center, the Bridgemarket, and the Chelsea Piers—the City is enjoying an unprecedented rate of renewal and expansion.

- Most of the action happens on a tiny island, Manhattan, which is only 22.7 miles square—probably smaller than your home town. The total area of all five boroughs of New York City (Manhattan, Brooklyn, Queens, the Bronx, and Staten Island) is just 301 square miles. Yet the City has 6,374.6 miles of streets, and 34.3 million tourists from every nation on Earth visited last year. They spent $20.6 billion.

- With 714 miles of track, 469 stations, and 6,089 subway cars, NYC's subway system is the world's largest. The subways run twenty-four hours a day and carry 1.2 billion passengers a year, while the City's public bus system consists of 300 routes and carries 600 million people a year (by far the most in the nation) on 4,200 buses.

- With immigrants continuing to pour in, the City boasts more than 100 ethnic newspapers, including twenty-five catering to the Russian community alone. And the public schools are microcosms of the world's population, with multiracial, multilingual student bodies. The languages spoken in the hallways range from Spanish, Arabic, Urdu, and Korean to Chinese, Hindi, Hebrew, and Russian.

- A major boost to the City's image, economy, and celebrity status, the film industry plays a major role in the New York economy. There are sixty to ninety productions filmed daily, with a total of 22,851 aggregate shooting days. Just walk around the City any day of the week and you're bound to bump into a film crew, walk onto a set, or spy a star.

- Culturally, you can't do better than 150 museums, thirty-eight Broadway playhouses, scores of off-Broadway and off-off-Broadway productions, more galleries even than museums, hundreds of dance clubs, music clubs, and poetry readings—and that's just the tip of the *mainstream* iceberg.

NEW YORK WEATHER

Average Temperatures

January
Low: *26 degrees F*
High: *38 degrees F*

April
Low: *44 degrees F*
High: *61 degrees F*

July
Low: *68 degrees F*
High: *85 degrees F*

October
Low: *50 degrees F*
High: *66 degrees F*

Average Rainfall
January: *3.11 inches*
July: *3.67 inches*

Snowfall
January: *7 inches*
July: *0 inches*

Great Cities Don't Grow on Trees

Since its inception, New York has been a key locale, primarily because of its strategic location.

- The area we now call the City was first inhabited by Native Americans and later discovered by a European, Giovanni da Verrazano, in 1524. In 1609, when Englishman Henry Hudson (employed by the Dutch East India Company) reported back on the beauty of Manhattan and its ample natural treasures (furs, birds, fruits), his descriptions of New York made an indelible impression on Europe.

- The first industry on the island, when the town was known (until 1664) as New Amsterdam, was the Dutch fur trade. The legend goes that the Dutch settlers purchased Manhattan from its original Native American inhabitants for approximately $24 in beads and trinkets. Later, under British rule (then known as New York), Manhattan gained prominence because of the shipping opportunities it afforded—its perfect natural harbor, extensive riverfront, and easy ocean access.

- In 1783 the British surrendered to the revolutionary colonists. New York City was the nation's capital from 1789 to 1790.

- Already a melting pot in the 1700s, New York has continued to attract immigrants from cultures and countries all around the world. Ellis Island Immigration first started registering immigrants on Friday, January 1, 1892. Famous immigrants who passed through its doors include Bob Hope, Marcus Garvey, Irving Berlin, and the von Trapp family.

- It wasn't until 1898 that the five boroughs—Manhattan, Queens, the Bronx, Brooklyn, and Staten Island—were incorporated into the entity of Greater New York.

- Babe Ruth hit his first home run in Yankee Stadium in the first game he ever played there.

- Scheduled to dock in New York at the end of her maiden voyage, *Titanic*'s tragedy prevented her from ever reaching New York's shores. Of the 2,200 passengers aboard the *Titanic*, 675 were rescued by a Cunard liner, which ironically delivered the passengers to the very same dock at which the *Titanic* was supposed to arrive.

Looking Ahead

The City That Never Sleeps is also the city that never rests on its laurels. Never still or silent, the City is always changing and evolving.

New York is looking to the new millennium with grand ambitions. From expanding and updating the classics, like the Museum of Modern Art and Radio City Music Hall, to revitalizing long-neglected neighborhoods like Harlem, the City's growth and booming economy promise to preserve New York's position as a world leader among cities.

- Harlem, a thriving cultural center during the '20s and '30s, is now on the up and up. New construction of shopping centers and suburban-sized grocery stores is under way, along with scheduled face-lifts for famous favorites like the Apollo Theater, Minton's Playhouse, the Art-Deco Lenox Lounge, and the Renaissance Ballroom. And many of the beautiful, aging brownstones that line the streets are being spruced up by residents.

- Construction will soon begin on New York Studios, a multi-million-dollar, Hollywood-style sound stage complex at the Brooklyn Navy Yard. The site, which has in the past often been used for film location shoots, will feature eleven sound stages ranging in size from 12,000 to 40,000 feet.

- The Port Authority of New York and New Jersey is planning $2.5 billion in construction and projects at Newark and Kennedy International Airports, intended to ease congestion, shorten passenger waits, and create thousands of jobs.

- A $484-million project is underway to convert the majestic Farley Post Office Building (the twin of the original Penn Station) into a Penn Station annex. Construction is scheduled to last about two-and-a-half years, and the results promise to be spectacular.

- The new Rose Center for Earth and Space is the Museum of Natural History's greatest addition in decades—and one of the City's greatest architectural accomplishments. In addition to the completely revamped Hayden Planetarium, other new attractions include the Gottesman Hall of Planet Earth, the Cullman Hall of the Universe, and the Big Bang Theater, where visitors are transported back to the beginning of time.

- Times Square, no longer the seedy area it was only ten years ago, will keep getting brighter, cleaner, and safer with each passing year. Planned developments in the area include new hotels like the Doubletree and the Westin New York (with nearly 450 and 850 rooms, respectively); the Forest City Ratner entertainment complex (which will include twenty-five movie screens, shops, and Madame Tussaud's Wax Museum), B.B. King's 550-seat Blues Room music club and restaurant; the World Wrestling Federation's WWF New York theme restaurant; corporate headquarters of media companies including Viacom, MTV, VH-1, ABC-TV's *Good Morning America*, Condé Nast Publishing, and Reuters; the new ESPN Zone dining and entertainment complex; and the $25-million, eight-story NASDAQ sign—the world's largest video screen.

- The Museum of American Folk Art is in the process of constructing a $20-million, six-story, 30,000-square-foot building (to be completed by the end of 2001). It is the City's first major new art museum construction since 1966.

- The Museum of Jewish Heritage—A Living Memorial to the Holocaust (established in 1997) is planning an 80,000-square-foot expansion (costing $45 million) to be completed by 2002.

- The MTA recently approved a five-year, $17.2-billion plan, which will include new trains, buses, and two entirely new subway lines. The new construction will include a rail link to La Guardia Airport.

- The $24 million, 98,000-square-foot Bridgemarket complex is opening in a spectacular vaulted hall, which sits under Manhattan's 59th Street Bridge.

The Tools to Make It Happen

Now that you're ready to take the next step, this book will give you the tools you need to take it like a local. I wish somebody had written this book (and given it to me!) when I first moved to New York City. Lucky for you, though, I've spent years making every conceivable mistake, so you don't have to.

- Section One includes information on neighborhoods in and around Manhattan, as well as in the major suburbs and beyond. There's information on renting and buying apartments, advice from experts, and tips from locals. This section answers the most commonly asked newcomer questions: Where should I live and what can I afford? Are the neighborhoods within NYC really *that* different from one another? Do certain neighborhoods have all the good schools? How do I find a roommate? Where do I live while I'm looking for an apartment?

- Section Two offers information on moving and critical details for getting yourself established once you've signed the lease (or mortgage).

- Section Three is about what to see and do, where and how to get involved in volunteer projects, how to join a local sports league, the best restaurants around town, and when and how to capitalize on the best free events the City has to offer. There's also a calendar of events (don't miss the July 4 fireworks), details on navigating the City via public transportation, and weekend escapes (and how to get to them) if you need a change of scenery or pace (skiing in Vermont, the Connecticut shoreline, etc.).

- Section Four has the essentials: Lists of important places around the City—like hospitals and specialty dry cleaners—and schools from preschool through college, university, and graduate education.

- Section Five is all about finding a job, whether you've been employed before or you're starting out fresh. What newspapers offer the best resources? How and to whom can a headhunter be helpful, and which ones are trustworthy? How best can you utilize the people and tools that professional organizations offer? How can you make temping a reliable option?

Now get going. You've got a lot of work to do!

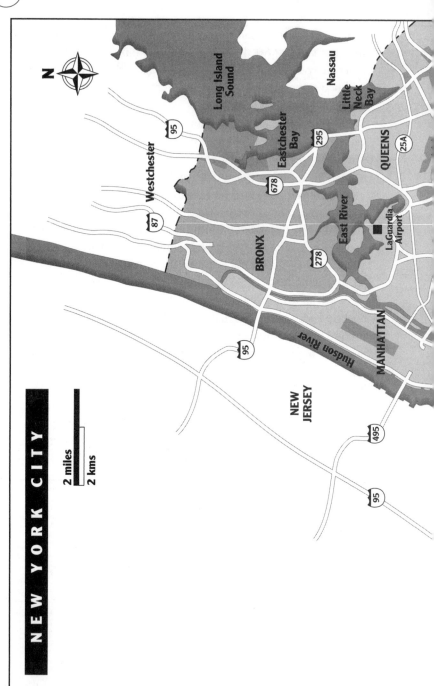

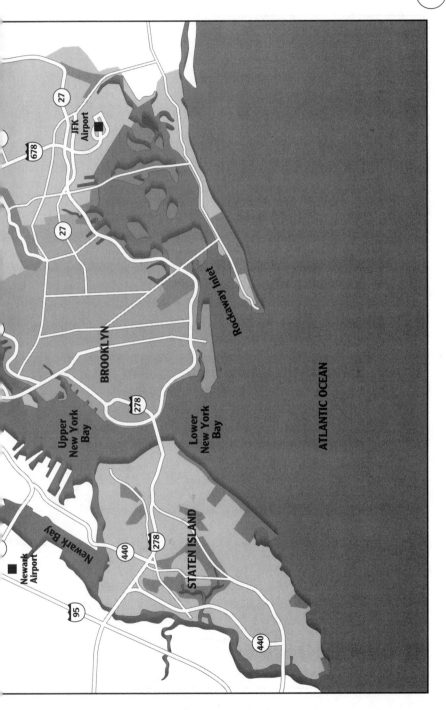

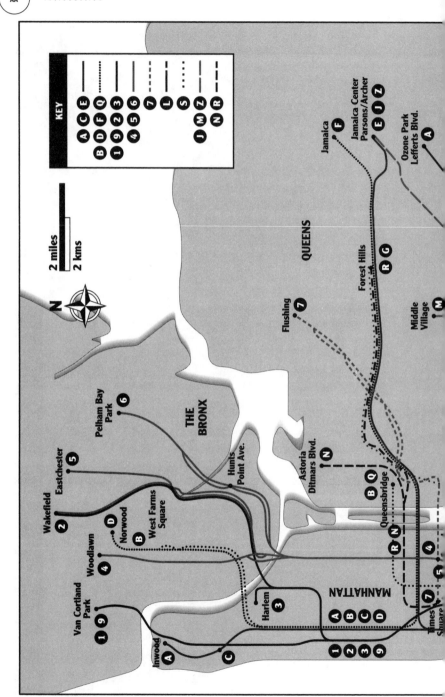

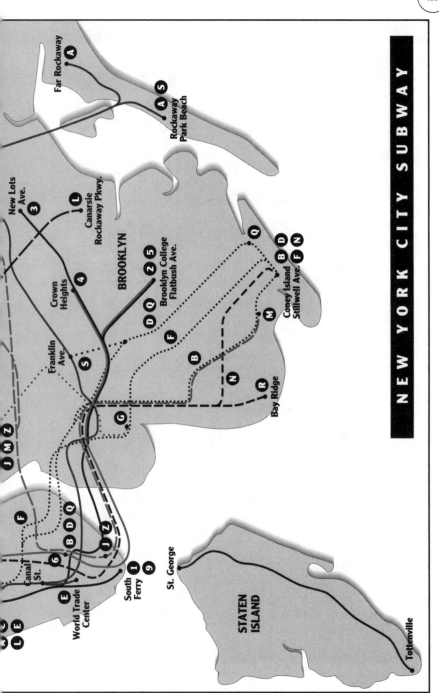

NEW YORK CITY SUBWAY

NEW YORK CITY SUBWAY

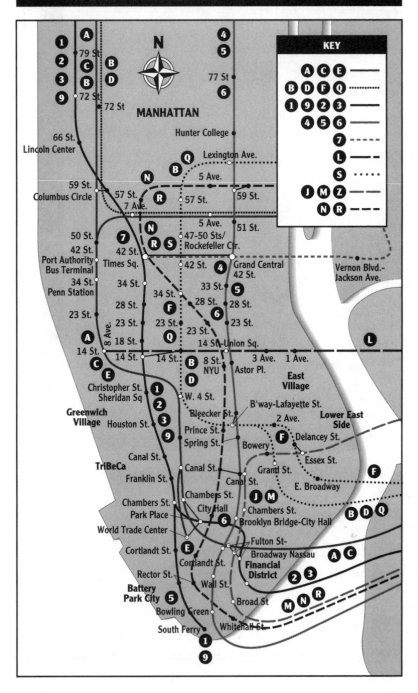

Places to Live

CHAPTER 1

Neighborhood Descriptions

Apart from the actual decision to relocate, perhaps the most significant and challenging decision you'll have to make when you relocate to New York is where you'll live. New York is geographically small, but your day-to-day life will center around two even smaller areas: the neighborhood where you live and the one where you work. Many aspects of your life (the restaurants you frequent, your health club, the services you utilize, and to some extent the friends you make) will flow from your choice of neighborhood, and even from your choice of block (New Yorkers often say "block" instead of "street") and building. Still, all is not what it seems on the surface, and your ultimate choice of neighborhood may be very different than your first instinct might lead you to think.

In an ideal New York City, you'd be able to get a large, airy, sunny apartment in your neighborhood of choice for exactly the amount of money you're willing and able to spend. But, in the real New York City, even multimillionaires have to make some compromises—and the rest of us have to compromise a whole lot. The delicate balance between the need for a space in which you'll be happy and the need for a few dollars left over to cover other essentials (like food) is an elusive target for every New Yorker.

When considering a neighborhood, you'll want to weigh the following primary factors:

- Your personality and the personality of the neighborhood
- Cost of housing
- Availability of desirable housing
- Safety
- Proximity to work

Consider these factors against the backdrop of three very important distinguishing factors about the neighborhoods in New York City (as opposed to neighborhoods almost everywhere else):

First, although the human brain uses generalizations to make sense of the world, the neighborhoods of New York City are mind-boggling in their diversity, and they resist generalization tooth and nail. Although it's possible to characterize neighborhoods based on the characteristics of the majority of their residents, the simple truth is that every kind of person imaginable lives in just about every neighborhood of New York. Sure, some neighborhoods have greater percentages of families or gays or specific ethnic groups, but without question you'll find everyone living everywhere.

For example, Chelsea is known as a gay neighborhood, but plenty of young, upwardly mobile, heterosexual, thirtysomething couples with kids choose to live there, perhaps because they work downtown and found a good apartment in the London Terrace complex or perhaps because they just like their neighbors. The stereotype of the Upper East Side is that it's stodgy and wealthy, but some young artists choose to live on the Upper East Side rather than in SoHo because, ironically, there are more housing bargains to be found on the Upper East Side. Not every building can be on Fifth Avenue facing Central Park—the side streets are full of deals—plus, though the artists may be downtown, the museums are uptown. You'll find plenty of corporate lawyer- and investment banker–types living in the working-class neighborhoods of Carroll Gardens in Brooklyn, or Astoria in Queens, because there's more space for the money and the commute to Wall Street from Brooklyn (and to Midtown from Queens) is better than from many neighborhoods within Manhattan. And Staten Island is not just for the big-hair crowd (like Melanie Griffith and Joan Cusack in *Working Girl*)—there are plenty of young professionals who choose to live in the apartments near the Staten Island ferry because they work downtown, the view is great, the rent is lower, they get more space, and all they have to do is walk off the boat and one block to the office—an easy commute by all accounts.

Even within a specific building, it's hard to generalize. Almost every brownstone in New York has one highly desirable ground-floor garden apartment with a backyard—and a nearly identical apartment (with no yard) on the fifth floor, which can only be reached by climbing five flights of stairs. These are two apartments in the *same building* with the *same internal square footage, same exposure,* and *same address*—yet one may cost three times as much as the other! While the garden apartment may be occupied by a lawyer and a doctor, their newborn baby, and a golden retriever, the fifth-floor walk-up may be shared by three aspiring actors or models.

Second, and this always takes newcomers a while to grasp, neighborhoods in New York change dramatically in just a few feet. For example, in the case of East 96th Street, one of the most genteel neighborhoods in America (Carnegie Hill) ends on the south side of the street, and one of the most rough-and-tumble (East Harlem) begins on the north side. It's hard to believe it until you've seen it, and even then it takes time for this reality to sink in. There are subtle and not-so-subtle dividing lines all over New York, and it takes a practiced eye to see them. Apartments in New York can be bigger or smaller, more or less desirable, cheaper or more expensive all based on these subtle dividing lines.

Third, New York City's neighborhoods are continually in a state of flux. Most of the Upper West Side was a slum in 1970. Now it's perhaps the most desirable (judging by popularity) neighborhood in town. TriBeCa, a former manufacturing district, is going residential. Only a decade ago, it would have been almost unthinkable for a newcomer to live in the neighborhood now known as Clinton—which used to be called Hell's Kitchen. Now it's one of the first you should consider for a good combination of value, location, and—increasingly—safety.

You can't expect to know where you want to live right away, and for the majority of people who choose to relocate to New York (young folks with no kids), that's not a problem. The thing to do is find yourself a space with which you'll be happy for the money you have and then spend the next year exploring the town and looking for a more permanent dwelling.

Basic New York City Geography

New York City is made up of five boroughs: Manhattan, Queens, the Bronx, Staten Island, and Brooklyn. There is also an emerging "sixth borough," which consists of the nearby New Jersey cities of Hoboken and Jersey City (discussed later in this chapter, in "The Suburbs"). But when most people think of "the City" they're visualizing Manhattan, and Manhattan is the likely destination for the over-whelming majority of newcomers. Most newcomers figure, Why move to the City if you're not going to live in the City? Thus, the primary focus of this chapter will be on the multitudes of neighbor-hoods within Manhattan. Still, you can almost always get more space for your money when you move outside of Manhattan. Because of this, this chapter also discusses the close-in, commutable communi-ties of the other four boroughs. There are many other lovely neigh-borhoods within those boroughs, but they are not of primary concern to newcomers. Also, this chapter contains an overview of neighborhoods and suburbs in Northern New Jersey, Long Island, Westchester/Rockland, and Southern Connecticut (the "tri-state area") and beyond, which (with the exception of Hoboken and Jersey City) are mostly of interest to families with children who want a house with a yard. The areas covered in this chapter are

New York City
- Manhattan
- Upper East Side
- Upper West Side
- West of Midtown
- East of Midtown
- Greenwich Village/SoHo
- East Village/Lower East Side
- TriBeCa/Downtown
- Washington Heights/Inwood

Boroughs
- Brooklyn: Brooklyn Heights/Cobble Hill/Carroll Gardens/Park Slope

- Queens: Astoria
- Staten Island
- The Bronx: Riverdale

Suburbs
- Westchester/Rockland
- Long Island
- Northern New Jersey
- Southern Connecticut

Outside the Area
- Upstate New York
- Southern and Central New Jersey
- Western and Upstate Connecticut
- The East End of Long Island

Crime in New York City

By now it's hardly news that safety in New York City has been improving by leaps and bounds over the past few years—and that trend shows no signs of abating. In the last year of the millennium, the number of murders in the city decreased another 23 percent, and the actual number of killings—743 (a very small number given the total population)—was the lowest in more than thirty years. All major categories of crime—including rape, robbery, and car theft—have been continuing their downward trends as well.

What most people don't realize, however, is that it is now safer to live in New York City than in most of the other cities in America—and New York is unquestionably the safest large city in America. Major new crime-fighting initiatives in the areas of statistics gathering, DNA testing, school safety, domestic violence, aggressive driving, and criminal justice reform promise to continue improving New York's reputation as a safe, livable city. Plus, it's important to remember that the bulk of New York City's violent crimes occur in neighborhoods that won't be under consideration in this book. In a safe neighborhood like Carnegie Hill, where my husband and I have lived for several years, any incident of violent crime (and there are very few) is major news in the community—just as it would be in any small town anywhere in America.

But crime is not just a question of numbers. Some crime is unavoidable, but most can be prevented through a combination of vigilance and common sense. Don't let yourself be a statistic. Be aware of your surroundings, don't get into situations or confrontations that you can't handle, and don't be afraid to call for help. Keep your doors locked and your eyes open. Plan for safety, and your safety will almost certainly be assured.

Also, safety is often in the eye of the beholder. Some neighborhoods, like the Lower East Side, may be perfectly safe for groups of young males sharing an apartment—but those same neighborhoods might not be as comfortable for families with young children or women living alone (although that neighborhood is improving so rapidly that, next year, it might be far more desirable). Up-and-coming, formerly unsafe (but not totally safe yet) neighborhoods are favorite destinations for young people who, in exchange for a big apartment with a small rent, are often willing to forgo conveniences (like twenty-four-hour markets or a big selection of nearby restaurants and dry cleaners) and dodge the sketchy characters that might be loitering around the area. Obviously, not everyone would make this choice.

Noteworthy in the Neighborhood

Were I writing this book about any other city, I'd tell you where in each neighborhood you could find a dry cleaner, a supermarket, and a health club. But any neighborhood in New York is likely to have at least 150 dry cleaners, thirty supermarkets (not to mention a couple of hundred smaller markets), and a dozen health clubs—not to mention scores of hair salons, nail salons, acupuncturists, acupressurists, chiropractors, and palm readers. Just about every service imaginable is going to lie within a few blocks of your front door if you live in Manhattan—and the rest you can get delivered.

So, instead of listing basic services, I've tried to include just a few significant landmarks and points of interest for each neighborhood. These are the sites that I think typify and characterize each neighborhood—to the extent that's possible. This is by no means a comprehensive listing—it's just a tool to help you get started thinking about each neighborhood.

Other services and attractions: For information about restaurants, arts, entertainment, events, and transportation in and around the City, see the listings in chapters 6 and 7. For essential services, such as hospitals, see chapter 9. And for schools, please consult the listings in chapter 10.

Understanding the Neighborhood Statistics

Averages can be deceiving, especially in a city of extremes, and you're unlikely ever to meet an average person in New York City. Thus, when talking about New York City, statistics can never tell the whole story— and, worse, they can be misleading.

The smallest geographic unit in New York City for which statistics are tracked is the Community District. For the most part, the community districts (which are, essentially, the smallest units of neighborhood governance) correspond to established neighborhoods. But many community districts contain two or more distinct neighborhoods (one affluent and one working-class, one extremely safe and one questionable), and even within a specific neighborhood there are pockets of poverty and wealth, crime and safety. Moreover, some individual apartment complexes (Lincoln Towers, Battery Park City, Stuyvesant Town) are so large (with tens of thousands of residents) that they constitute their own neighborhoods. As with everything in New York City, there is no substitute for close-up examination of the specific neighborhood, block, and building you're considering.

The demographic statistics following (population, ethnicity, age, gender) come from New York's Department of City Planning and are based on the most recent census (and therefore may not conform to some of the statistics used later in this book). There has been no census in New York since 1990 (the 2000 census is being compiled as this book is in press), so many of the demographic statistics listed here will have changed somewhat—but they are still largely accurate.

The official city statistics regarding average rents and apartment purchase prices are all but irrelevant to the newcomer. For example, you'll be surprised to learn that the average monthly rent for an apartment in Manhattan is $478. But don't get your hopes up. Unless you moved into an apartment forty years ago and are protected by rent-control laws (as many New Yorkers are), or you live in city-owned low-income housing, this $478 apartment for all intents and purposes does not exist. And, of course, all those artificially underpriced apartments have jacked up the rents on the rest of the City's apartments. So, if you ask Douglas Elliman, New York City's largest realtor, what the average rent is on actual, available apartments, you'll learn that $1,200 per month is pretty much the lower limit for a clean, safe, small studio apartment in a good building—and that a similar two-bedroom apartment will run you $2,600 to $4,000 or more. The government's housing purchase price statistics are somewhat more reliable, but also can be deceptive.

Douglas Elliman has gathered housing cost statistics for some neighborhoods; those statistics have been included here (purchase-price statistics are available only for neighborhoods with significant condo and co-op markets, of course). Where no reliable, real-world statistics are available, government statistics have been provided—but please take these with a grain of salt. The reality for the average newcomer could easily be double or triple whatever cost the government indicates.

Crime statistics in New York are likewise very complex (and political). Rather than bury you in raw data, I've chosen simply to give a summary of the safety picture for each neighborhood (which, ultimately, given all the conflicting data, represents my judgment as a New Yorker combined with the judgment of several experts with whom I spoke). With regard to income, I have done the same—painting neighborhoods with broad brushstrokes as "affluent," "middle-class," or "working-class." Commuting times are mostly for mass transit (which is, typically, how New Yorkers commute). They are based on discussions with neighborhood residents and on actual tests by me. These times also assume good weather and apply only if you live and work within a short walk of mass transit on each end of your trip.

Neighborhoods in New York City

Just to give you an overall feel for New York City, and to set a benchmark for comparison when evaluating neighborhood statistics, following is a portrait of the population for all five of New York's boroughs taken together.

New York City (Five Boroughs) Statistical Profile

Total Population:　7,322,564

Population by Ethnicity

White	3,163,125 (43.2%)
Black	1,847,049 (25.2%)
Hispanic	1,783,511 (24.4%)
Asian	489,851 (6.7%)
American Indian	17,871 (.2%)
Other	21,157 (.3%)

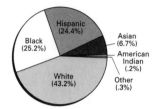

Population by Age

Median age　33.7

18 years & over	5,635,846 (77%)
21 years & over	5,322,707 (72.7%)
62 years & over	1,143,559 (15.6%)

Population by Gender

Female	3,884,877 (53.1%)
Male	3,437,687 (46.9%)

Manhattan Neighborhoods

This is it—the City. As far as the average citizen of Earth is concerned, New York and Manhattan are synonymous (although, because of films like *Saturday Night Fever*, Brooklyn does enter into some people's consideration). As a newcomer, absent extraordinary circumstances, you'll likely choose Manhattan as the site of your first apartment. Thus, most of this chapter is devoted to a discussion of neighborhoods in Manhattan.

MANHATTAN

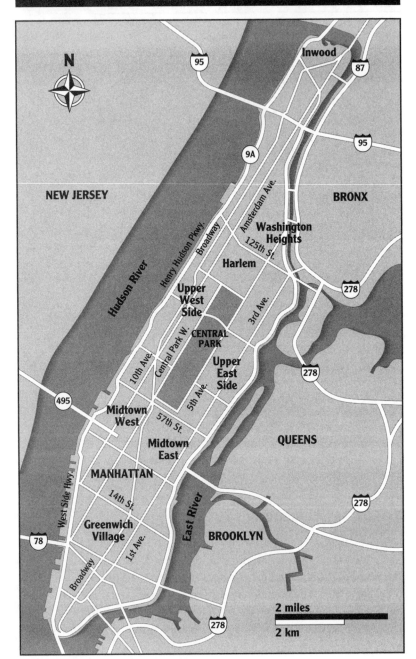

N

95

Inwood

87

95

9A

NEW JERSEY

BRONX

Henry Hudson Pkwy.

Broadway

Amsterdam Ave.

Washington
Heights

125th St.

Harlem

Hudson River

278

Upper
West
Side

3rd Ave.

10th Ave.

Central Park W.

CENTRAL
PARK

Upper
East
Side

5th Ave.

278

495

Midtown
West

57th St.

Midtown
East

QUEENS

MANHATTAN

West Side Hwy.

14th St.

East River

78

Greenwich
Village

1st Ave.

BROOKLYN

278

Broadway

278

2 miles

2 km

Manhattan Geography Cheat Sheet

Though it has a few twists and turns, once you understand the basics Manhattan is one of the easiest places in the world to navigate and understand—far more so than many smaller cities.

Manhattan is an island, and it points north–south (technically it's on a bit of an east-leaning angle—but we ignore that for the purpose of orientation and navigation). Thus, *up* is north (uptown), *down* is south (downtown), *left* is west, and *right* is east. Central Park lies almost dead center on this island, and that big street running north–south along the east (right) side of Central Park is Fifth Avenue—the dividing line between the East Side and the West Side.

If you started at the Hudson River (on the west side of the island) and walked along, say, 50th Street, you'd start by seeing buildings with high numbers: 401 West 50th Street and the like (by the way, odd numbers are always on the south side of the street; even numbers on the north). As you walked east, you'd see those numbers decline until, as you approached Fifth Avenue, the numbers would reach 1 West 50th. Then, on crossing Fifth Avenue, you'd encounter 1 East 50th Street, and the numbers would begin counting up until you reached the extreme east end of the island, otherwise known as the East River. The highway-like road along the East River is the FDR Drive; the one along the Hudson River is called the Henry Hudson Parkway, West Side Highway, or West Street, depending on exactly which portion you're on. Over the Hudson River to the west, that's New Jersey. Over the East River, to the east, you've got Brooklyn and Queens. And of course you know the Bronx is up and the Battery (the southern tip of Manhattan) is down. And south of that is Staten Island.

Most of Manhattan (aside from the historic downtown areas) is organized on an eminently sensible grid: Avenues run north–south; streets run east–west. Street numbers climb as you go north. Because the island is not a perfect square, and because it developed over many years and under several regimes (Dutch, English, American, Giuliani), avenues do occasionally end or change their names. Eighth Avenue becomes Central Park West at 59th Street (where Central Park begins).

As a rough guide (we'll get more specific as we examine each neighborhood), Midtown is the area between 34th and 59th Streets. North of Midtown is what we call Uptown. South of Midtown is what we call . . . Downtown. In New Yorkese, though, uptown and downtown (lower case) are also used as directions, so 92nd Street is downtown from 93rd Street even though both streets are Uptown—you'll get the hang of it.

So the bulk of Manhattan is easy to grasp. However, navigation-wise, all bets are off once you reach Greenwich Village, below 8th Street. These meandering streets (which follow all sorts of natural and political boundaries) date back to the seventeenth and eighteenth centuries, before the grid was established. You'll need a map or a very good memory to get around Downtown. Farther downtown, below Houston Street (please—it's "how-ston" not "hew-ston"), streets have names and not numbers.

Any questions?

A Word on Uptown Versus Downtown

There was a time, not too long ago, when there were Uptown people and Downtown people, as indicated by use of those terms in another way—as adjectives to describe people: "Uptown" meaning snooty, ritzy, or unattainable (as in the Billy Joel song "Uptown Girl") and "Downtown" meaning hip, countercultural, and interesting (like the MTV vee-jay, "Downtown" Julie Brown). I still know some folks—wannabe hipster types and old-timers mostly—who won't go above or below (respectively) 14th Street except in the case of a dire emergency (and maybe not even then). The Downtown crowd thought the Uptown crowd was stuffy, snobbish, and shallow. The Uptown crowd thought the Downtown crowd was self-consciously hip, artsy, and pseudo-intellectual.

These days, neighborhood boundaries have been so eroded and crossover populations have become so common that it's hard to maintain this hard-line distinction between Uptown and Downtown. Plus, you now have a fair number of people living in the middle—in newly developed neighborhoods that are culturally affiliated with neither extreme. There's still an artsy attribute to Downtown Manhattan, and there's still a clean-cut conformism about the Uptown neighborhoods—but don't be fooled into thinking that these are hard-and-fast rules anymore. As a newcomer, you should cast prejudices aside, keep all your options open, and decide for yourself.

Manhattan Borough Statistical Profile

Total Population: 1,487,536

Population by Ethnicity

White	726,755 (48.9%)
Black	261,120 (17.6%)
Hispanic	386,630 (26%)
Asian	106,306 (7.1%)
American Indian	2,793 (.2%)
Other	3,932 (.3%)

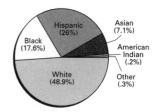

Population by Age

Median age   35.9

18 years & over	1,240,709 (83.4%)
21 years & over	1,186,112 (79.7%)
62 years & over	236,114 (15.9%)

Population by Gender

Female	786,963 (52.9%)
Male	700,573 (47.1%)

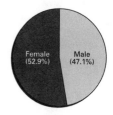

Average Housing Costs

Co-op:	$411,711
Studio:	$108,087
1-bedroom:	$205,255
2-bedroom:	$538,056
3-bedroom:	$1,486,668
4-bedroom:	$3,422,637

Rental Price Index

Studio:	*$1,200–$1,800*
1-bedroom:	*$1,500–$2,200*
2-bedroom:	*$2,600–$4,000*

2-bedroom $2,600–$4,000

1-bedroom $1,500–$2,200

Studio $1,200–$1,800

UPPER EAST SIDE

New Yorkers are fiercely loyal to their neighborhoods, and I must confess I arranged the layout of this section so that my neighborhood would come first. And here we have lesson number one: Every neighborhood contains numerous subdivisions, and subdivisions of subdivisions. You see, I don't really live on the Upper East Side. Sure, as a strict matter of geography, I live there. But I prefer to say I live in Carnegie Hill, a small slice of the Upper East Side that runs from 86th to 96th Streets, and from Fifth to Lexington Avenues. To be exact, within Carnegie Hill, I live near Madison Avenue in the 90s—a very specific area within Carnegie Hill that is characterized by sidewalk cafés (you'll see my neighbors Paul Newman and Joanne Woodward, as well as Ralph Lauren, Calvin Klein, and Michael J. Fox, at nearby restaurants), a family atmosphere, and proximity to Central Park. Other folks who live in Carnegie Hill might live on Park Avenue or Fifth Avenue (those are the rich people, for the most part)—but they're not really my neighbors. Even within my block, I live in a sub-community: I live in one of Ken's buildings. Ken is my landlord, and he owns a number of buildings (mostly old townhouses that, like many of the beautiful landmark townhouses in Carnegie Hill, have been divided into apartments) in the neighborhood. Though we New Yorkers live in a gigantic metropolis, we tend to define ourselves in

UPPER EAST/UPPER WEST SIDES

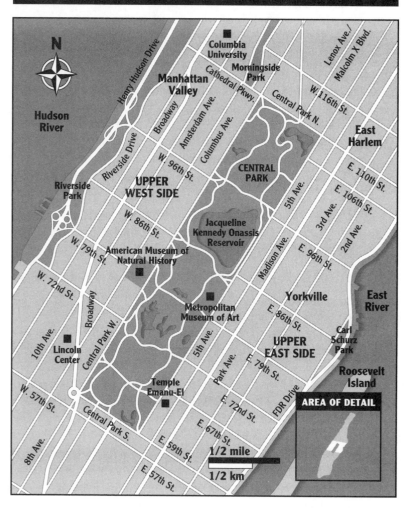

N

Hudson River

Columbia University

Morningside Park

Manhattan Valley

Cathedral Pkwy.

Henry Hudson Drive

Broadway

Amsterdam Ave.

Columbus Ave.

Central Park N.

W. 116th St.

Lenox Ave./ Malcolm X Blvd.

East Harlem

Riverside Drive

W. 96th St.

CENTRAL PARK

E. 110th St.

E. 106th St.

Riverside Park

UPPER WEST SIDE

5th Ave.

3rd Ave.

2nd Ave.

W. 86th St.

Jacqueline Kennedy Onassis Reservoir

Madison Ave.

E. 96th St.

W. 79th St.

American Museum of Natural History

W. 72nd St.

Broadway

Metropolitan Museum of Art

Yorkville

E. 86th St.

East River

10th Ave.

Central Park W.

5th Ave.

UPPER EAST SIDE

Carl Schurz Park

Lincoln Center

E. 79th St.

Park Ave.

Roosevelt Island

W. 57th St.

Temple Emanu-El

E. 72nd St.

FDR Drive

AREA OF DETAIL

Central Park S.

E. 67th St.

E. 59th St.

1/2 mile

8th Ave.

E. 57th St.

1/2 km

precise terms that create communities. So, if you live in one of Ken's buildings, and you meet someone who lives in another of Ken's buildings, you're already nine-tenths of the way toward being friends.

The rest of the Upper East Side (if I must talk about it) is also quite nice and houses some of the wealthiest people in America.

Moving east from Carnegie Hill, there's Yorkville, which used to be a German neighborhood (you'll still find a few German shops along First Avenue near 86th Street) but is now home to numerous high-rise apartment buildings that serve as homes to a growing number of young professionals.

South of 86th Street lies the genuine Upper East Side, where you'll find many of New York's best co-ops and condos along Park Avenue, Fifth Avenue, and East End Avenue. These are some of the most expensive properties anywhere. The Upper East Side is very safe and is therefore perfect for families. It has interesting shops and boutiques, many of the best private and public schools, easy access to Central Park and most of New York's major museums. Some people say the Upper East Side is too predictable—but residents value it for just that reason.

Still, despite the Upper East Side's reputation as a wealthy area (the East 60s and 70s are, statistically speaking, one of the two or three wealthiest communities in America), I and many others like me (writers, younger people starting out in their careers, and even some artists) live here, and I assure you we're not rich. As with all neighborhoods, there are housing bargains to be had on the Upper East Side—and in fact they're easier to find here than in many other areas because this neighborhood has yet to become as popular as the Upper West Side or Downtown.

Finally, as a matter of political organization (if not cultural similarity), the unusual area of Roosevelt Island is technically part of this district. An island in the middle of the East River, Roosevelt Island holds a series of middle-class apartment complexes, some of which provide excellent views of Manhattan. Roosevelt Island feels like its own city, and is unlike anything in Manhattan or the boroughs. There is no automobile traffic, and everything (including the shops) is centrally planned. The famous Roosevelt Island Tramway (a cable car running from Manhattan to Roosevelt Island) is still in use, although the construction of a subway station on the island has made it largely outdated. The only bridge connection to the mainland is to Queens—there is no bridge to Manhattan from Roosevelt Island.

Neighborhood Statistical Profile

Total Population: 210,880

Population by Ethnicity

White	*183,979 (87.2%)*
Black	*6,256 (3%)*
Hispanic	*11,748 (5.6%)*
Asian	*8,517 (4%)*
American	
* Indian*	*154 (.1%)*
Other	*226 (.1%)*

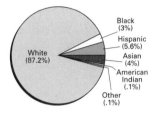

Population by Age

Median age   39.6

18 years & over	*189,181 (89.7%)*
21 years & over	*185,891 (88.2%)*
62 years & over	*38,789 (18.4%)*

Population by Gender

Female	*118,218 (56.1%)*
Male	*92,662 (43.9%)*

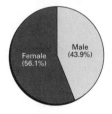

Average Housing Costs

Co-op:	*$636,113*
Studio:	*$102,240*
1-bedroom:	*$197,215*
2-bedroom:	*$590,002*
3-bedroom:	*$1,608,535*
4-bedroom:	*$3,773,122*

2-bedroom $2,700-$3,500

1-bedroom $1,700-$2,200

Studio $1,200-$1,500

Rental Price Index

Studio:	*$1,200–$1,500*
1-bedroom:	*$1,700–$2,200*
2-bedroom:	*$2,700–$3,500*

Other Statistics

Crime Picture:	*This is considered an extremely safe neighborhood.*
Income Picture:	*This is one of the most affluent neighborhoods in the world.*

Commuting Times:

Midtown East	*10–20 minutes*
Midtown West	*25–35 minutes*
Wall Street	*30–40 minutes*

Noteworthy in the Neighborhood

Madison Avenue Shopping District (Barney's, Polo, and most designer boutiques)

Central Park (Conservatory Garden, Reservoir, Metropolitan Museum, Zoo)

Museum Mile (Metropolitan Museum of Art, Guggenheim, Cooper-Hewitt, Jewish Museum, International Center of Photography, and others)

Gracie Mansion (Mayor's residence)

Numerous distinguished private clubs (Harmonie Club, Metropolitan Club, Lotos Club)

Temple Emanu-El (largest—bigger than St. Patrick's Cathedral—and oldest Reform Jewish congregation), 1 East 65th Street (Fifth Avenue), (212) 744-1400

Asia Society (art collection assembled by John D. Rockefeller), 725 Park Avenue (70th Street), (212) 288-6400

Frank E. Campbell Funeral Chapel (most prestigious in world, James Cagney, John Lennon, Mae West, and Tennessee Williams as "customers"), 1076 Madison Avenue (81st Street), (212) 288-3500

92nd Street Y (major Jewish cultural and community center), 1395 Lexington Avenue (92nd Street), (212) 427-6000

Synod of Bishops of the Russian Orthodox Church Outside Russia (dramatic 1917 Georgian mansion, now a cathedral), 75 East 93rd Street (Park & Madison Avenues), (212) 534-1601

Islamic Center of New York (New York's first major mosque, designed by Skidmore, Owings, and Merrill), 1711 Third Avenue (96th Street), (212) 722-5234

UPPER WEST SIDE

If you stood at the corner of 68th Street and Columbus Avenue (near where my husband grew up) in 1970 and then traveled via time machine to the same corner in the year 2000, you'd assume your time machine had taken you to the wrong place. What was basically a slum in 1970 is now the site of one of New York's most luxurious new apartment buildings (which also houses the exclusive Reebok Sports Club and the Sony IMAX theater). The transformation of the Upper West Side, triggered by the construction of Lincoln Center in the 1960s and bolstered by frantic luxury high-rise construction in the 1980s and 1990s, has made this neighborhood one of the world's great urban reclamation stories.

The Lincoln Square area (the complex of high-rise buildings surrounding Lincoln Center) is the southernmost part of the Upper West Side, and has the most of the newest buildings. The more traditional residential area, from the high 60s to the 90s, has some new construction but also many glorious old buildings along Central Park West (most notably the Dakota) and Riverside Drive (with great views of the river and proximity to Riverside Park), with many attractive brownstones in the middle. Also of interest here is the gigantic Lincoln Towers apartment complex in the West 60s and 70s, which offers some of the more reasonably priced apartments for sale in the area. The northernmost part of the neighborhood is known as Manhattan Valley, which fills the gap between the Upper West Side and Columbia

University. This is the most recently improved part of the area, and it offers the best housing values.

The traditional residents of the Upper West Side are quite diverse, ranging from professors at Columbia University and Fordham Law School to wealthy residents on Central Park West to an eclectic group of older tenants left over from the days when the neighborhood was inexpensive and not entirely safe. Today, good private schools, access to Central Park and Riverside Park, a wealth of restaurants and shops, and proximity to cultural attractions make the Upper West Side the choice of many young professionals. The neighborhood is also home to many young Modern Orthodox Jews who are attracted by the Lincoln Square Synagogue and an abundance of kosher restaurants in the 70s and, of course, the presence of many other members of their faith. There has always been a strong Jewish influence in this neighborhood (New York's oldest congregation is here), and the phrase "Upper West Side intellectual" was traditionally code for "Jewish intellectual." Indeed, it is often said that the major difference between the Upper West Side and the Upper East Side is that the Upper West is more Jewish and the Upper East is more WASP-y. But, in reality, there are plenty of representatives of each group on either side of the park.

If there is a downside to the dramatic improvement of the Upper West Side, it is that the neighborhood is crowded. Parking is next to impossible and restaurants are always packed. Old-timers in the neighborhood bemoan the loss of space and light, but few would go back to the way things were.

Neighborhood Statistical Profile

Total Population: 210,993

Population by Ethnicity

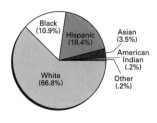

White	141,029 (66.8%)
Black	22,965 (10.9%)
Hispanic	38,737 (18.4%)
Asian	7,452 (3.5%)
American Indian	379 (.2%)
Other	431 (.2%)

Population by Age

Median age   37.9

18 years & over   *184,210 (87.3%)*

21 years & over   *179,141 (84.9%)*

62 years & over   *33,897 (16.1%)*

Population by Gender

Female   *111,264 (52.7%)*

Male   *99,729 (47.3%)*

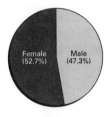

Average Housing Costs

Co-op: *$485,840*

Studio: *$117,818*

1-bedroom: *$218,590*

2-bedroom: *$572,193*

3-bedroom: *$1,376,082*

4-bedroom: *$3,343,536*

Rental Price Index

Studio: *$1,200–$1,500*

1-bedroom: *$1,700–$2,200*

2-bedroom: *$2,700–$3,500*

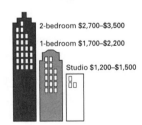

Other Statistics

Crime Picture:	*This is considered a very safe neighborhood, although the north and south ends of the area are still developing.*
Income Picture:	*This is an affluent and upwardly mobile neighborhood.*
Commuting Times:	
Midtown East	*25–35 minutes*
Midtown West	*10–20 minutes*
Wall Street	*35–45 minutes*

Noteworthy in the Neighborhood

Central Park (Reservoir, The Lake, Strawberry Fields, Sheep Meadow, Tavern on the Green)

Lincoln Center (New York's major center of the performing arts, including the Metropolitan Opera House, Avery Fisher Hall, and New York State Theater)

Christ and St. Stephen's Church (uncharacteristically rural church in the middle of a developed city block), 120 West 69th Street (Columbus & Broadway), (212) 787-2755

Lincoln Square Synagogue (1970 Hausman & Rosenberg building, now a leader of the Modern Orthodox movement), 200 Amsterdam Avenue (69th Street), (212) 874-6100

Beacon Theater (gorgeous old 2,700-seat theater used for a variety of performances), 2124 Broadway (75th Street), (212) 496-7070

New-York Historical Society (spelled with a hyphen, it's one of the best American collections around), 170 Central Park West (76th & 77th Streets), (212) 873-3400

American Museum of Natural History (the premier natural history museum and research institute, now with a dramatic new planetarium), Central Park West at 79th Street, (212) 769-5000

WEST OF MIDTOWN: CLINTON AND CHELSEA

Chelsea is not unlike many other young, affluent areas of New York. You'll see attractive couples out for the evening or just walking hand in hand down the street. But in Chelsea, the couples are often men.

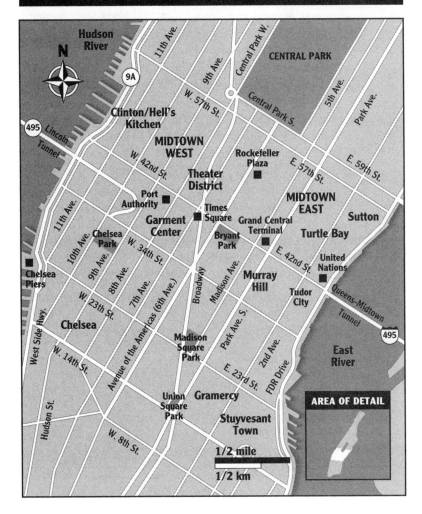

MIDTOWN EAST AND WEST

New York has a substantial gay population, and the City is historically very tolerant of gays—it would be exceptionally poor form to speak homophobically in Manhattan. And, while Chelsea is probably the most visibly gay neighborhood in New York right now, it is also home to many happily coexisting people of all stripes and preferences.

Chelsea is near the Garment Center and encompasses the Flower District. The streets feel open, and there are few high-rise buildings (except for a few large complexes like the Chelsea Towers). There are many attractive walk-up buildings and brownstones, plus a few loft buildings. An array of new stores has opened along Sixth Avenue in recent years, restaurants and shops now line Eighth Avenue, and the western part of Chelsea contains several up-and-coming art galleries. The Chelsea Piers athletic and recreation complex has completed the neighborhood, providing a facility unlike any other in the world. This is a rapidly improving neighborhood, and there may not be all that many housing bargains left, but it's worth a try.

North of Chelsea is what is now called Clinton—and used to be called Hell's Kitchen. In the early 1990s, a few prestigious corporations and law firms, tired of paying Midtown rents, struck out into Midtown West and relocated their corporate headquarters into this neighborhood, which was formerly made up of porn shops, slums, and some artists' residences (mostly actors and dancers). The presence of these large companies spurred housing growth, and in just the past three or four years this neighborhood has really turned the corner. Although not as reliably safe as the Upper West Side or Chelsea, it is a fine neighborhood for young people and continues to improve each year. There has been some new high-rise condo construction, but most of the housing is in smaller prewar buildings and lofts.

Neighborhood Statistical Profile

Total Population: 84,431

Population by Ethnicity

White	*53,544 (63.4%)*
Black	*6,674 (7.9%)*
Hispanic	*19,700 (23.3%)*
Asian	*4,132 (4.9%)*
American Indian	*183 (.2%)*
Other	*198 (.2%)*

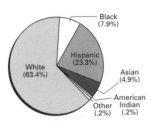

Population by Age

Median age   37.2

18 years & over	*76,151 (90.2%)*
21 years & over	*73,872 (87.5%)*
62 years & over	*13,444 (15.9%)*

Population by Gender

Female	*40,853 (48.4%)*
Male	*43,578 (51.6%)*

Average Housing Costs

Average apartment value: $500,001
   (government statistics)
Average rent: $496
   (reality will be higher)

Other Statistics

Crime Picture:	*Traditionally a marginal area, this is now a safe (and improving daily) neighborhood—although there are some still-developing areas around the fringes.*
Income Picture:	*This area ranges from affluent to working-class, depending on specific location.*
Commuting Times:	
Midtown East	*15–25 minutes*
Midtown West	*5–15 minutes*
Wall Street	*30–40 minutes*

Noteworthy in the Neighborhood

Broadway Theater District (most of the major theaters are here)

Flower District (wholesale and retail), Avenue of the Americas from 27th to 30th Streets

Antiques (this is a major center of antiques in New York City), Ninth Avenue from 20th to 22nd Streets

Chelsea Piers (gigantic sports and recreation complex), West Street from 17th to 23rd Streets, (212) 336-6666

Javits Center (New York's largest convention center), 655 West 34th Street (Eleventh & Twelfth Avenues), (212) 216-2000

Port Authority (the main bus terminal for New York), Eighth and Ninth Avenues from 40th to 42nd Streets, (212) 564-8484

Intrepid Air and Space Museum (beautifully preserved WWII aircraft carrier), 46th Street & Twelfth Avenue, (212) 245-0072

EAST OF MIDTOWN:
TURTLE BAY, MURRAY HILL, GRAMERCY

To the east and south of midtown Manhattan you'll find a mixed bag of neighborhoods, each with its own personality. Turtle Bay, Murray Hill, and Gramercy are the most well defined of these neighborhoods, although there are also several large apartment complexes, like Tudor City, Peter Cooper Village, and Stuyvesant Town, that are neighborhoods in their own right (they are, individually, larger than many small towns).

Murray Hill is centrally located and provides good access to most areas of Manhattan. Many people choose to live here so they can walk to work, and therefore the neighborhood is rife with professionals (although not necessarily young ones). There are townhouses near Park Avenue, high-rises near First Avenue, and Third Avenue is an emerging restaurant and entertainment venue. Turtle Bay is a small area north of the United Nations, with a fiercely devoted populace (including its own newspaper). Despite the office buildings that tower over the neighborhood, it is home to many interesting restaurants and people. Also near Turtle Bay are the areas of Sutton Place and Beekman Place, which are genteel and affluent. There are many consulates nearby, and proximity to Midtown offices is extraordinary.

Gramercy Park is centered around a beautiful private park (the only one in the City) open only to residents of buildings in the neighborhood. It's a quiet neighborhood because the park cuts up the streets and prevents most through-traffic. The park is surrounded by nineteenth-century townhouses, and there are many attractive small buildings nearby. Prices are highest closest to the park.

Neighborhood Statistical Profile

Total Population: 133,748

Population by Ethnicity

White	*108,798 (81.3%)*
Black	*5,730 (4.3%)*
Hispanic	*8,984 (6.7%)*
Asian	*9,950 (7.4%)*
American Indian	*147 (.1%)*
Other	*139 (.1%)*

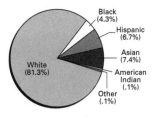

Population by Age
Median age   40.9

18 years & over	*123,820 (92.6%)*
21 years & over	*120,816 (90.3%)*
62 years & over	*26,384 (19.7%)*

Population by Gender

Female	*73,222 (54.7%)*
Male	*60,526 (45.3%)*

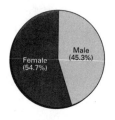

Average Housing Costs

Co-op:	*$451,853*
Studio:	*$102,970*
1-bedroom:	*$205,103*
2-bedroom:	*$551,793*
3-bedroom:	*$1,314,562*
4-bedroom:	*$2,657,667*

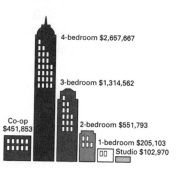

4-bedroom $2,657,667

3-bedroom $1,314,562

Co-op $451,853

2-bedroom $551,793

1-bedroom $205,103

Studio $102,970

Rental Price Index

Studio:	*$1,200–$1,500*
1-bedroom:	*$1,700–$2,200*
2-bedroom:	*$2,700–$3,500*

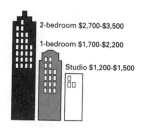

2-bedroom $2,700-$3,500

1-bedroom $1,700-$2,200

Studio $1,200-$1,500

Other Statistics

Crime Picture: *This is considered a very safe neighborhood.*

Income Picture: *This is an affluent area.*

Commuting Times:

Midtown East	*5–15 minutes*
Midtown West	*15–25 minutes*
Wall Street	*25–35 minutes.*

Noteworthy in the Neighborhood

Union Square Park (including the Union Square Greenmarket), from 14th to 17th Streets bounded by Union Square East and Union Square West

Theodore Roosevelt Birthplace (one of New York's most charming attractions), 28 East 20th Street, (212) 260-1616

Flatiron Building (called "flatiron" for its shape, this was New York's first self-sufficient skyscraper), 175 Fifth Avenue (22nd and 23rd Streets)

Pierpont Morgan Library (America's finest collection of Medieval and Renaissance manuscripts, and then some), 29 East 36th Street (Park & Madison Avenues) (212) 685-0610

GREENWICH VILLAGE AND SOHO

The areas of Greenwich Village (pronounced "greh-nitch") and SoHo (an acronym for South of Houston Street) are two of the most sought after neighborhoods in the City right now. This is somewhat ironic to me, because for most of my life these were known as alternative, bohemian neighborhoods. But the artists gave way to the more well-to-do and professional types (and some got rich selling their art), and it's now more expensive to live in Greenwich Village or SoHo than almost anywhere else in New York.

By Greenwich Village I mean what some people now call the West Village (there is now also an East Village, which is discussed in a separate section). The center of the neighborhood, physically and spiritually, is New York University. The residential streets in the center of the

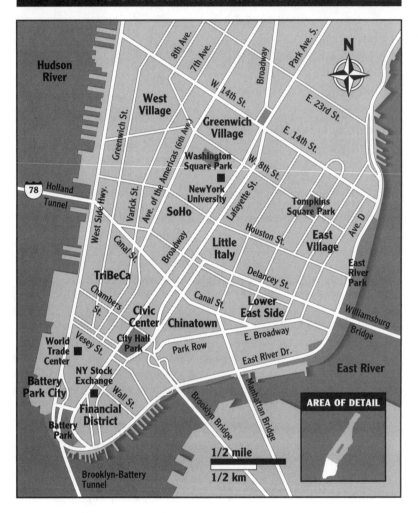

LOWER MANHATTAN

Village are elegant and full of attractive old brick townhouses, plus some apartment buildings. If you're thinking funky and unusual, you've got the wrong image—many of the streets in the Village are as dignified as they come. The neighborhood is also popular with students and alternative types, but they have been pushed farther and farther west, where funkiness is more of a possibility.

SoHo, home to the greatest concentration of galleries in the City, is another artists' neighborhood that has undergone extensive gentrification. Pricewise, SoHo is downright prohibitive, and the artists have been pushed south into TriBeCa and, more often, out into the boroughs (especially the industrial areas of Brooklyn). SoHo is a great and fun area, though, with incredible restaurants and a bustling nightlife.

The gentrification of SoHo has, as is often the case, caused an outward push. Now, the nearby areas of NoHo (North of Houston), Little Italy (which no longer houses many Italians), and Nolita (a relatively new designation meaning North of Little Italy) are fast becoming desirable residential areas as well.

Neighborhood Statistical Profile

Total Population: 94,105

Population by Ethnicity

White	*73,381 (78%)*
Black	*2,941 (3.1%)*
Hispanic	*5,899 (6.3%)*
Asian	*11,605 (12.3%)*
American	
Indian	*140 (.1%)*
Other	*139 (.1%)*

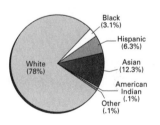

Population by Age

Median age	*37.3*
18 years & over	*86,248 (91.7%)*
21 years & over	*81,772 (86.9%)*
62 years & over	*13,947 (14.8%)*

Population by Gender

Female	*46,832 (49.8%)*
Male	*47,273 (50.2%)*

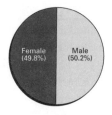

Average Housing Costs

Co-op:	*$282,965*
Studio:	*$122,145*
1-bedroom:	*$243,695*
2-bedroom:	*$520,195*
3-bedroom:	*$1,348,750*
4-bedroom:	*$1,490,000*

Rental Price Index

Studio:	*$1,250–$1,800*
1-bedroom:	*$1,500–$2,000*
2-bedroom:	*$2,600–$4,000*

Other Statistics

Crime Picture:	*This is considered a very safe neighborhood, although the fringe areas can be questionable.*
Income Picture:	*At its core, this is an affluent area, although there are pockets of lower income.*
Commuting Times:	
Midtown East	*25–35 minutes*
Midtown West	*15–25 minutes*
Wall Street	*20–30 minutes*

Noteworthy in the Neighborhood

Numerous playhouses, music venues, galleries, and boutiques

Washington Square Park (largest public space downtown, the focal
point being the large Memorial Arch), from West 4th Street
to Waverly Place and University Place to MacDougal Street

New York University (major institution of higher learning and a
defining voice in the neighborhood), from West 3rd Street to
Waverly Place and Mercer Street to La Guardia Place, (212)
998-4636

Film Forum (New York's premier art house movie theater), 209 West
Houston Street (Sixth Avenue & Varick Street), (212) 627-
2035

EAST VILLAGE,
LOWER EAST SIDE, AND CHINATOWN

A few years ago, I wouldn't have included these neighborhoods in this
book—save perhaps for the East Village as a place for nonconformists.
But today these are some of the most promising areas for newcomers
on limited budgets.

The designation "East Village" was created to bestow some legiti-
macy on this formerly run-down part of the Lower East Side. And it
worked. The neighborhood is now improving steadily, and even the
dreaded "Alphabet City" (the area jutting out into the river, where the
extra avenues are designated by letters) has been cleaned up dramatically by recent police action. Housing is mostly old and small, but
there are bargains to be had. The area is especially popular with the
young, anti-establishment crowd.

The Lower East Side is one of Manhattan's last bastions of bargain
housing, and the supply is rapidly dwindling as people catch on and
the neighborhood becomes safer and more desirable. Traditionally the
landing point for new immigrants to the City, the Lower East Side still
has more ethnic character than most neighborhoods. But the latest
immigrants are more likely to be American than foreign.

Likewise, many non-Chinese are finding good housing in Chinatown. Although, safety-wise, I'd still not recommend these areas for families with young children or for women living alone, it's only a matter of a very short time before they become safe for these folks too.

Neighborhood Statistical Profile

Total Population: 161,617

Population by Ethnicity

White	*47,392 (29.3%)*
Black	*13,387 (8.3%)*
Hispanic	*52,217 (32.3%)*
Asian	*47,883 (29.6%)*
American	
Indian	*385 (.2%)*
Other	*353 (.2%)*

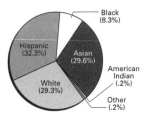

Population by Age

Median age	*34.2*
18 years & over	*129,365 (80%)*
21 years & over	*121,650 (75.3%)*
62 years & over	*25,990 (16.1%)*

Population by Gender

Female	*81,160 (50.2%)*
Male	*80,457 (49.8%)*

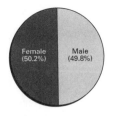

Average Housing Costs

Average apartment value:	*$268,750*
(government statistics)	
Average rent:	*$348*
(reality will be higher)	

Other Statistics

Crime Picture: *This is considered a developing neighborhood; caution is recommended although there are many safe areas.*

Income Picture: *This is a middle- and working-class area.*

Commuting Times:

Midtown East	*15–25 minutes*
Midtown West	*25–35 minutes*
Wall Street	*15–25 minutes*

Noteworthy in the Neighborhood

Major center of alternative culture, including music and boutiques

St. Mark's Place (the most visible representation of East Village culture), from Avenue A to Third Avenue

Cooper Union (famous private college that is the oldest steel-beam building in America), 7 East 7th Street (Fourth Avenue), (212) 353-4100

Orchard Street (center of the old Jewish Lower East Side, now a pedestrian mall on weekends), from Delancey Street to Houston Street

Mott and Canal Streets, the gateway to Chinatown, is a destination that virtually every tourist to New York visits.

TRIBECA AND LOWER MANHATTAN

Nobody used to live in lower Manhattan, except for traders and investment bankers who lived at their offices. For the longest time, this was strictly a commercial district. But, over the past few years, the dominos have fallen, first in TriBeCa, then with the construction of Battery Park City, and, finally, with new development right near Wall Street, in the heart of the Financial District.

TriBeCa (an acronym for Triangle below Canal Street), with its large-windowed cast-iron buildings, now looks more like SoHo than like the industrial neighborhood it once was. The warehouses and small factories are being reborn as residential apartments—expensive ones. The restaurant situation is excellent, spurred by low rents in the 1980s and now sustained by a desirable clientele despite climbing rents. Not as artsy as SoHo, TriBeCa nonetheless has an exceptionally active nightlife, an attractive park (Duane Park), a bike path along the Hudson River, a fair number of clothing and design shops, plus some galleries. Access to basic services has improved greatly over the past few years, such that this is now a fully functioning and very popular residential neighborhood.

Battery Park City, a ninety-two-acre site adjacent to the World Financial Center and World Trade Center complexes, is an easy walk from the downtown business district. It is a carefully planned development of apartment complexes, with private security, bronze sculptures, a 1.2-mile esplanade, Hudson River breezes, and a beautiful marina. Shops and restaurants are still somewhat rudimentary compared with the rest of the City, but residents find them sufficient given the neighborhood's other benefits. Some apartments have incredible views of the harbor or of Downtown.

And, today, it is possible to live right in the shadow of Wall Street. New apartment complexes (some in renovated former office buildings) are springing up in the Financial District, and the investment bankers and traders—who arguably live there already—are starting to move in. Unlike some emerging neighborhoods, this area is not characterized by low prices. Expect to pay top dollar for newly renovated apartments in full-service buildings. Neighborhood services are still rudimentary, but the video stores, twenty-four-hour markets, and dry cleaners are slowly gaining a foothold.

Neighborhood Statistical Profile

Total Population: 25,366

Population by Ethnicity

White	18,097 (71.3%)
Black	2,502 (9.9%)
Hispanic	2,231 (8.8%)
Asian	2,425 (9.6%)
American Indian	67 (.3%)
Other	44 (.2%)

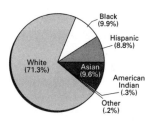

Population by Age

Median age	34.8
18 years & over	22,112 (87.2%)
21 years & over	21,350 (84.2%)
62 years & over	2,409 (9.5%)

Population by Gender

Female	11,378 (44.9%)
Male	13,988 (55.1%)

Average Housing Costs

Co-op:	$679,368
Studio:	$164,786
1-bedroom:	$440,953
2-bedroom:	$804,863
3-bedroom:	$1,117,500
4-bedroom:	$2,200,000

2-bedroom $2,600–$4,000

1-bedroom $1,500–$2,000

Studio $1,250–$1,800

Rental Price Index

Studio:	*$1,250–$1,800*
1-bedroom:	*$1,500–$2,000*
2-bedroom:	*$2,600–$4,000*

Other Statistics

Crime Picture: This is considered a safe neighborhood, although somewhat deserted at night.

Income Picture: This is an upwardly mobile area, with some pockets of
lower income.

Commuting Times:

Midtown East	*30–40 minutes*
Midtown West	*25–25 minutes*
Wall Street	*5–10 minutes*

Noteworthy in the Neighborhood

Center of the nation's financial markets (New York Stock Exchange,
World Trade Center, World Financial Center)

Site of many historic landmarks (Brooklyn Bridge, Trinity Church,
Woolworth Building)

Headquarters of government (City Hall, Municipal Building, Federal
Building) and courts (State and Federal)

Departure point for ferries to Statue of Liberty and Ellis Island

Fraunces Tavern (where Washington said farewell to his officers), 54
Pearl Street (at Broad Street)

South Street Seaport and Pier 17 (shopping, dining, and outdoor
events)

Many artsy and ethnic attractions in TriBeCa

WASHINGTON HEIGHTS AND INWOOD

At the northern tip of Manhattan, on the island's highest ground, are two peaceful, mostly working-class neighborhoods that offer some very attractive housing values for those willing to strike out into uncharted territory. People think of anything north of Columbia

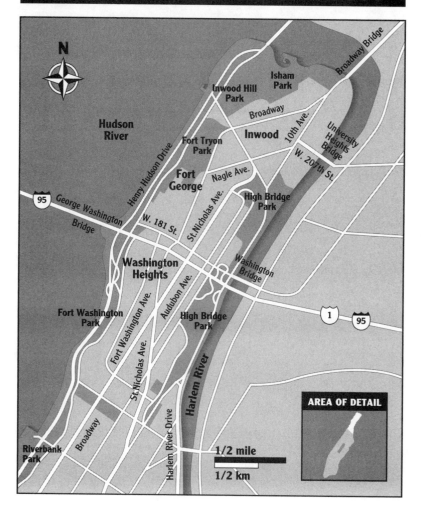

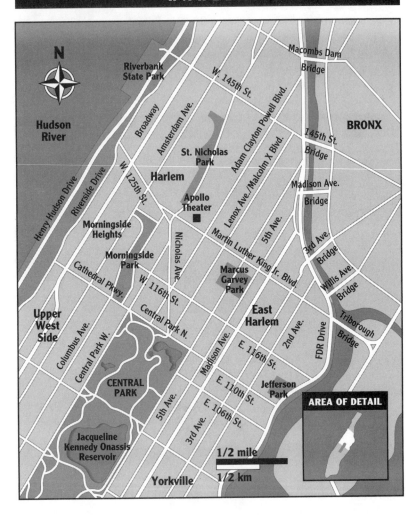

HARLEM

University as "Harlem," but once you get north of Harlem (which itself is an improving neighborhood—but not in time for this edition of this book), you come back to relative safety and tranquillity.

Washington Heights and Inwood are visually stunning, with the George Washington Bridge and the major Manhattan waterways framing the area. Housing is good, with many buildings newly reno-vated. These areas are ideal bastions for artists, musicians, and actors—as well as professionals—who want to escape the City's urban core and save some money, but don't actually want to go suburban. Inwood is traditionally considered safer and more desirable than Washington Heights, but each is a collection of better and worse areas, so it's important to choose your location carefully. In general, the bet-ter parts are to the west of Broadway (one of the major commercial thoroughfares in the area; the other is 181st Street). In the entire area, however, crime has been declining steadily for the past few years.

Most people find their apartments here by word of mouth—the neighborhoods are still to some extent tough nuts to crack. But it may be worth the effort if the area strikes your fancy.

Neighborhood Statistical Profile

Total Population: 198,192

Population by Ethnicity

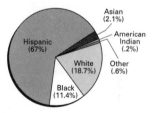

White	37,021 (18.7%)
Black	22,562 (11.4%)
Hispanic	132,722 (67%)
Asian	4,217 (2.1%)
American Indian	393 (.2%)
Other	1,277 (.6%)

Population by Age

Median age   31.9

18 years & over	146,259 (73.8%)
21 years & over	137,271 (69.3%)
62 years & over	26,460 (13.4%)

Population by Gender

Female   *105,097 (53%)*

Male   *93,095 (47%)*

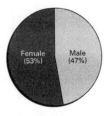

Average Housing Costs

Average apartment value: *$155,825*
     (government statistics)

Average rent: *$387*
     (reality will be higher)

Other Statistics

Crime Picture: *This is a mixed neighborhood but there are some very safe areas; you have to choose your block and building carefully.*

Income Picture: *This is a working-class area.*

Commuting Times:

     Midtown East   *40–50 minutes*

     Midtown West   *35–45 minutes*

     Wall Street   *50–60 minutes*

Noteworthy in the Neighborhood

Fort Tryon Park (includes the Cloisters, which houses the Medieval collection of the Metropolitan Museum of Art), from 192nd to Dyckman Streets and Broadway to Riverside Drive

Yeshiva University (major center of Jewish learning), 186th Street and Amsterdam Avenue, (212) 960-5400

Baker Field (Columbia University's football stadium—the only one in Manhattan), 218th Street between Broadway and Seaman Avenue, (212) 567-0404

George Washington Bridge (visual focal point of the neighborhood, carrying traffic to New Jersey), at 178th Street

Little Red Lighthouse (circa 1921 lighthouse in Fort Washington Park), under the George Washington Bridge

Brooklyn

If Brooklyn broke from New York and became its own city, as it once was, it would still be one of the largest in the world. It dwarfs

BROOKLYN

Manhattan in both population and area. The parts of Brooklyn that lie closest to Manhattan are very popular, especially with those who work in downtown Manhattan, because of their good housing value and relative safety.

BROOKLYN HEIGHTS

Brooklyn Heights, the area directly over the Brooklyn Bridge and north of Atlantic Avenue, has become so popular with Manhattan professionals that the folks in the rest of Brooklyn don't acknowledge the Heights as part of the real Brooklyn anymore. And, walking around Brooklyn Heights, one would be forgiven for assuming it's a nice residential neighborhood of Manhattan—although the buildings are lower and it's impossible to get views of Manhattan this good from within Manhattan.

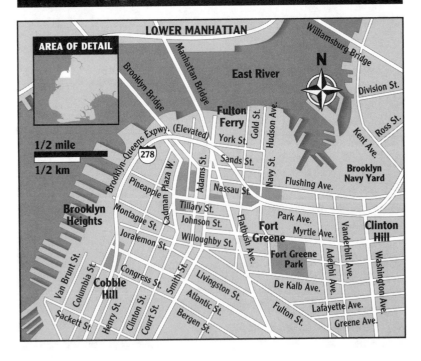

The Brooklyn Heights Esplanade, a magnificent walkway above the Brooklyn–Queens Expressway, affords incomparable vistas of downtown Manhattan, Governors Island, and the Statue of Liberty to the south, and the Manhattan Bridge, Brooklyn Bridge, the Chrysler Building, and the Empire State Building to the north. Brooklyn Heights was declared, in 1965, the City's first historic district (there are now many others), and Civil War–era architecture dominates. Montague Street is the main commercial street in the Heights, and is rife with shops and restaurants (and, these days, unfortunately, traffic).

It's a quicker commute from Brooklyn Heights to Wall Street than from almost any residential neighborhood in Manhattan, yet Brooklyn Heights offers less expensive housing than Manhattan (although prices are rising), plus an active restaurant and entertainment scene. When the weather is nice, Heights residents walk (or bike) to Manhattan via the Brooklyn Bridge pedestrian walkway.

The nearby areas of Boerum Hill, Fort Greene, and Clinton Hill are likewise becoming gentrified and are worth a look.

Neighborhood Statistical Profile

Total Population: 94,534

Population by Ethnicity

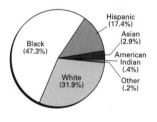

White	30,144 (31.9%)
Black	44,670 (47.3%)
Hispanic	16,407 (17.4%)
Asian	2,787 (2.9%)
American Indian	339 (.4%)
Other	197 (.2%)

Population by Age

Median age   32.8

18 years & over	76,229 (80.6%)
21 years & over	71,815 (76%)
62 years & over	11,123 (11.8%)

Population by Gender

Female   48,363 (51.2%)
Male   46,171 (48.8%)

Female
(51.2%)

Male
(48.8%)

Average Housing Costs

Average apartment value: $263,300
    (government statistics)
Average rent: $449
    (reality will be higher)

Other Statistics

Crime Picture: This is considered a safe neighborhood.
Income Picture: This is a middle-class area, with some affluent residents.
Commuting Times:
    Midtown East   30–40 minutes
    Midtown West   35–45 minutes
    Wall Street   10–20 minutes

Noteworthy in the Neighborhood

Atlantic Avenue (center of Middle Eastern culture in New York)

Brooklyn Borough Hall (similar to City Hall in Manhattan),
    (718) 802-3700

Brooklyn Academy of Music (known by locals as "BAM"),
    30 Lafayette Avenue (St. Felix Street & Ashland Place),
    (718) 636-4100

COBBLE HILL, CARROLL GARDENS, PARK SLOPE

Cobble Hill is much like Brooklyn Heights (it too is a historic district—declared in 1969—with similar architecture), but is on the south side of Atlantic Avenue. Those who live in Cobble Hill, however, consider it a more neighborly and less apartment-oriented area. Truly

PARK SLOPE

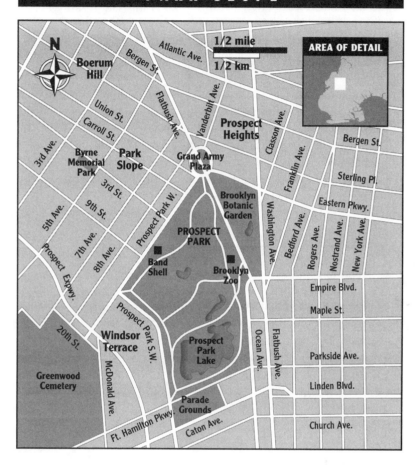

N

1/2 mile

1/2 km

AREA OF DETAIL

Boerum Hill

Bergen St.

Atlantic Ave.

Union St.

Carroll St.

Flatbush Ave.

Vanderbilt Ave.

Prospect Heights

Classon Ave.

Bergen St.

3rd Ave.

Byrne Memorial Park

Park Slope

Grand Army Plaza

Franklin Ave.

Sterling Pl.

5th Ave.

3rd St.

9th St.

Prospect Park W.

Brooklyn Botanic Garden

Washington Ave.

Eastern Pkwy.

Bedford Ave.

Rogers Ave.

Nostrand Ave.

New York Ave.

Prospect Expwy.

7th Ave.

8th Ave.

PROSPECT PARK

Band Shell

Brooklyn Zoo

Empire Blvd.

Maple St.

20th St.

Prospect Park S.W.

Windsor Terrace

Prospect Park Lake

Ocean Ave.

Flatbush Ave.

Parkside Ave.

Greenwood Cemetery

McDonald Ave.

Linden Blvd.

Ft. Hamilton Pkwy.

Parade Grounds

Caton Ave.

Church Ave.

an oasis, Cobble Hill has one of the lowest crime rates in the city, and boasts many trees and the attractive Cobble Hill Park. Transportation to Manhattan is excellent, with four subway lines making stops in the neighborhood.

Carroll Gardens, to the south of Cobble Hill, burst on the scene as an emerging commuter neighborhood very recently, and now has scores of good restaurants and plenty of activity along its avenues. This friendly neighborhood, centered around Carroll Park (which features a monument honoring neighborhood residents killed in World War I), has always been a nice place to live. Now, with this current wave of expansion, it's an even more desirable place to look for housing.

To the east of Cobble Hill and Carroll Gardens, a little farther from Manhattan (but still quite close by subway) is Park Slope. Those who live here are unusually loyal to the neighborhood (even for New Yorkers). The salient landmark, Prospect Park, is reminiscent of Central Park (same designers) albeit not as large (nor as crowded). Prospect Park has many interesting churches and brownstone row houses, plus diverse shopping along Seventh Avenue and a growing number of ethnic and eclectic restaurants. Neo-Renaissance and neo-Classical architecture are dominant, and this is one of the most architecturally attractive neighborhoods in the City.

Neighborhood Statistical Profile

Total Population: 102,228

Population by Ethnicity

White	56,213 (55%)
Black	16,176 (15.8%)
Hispanic	26,002 (25.4%)
Asian	3,323 (3.3%)
American Indian	252 (.2%)
Other	262 (.3%)

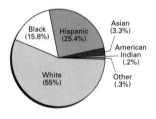

Population by Age

Median age   32.7

18 years & over	81,594 (79.8%)
21 years & over	78,137 (76.4%)
62 years & over	12,391 (12.1%)

Population by Gender

Female   *54,112 (52.9%)*

Male   *48,116 (47.1%)*

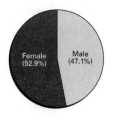

Average Housing Costs

Average apartment value: *$294,900*
(government statistics)

Average rent: *$508*
(reality will be higher)

Other Statistics

Crime Picture: *This is considered a safe neighborhood, with some areas being safer than others.*

Income Picture: *This is a middle- and working-class area, with some affluent residents.*

Commuting Times:

Midtown East   *30–40 minutes*

Midtown West   *35–45 minutes*

Wall Street   *10–20 minutes*

Noteworthy in the Neighborhood

Prospect Park (designed by Olmstead and Vaux, of Central Park fame)

Grand Army Plaza (leading up to Prospect Park, with several interesting monuments)

Brooklyn Museum (one of New York's best collections), 200 Eastern Parkway (Washington Avenue), (718) 638-5000

Queens (Astoria)

Queens is the City's largest and most ethnically diverse borough (many of the residents of the old ethnic neighborhoods of Manhattan or their children now live in Queens), and right now may very well be the most ethnically diverse place in the world. The borough presents a dizzying array of housing options, most of which are solidly working class (it is often said that every cab driver lives in Queens), but one neighborhood in particular—Astoria—is fast gaining popularity with professionals who work in Manhattan.

QUEENS

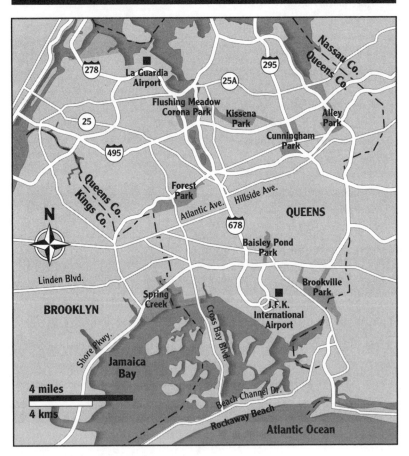

ASTORIA/LONG ISLAND CITY

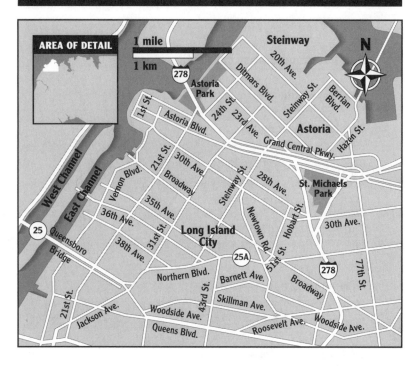

Formerly a center of filmmaking, and now (depending on which street you cross) a Greek, Yugoslavian, Russian, Asian, and Middle Eastern neighborhood, Astoria is a quick subway commute to Midtown Manhattan and is attracting a young professional crowd that values space and savings. It's safe, you can live in an actual house if you want (although most people live in apartments carved out of former private homes), and the ethnic composition of the neighborhood makes for some great (and cheap) eating—at more than 200 restaurants—plus a dizzying array of nightlife and shopping along the major thoroughfares (like Steinway Street). Navigating Queens can be a challenge—there are "streets," "roads," "boulevards," and "avenues" stacked up in a seemingly random manner—but residents swear there's a simple logic to it all.

The adjacent area of Long Island City (debates rage about where one neighborhood ends and the other begins) is also developing nicely as a commuter residence.

Neighborhood Statistical Profile

Total Population: 188,549

Population by Ethnicity

White	*101,934 (54.1%)*
Black	*20,223 (10.7%)*
Hispanic	*48,797 (25.9%)*
Asian	*16,176 (8.6%)*
American	
Indian	*437 (.2%)*
Other	*982 (.5%)*

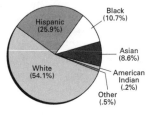

Population by Age

Median age	*33.4*
18 years & over	*154,747 (82.1%)*
21 years & over	*146,066 (77.5%)*
62 years & over	*29,566 (15.7%)*

Population by Gender

Female	*91,527 (48.5%)*
Male	*97,022 (51.5%)*

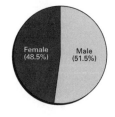

Average Housing Costs

Average home value: *$221,650*
     (government statistics)
Average rent: *$475*
     (reality will be higher)

Other Statistics

Crime Picture: *This is considered a safe neighborhood, but you must choose your location carefully.*

Income Picture: *This is a working-class area.*

Commuting Times:

Midtown East	*20–30 minutes*
Midtown West	*30–40 minutes*
Wall Street	*40–50 minutes*

Noteworthy in the Neighborhood

Formerly a center of the American film industry

American Museum of the Moving Image (incredible collection of pop culture), 36–01 35th Avenue (36th Street), (718) 784-0077

Kaufman Astoria Studios (still a functioning studio), 34–12 36th Street (24th Avenue), (718) 932-1510

Steinway Mansion (as in the pianos—the factory is still in Astoria), 18–33 41st Street (Berrian Boulevard)

Isamu Noguchi Garden Museum (housing more than 250 works by this renowned sculptor), 32–37 Vernon Boulevard

Staten Island

Staten Island is one of the least examined (and the least populous) of the boroughs, and residents like it that way. One of my friends, who grew up on Staten Island, says that if you tell people elsewhere in America that you "come from Staten Island," they have no idea what

STATEN ISLAND

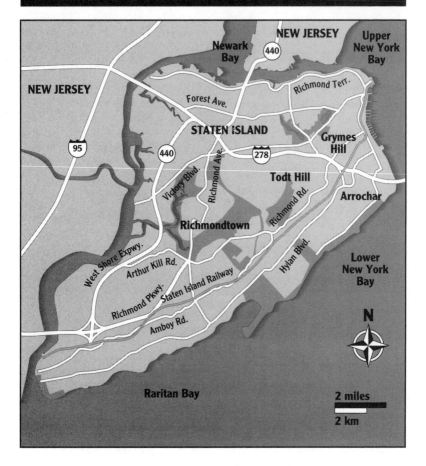

you're talking about—but they assume you're tough because of the syncopated sound of "STA-ten IS-land." Even New Yorkers tend to know little more than that Staten Island is "that place the Staten Island ferry goes."

But Staten Island, for the most part, is anything but tough. It's the most suburban and spacious part of the City by far, and residents can't imagine living anywhere else. Staten Island is so unlike the rest of the

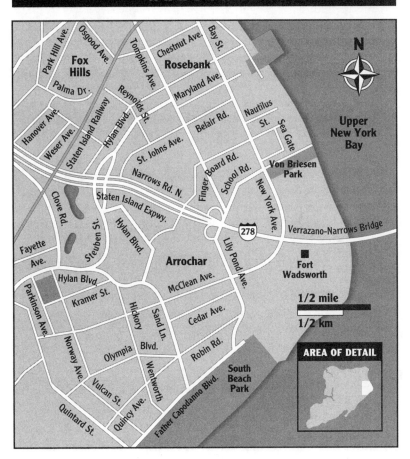

ARROCHAR

City that it occasionally threatens to secede from the larger political whole—an attempt that is not likely to succeed any time soon.

You can get to and from Staten Island by ferry from lower Manhattan (for free), or via several bridges (the most noteworthy being the Verrazano-Narrows Bridge, which connects Staten Island to Brooklyn.) There is no bridge directly to Manhattan. Within Staten Island, private automobiles are common, and there's also Staten Island

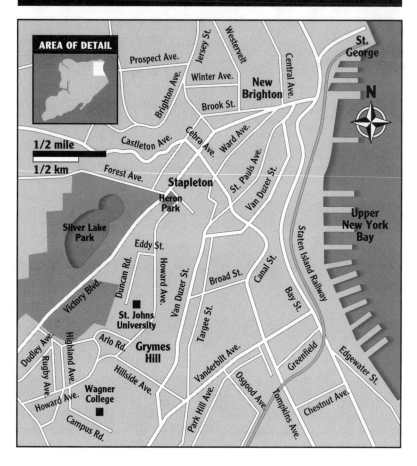

GRYMES HILL

Rapid Transit (similar to the subways in the rest of the City), and an extensive local and commuter bus network.

Almost exclusively residential, this sixty-one-square-mile island has everything from large apartment complexes near the ferry terminal (perfect for those who work on Wall Street), to a diverse array of apartments in converted private homes and townhouses, to large

RICHMONDTOWN

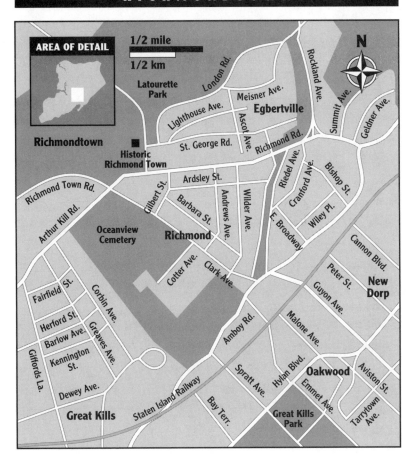

mansions with extensive grounds farther south. Nearest to Manhattan are a series of dramatic hills and slopes stretching from St. George to Richmondtown. In Todt, Emerson, and Grymes Hills, you can live in a multimillion-dollar home with a view of Manhattan or Brooklyn—or both. The local paper is the *Staten Island Advance*, which contains the most relevant housing ads.

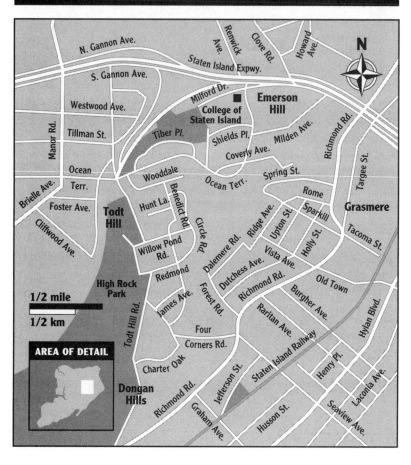

Neighborhood Statistical Profile

Total Population: 378,977

Population by Ethnicity

White	*303,081 (80%)*
Black	*28,172 (7.4%)*
Hispanic	*30,239 (8.0%)*
Asian	*16,483 (4.3%)*
American	
Indian	*611 (.2%)*
Other	*391 (.1%)*

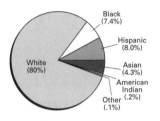

Population by Age

Median age   33.3

18 years & over	*284,915 (75.2%)*
21 years & over	*268,332 (70.8%)*
62 years & over	*51,576 (13.6%)*

Population by Gender

Female	*195,822 (51.7%)*
Male	*183,155 (48.3%)*

Average Housing Costs

Average apartment value: $186,300
      (government statistics)
Average rent: $509
      (reality will be higher)

Other Statistics

Crime Picture: This is considered a very safe area, with some variation
                        depending on specific regions.

Income Picture: This is a mostly middle-class area, with pockets of afflu-
                        ence and some poverty.

Commuting Times:

  Midtown East   45–55 minutes

  Midtown West   45–55 minutes

  Wall Street   25–35 minutes

  (assuming you live within 5–10 minutes of the ferry; longer otherwise)

Noteworthy in the Neighborhood

Snug Harbor Cultural Center (eighty-three-acre visual and perform-
     ing arts center), 1000 Richmond Terrace (Tyson Street), (718)
     448-2500

Verrazano-Narrows Bridge (world's longest suspension bridge—
     longer than the Golden Gate—and starting point of the NYC
     Marathon)

Historic Richmond Town (twenty-nine buildings dating from the
     seventeenth to nineteenth centuries), 441 Clarke Avenue
     (Richmond & Arthur Kill Roads), (718) 351-1611

Alice Austen House (the *Life* magazine photographer), 2 Hylan
     Boulevard (Bay Street), (718) 816-4506

Fresh Kills (New York's notorious—and huge—garbage dump)

The Bronx (Riverdale)

Although most areas of the Bronx (the smallest borough and the only
one beginning with a definite article) are not particularly desirable for
housing at this time, the enclave of Riverdale is one of the most beautiful places to live in all of New York City. More like a suburb than a
neighborhood of the Bronx (many people, even New Yorkers, assume
Riverdale is part of Westchester and not part of the City), Riverdale

BRONX

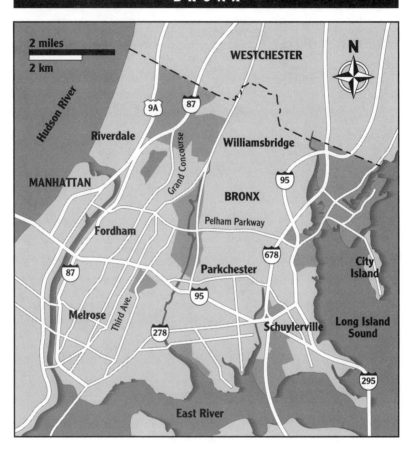

offers both houses and apartments in a spacious, mostly low-rise setting near the water. Narrow streets meander over rocky bluffs, past nineteenth-century landmark mansions overlooking Manhattan and the Palisades (a series of cliffs across the Hudson River, in New Jersey). On the outskirts of the neighborhood, there are some apartment complexes.

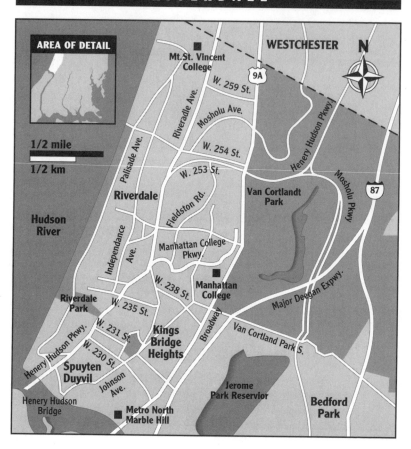

RIVERDALE

AREA OF DETAIL

WESTCHESTER N

Mt.St. Vincent College

1/2 mile

1/2 km

Riverdale Ave.

Mosholu Ave.

W. 259 St.

9A

W. 254 St.

W. 253 St.

Palisade Ave.

Riverdale

Van Cortlandt Park

Henery Hudson Pkwy.

Mosholu Pkwy

87

Hudson River

Fieldston Rd.

Independance Ave.

Manhattan College Pkwy.

Manhattan College

W. 238 St.

Riverdale Park

W. 235 St.

Henery Hudson Pkwy.

W. 231 St.

Kings Bridge Heights

Broadway

Major Deegan Expwy.

Van Cortland Park S.

W. 230 St.

Spuyten Duyvil

Johnson Ave.

Jerome Park Reservior

Bedford Park

Henery Hudson Bridge

Metro North Marble Hill

Because of the open spaces available in the Bronx, there are several prestigious high school campuses nearby (Fieldston, Horace-Mann, Riverdale Country Day, Bronx Science), as well as immense parks and even golf courses. There is a strong Jewish community, with three excellent Jewish schools and numerous synagogues.

CITY ISLAND

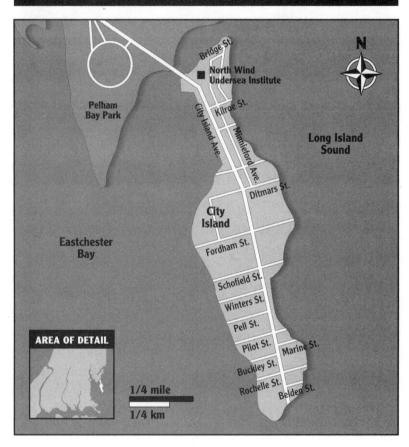

Although Riverdale residents head to Manhattan for serious dining and entertainment, Riverdale does offer a good selection of restaurants and even some cultural activities. Residents commute to Manhattan primarily by express bus and Metro North commuter train.

HIGH BRIDGE

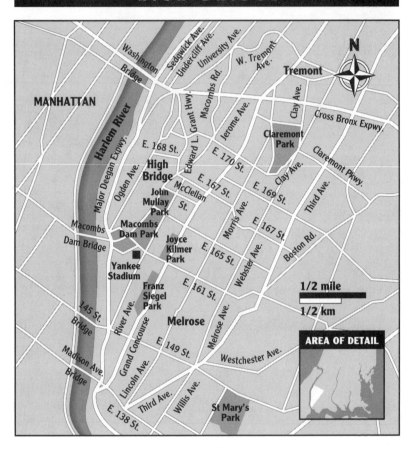

The nearby areas of Spuyten Duyvel (a collection of apartment buildings facing Manhattan and the Harlem River) and Marble Hill (which is technically part of Manhattan but, due to a redirection of the

MORRISANIA

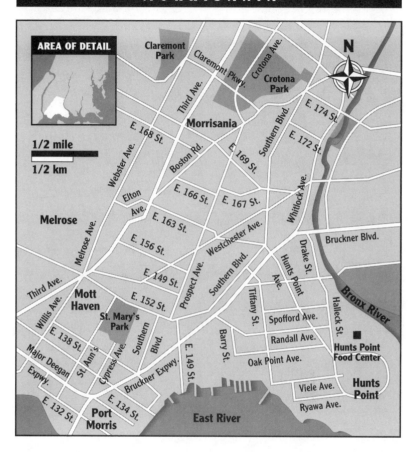

river, now sits physically in the Bronx) also provide some attractive housing options. Elsewhere in the Bronx, City Island seems more like a New England fishing community than like part of New York or any city.

PARKCHESTER

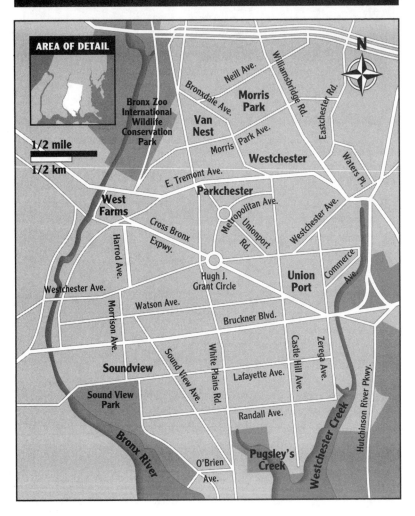

SCHUYLERVILLE

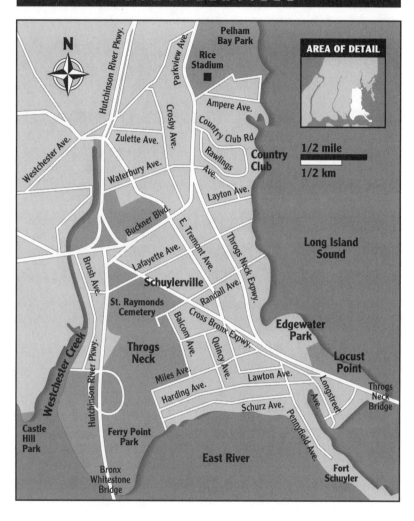

N

AREA OF DETAIL

Pelham
Bay Park

Rice
Stadium

Hutchinson River Pkwy.

Parkview Ave.

Ampere Ave.

Crosby Ave.

Country Club Rd.

Zulette Ave.

Rawlings Ave.

Country
Club

Westchester Ave.

Waterbury Ave.

1/2 mile

1/2 km

Layton Ave.

Buckner Blvd.

E. Tremont Ave.

Throgs Neck Expwy.

Long Island
Sound

Lafayette Ave.

Brush Ave.

Schuylerville

Randall Ave.

St. Raymonds
Cemetery

Cross Bronx Expwy.

Balcom Ave.

Quincy Ave.

Edgewater
Park

Throgs
Neck

Miles Ave.

Lawton Ave.

Locust
Point

Hutchinson River Pkwy.

Harding Ave.

Longstreet Ave.

Throgs
Neck
Bridge

Westchester Creek

Schurz Ave.

Pennyfield Ave.

Castle
Hill
Park

Ferry Point
Park

East River

Fort
Schuyler

Bronx
Whitestone
Bridge

UNIVERSITY HEIGHTS

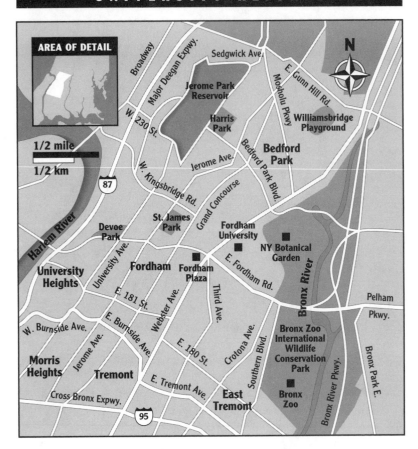

WILLIAMSBRIDGE

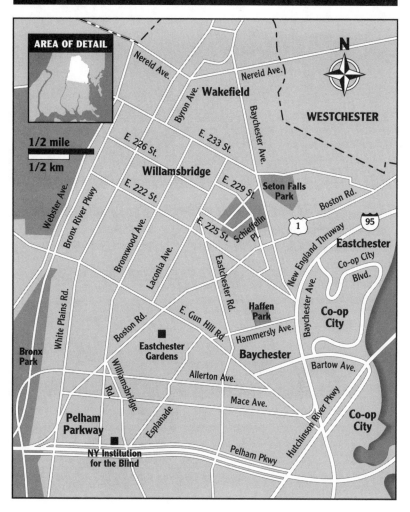

AREA OF DETAIL

N

1/2 mile
1/2 km

Nereid Ave.

Wakefield

Nereid Ave.

WESTCHESTER

Byron Ave.

Baychester Ave.

E. 233 St.

E. 226 St.

Willamsbridge

E. 229 St.

Seton Falls
Park

Boston Rd.

E. 222 St.

Webster Ave.

Bronx River Pkwy

Bronxwood Ave.

E. 225 St.

Schieffelin
Pl.

1

New England Thruway

95

Eastchester

Co-op City
Blvd.

Laconia Ave.

Eastchester Rd.

Baychester Ave.

Co-op
City

White Plains Rd.

Boston Rd.

E. Gun Hill Rd.

Haffen
Park

Hammersly Ave.

Baychester

Bronx
Park

Eastchester
Gardens

Allerton Ave.

Bartow Ave.

Williamsbridge Rd.

Mace Ave.

Hutchinson River Pkwy

Co-op
City

Pelham
Parkway

Esplanade

NY Institution
for the Blind

Pelham Pkwy

Neighborhood Statistical Profile

Total Population: 97,030

Population by Ethnicity

White	*57,310 (59.1%)*
Black	*11,364 (11.7%)*
Hispanic	*23,913 (24.6%)*
Asian	*4,051 (4.2%)*
American Indian	*169 (.2%)*
Other	*223 (.2%)*

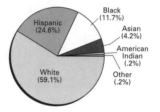

Population by Age

Median age   38.5

18 years & over	*78,337 (80.7%)*
21 years & over	*74,352 (76.6%)*
62 years & over	*23,414 (24.1%)*

Population by Gender

Female	*53,158 (54.8%)*
Male	*43,872 (45.2%)*

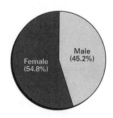

Average Housing Costs

Average apartment value: $251,850
        (government statistics)
Average rent: $453
        (reality will be higher)

Other Statistics

Crime Picture: *This is considered a very safe neighborhood, but it is an enclave within the Bronx so you must be careful when approaching neighborhood boundaries.*

Income Picture: *This is an affluent area.*

Commuting Times:

     Midtown East   *40–50 minutes*

     Midtown West   *40–50 minutes*

     Wall Street   *55–65 minutes*

Noteworthy in the Neighborhood

Wave Hill (twenty-eight-acre nineteenth-century mansion with beautiful gardens and greenhouses), 675 East 252nd Street (Independence Avenue), (718) 549-2055

Van Cortlandt House Museum (restored Georgian-Colonial mansion), Broadway at West 246th Street, (718) 543-3344

The Suburbs

Living outside of the city, especially for people who are relocating and are new to the area, adds a challenge to your life that you may not especially relish. It is important to try to keep your search focused on areas that will keep your commute time to a reasonable minimum. If you expect to work twelve-hour days, a ninety-minute commute (one hour and fifteen minutes on the train, then fifteen minutes within the City) will extend that day to fifteen hours or more. Carefully calculate whether that commute is going to make your life great or a living hell.

The suburbs in the tri-state area are comprised of towns that, in other parts of the country, would be considered major cities. Some of these, like Yonkers and Jersey City, which rank in the top 100 largest U. S. cities (numbers 94 and 71), would be the largest city in any state. Others, like White Plains and Stamford, are homes to powerhouse companies like IBM and GE. Deciding to live in one of these towns is a start, but you'll still have to narrow your scope, because within each of these towns, there are many neighborhoods to choose from. You still need to do your homework and enlist the help of a local, experienced realtor (ask for someone who's a specialist on relocating) who can be a real asset in helping you make a good choice.

The desirability of commuter suburbs in the tri-state area is primarily determined by one thing, and that's public transportation. You will find pockets of commuters in a town that has a train or bus line, and (especially in New Jersey) virtually no commuters living in the town next door if that town does not offer its residents transportation into the City. This one factor also makes a big difference in real estate prices. A town that is conveniently located on a train or bus line that runs into the City will command higher prices than one that is not.

PROS AND CONS OF LIVING IN THE SUBURBS

If you are considering living in the suburbs (with the exception of New Jersey towns like Hoboken and Jersey City, which are the New Jersey equivalents of Brooklyn Heights and Cobble Hill—just on the other side of the river), I will assume, for the purposes of clarity, a few things about you (forgive me): (1) You already have a job in the City, and (2) you have a family or are planning to begin one soon.

Hundreds of thousands of people commute thirty minutes to two hours into Manhattan from the outlying suburbs every day. The primary reason for this involves a lifestyle choice—these commuters want to live with their families in a house with a yard (it is primarily families who live in these areas). That is the bottom line. People have other reasons for living outside of the City, but when you get down to the heart of the matter, the ability to live in a house with a yard is most important. How badly do you want more space? Are you willing to commute up to two hours for it?

People choose to live in the suburbs for many reasons, like the schools are better and the children will be safer, but in making your decision, you should note that in recent years the City has gotten much safer and the suburbs less secure. It is no longer true that the best suburban neighborhoods are free of drugs and dealers, and that all of the neighborhood schools provide top-notch educations. As the City has improved, many suburbs have declined. I don't mean to scare you into thinking that the suburbs are dangerous or hazardous to your child's safety—plenty of children play out in their yards and attend the public schools—it just isn't universal anymore.

Clearly, by opting to live outside of the City, you will have far more space, inside and out (the closets alone make me green with envy), you will have mega–grocery stores, shopping malls, and discount shopping for added convenience. If you select your neighborhood with the school system in mind, chances are good that your child will attend the local public school. Getting your child to Little League on Saturday mornings won't be a struggle, and having a pet is a whole lot easier (and no one is telling you whether or not you can have one). And, if you're moving from a far less urban environment, you may find that living in the suburbs will be an easier transition for you and your family than living in the City would be.

But, you will have to face that commute every day, twice a day. You'll have to drive yourself and your children everywhere (and if you can't do it, you'll have to get someone else who can). You will also pay a premium for proximity to something (Manhattan) that you may not take advantage of on a regular basis (except for the purposes of your livelihood). If you have a child who is gifted in music or art, dance, or science, that child has fewer options in the suburbs than in the City. The City is so diverse; in living there, you and your children are exposed on a daily basis to dozens of different cultures, ethnicities, and lifestyles. My friend's four-year-old son wanted to know where Korea was because his friend from the neighborhood playground is from Korea. He is exposed to so much diversity of life at such a young age that the variety doesn't even cross his mind.

Make no mistake, living outside of the city, especially if only one member of the couple will be working and commuting, is a major lifestyle choice. Sure, you can still go to the opera, museums, and Broadway shows; you can still have dim sum in Chinatown or take a walk over the Brooklyn Bridge. But realistically, you'll do it less often and it will take more out of you than if it was right around the corner. So before you decide, lay out your list of pros and cons and figure out what lifestyle suits you and your family best.

Pros of Living in the Suburbs

- More space for your money
- Property, yard for children to play in, a place to plant a garden

- Shopping conveniences like bigger grocery stores, malls, and discount stores
- If you select a neighborhood with a strong school system, you'll be more likely to send your children to public school

Cons of Living in the Suburbs

- Commute time—you will see your family less
- Paying for proximity to something you don't have immediate access to
- You are dependent on your car(s)—you will have to drive everywhere
- You are more likely to live in a sheltered and homogeneous community

WHERE TO LIVE—REGIONS AND NEIGHBORHOODS

Where you decide to live outside of the City is a matter of taste and priorities. The general rule is that the farther away from the City you live, the more house and land you can get for your money. Factor in the communities with the best school systems, the most valued attractions, easy access to train and bus lines. In deciding on each of those factors, you are also adding or subtracting dollars from the price of your house. Because, just like all over the country and the world, you're not just buying a house, you're buying into the community, and that is something that you pay for no matter where you choose to live.

There are many communities, outside of New York City and within the tri-state area from which you can choose to live. They consist primarily of:

Westchester/Rockland (New York)

Long Island (New York)

Northern New Jersey

Southern Connecticut

Long Island includes the North Shore, South Shore, and East End. The North Shore of Long Island, made up of communities like Roslyn and

Great Neck, is the more affluent and desirable area. The South Shore is generally made up of working-class communities, and, while you may find some beautiful homes and get more house for your money, the South Shore is a less desirable area for choices of communities or schools. The East End of Long Island is, for anyone but the most ambitious (or masochistic), too far for easy commuting and is made up of communities like the famous, trendy, and very costly Hamptons.

The state of New Jersey is made up of a multiplicity of communities. There are the nearby urban communities like Hoboken and Jersey City. Unlike many other suburbs of New York City, these communities are made up of young, single, twenty- and thirtysomethings and have burgeoned as towns as a result of their residents' desire for more space and lower rents (and great views of the City). North and west of the George Washington Bridge (GWB) are the so-called bedroom communities, like Teaneck and Fair Lawn, which are as close as some commutes from within the City (and for which you will pay dearly as a result). The far-reaching suburbs, like Parsippany and Whippany, which are northwest of the City, are very suburban but no farther away than many commutes from Long Island. And the Northeast Corridor, from (but not including) Newark down to (but not including) Trenton is where you can get, and be surrounded by, a lot of land because the region used to be and still is used for agricultural production. On the New Jersey Transit Northeast Corridor train to Princeton, as you move away from the City, each town in which the train stops is its own community—a community in and around which you'll be likely to get more land than you could in the City. In general, you will get more house for your money in New Jersey than in the other states in the region.

Westchester and Southern Connecticut are the areas where the especially affluent people live. The coastal strip from Larchmont to Westport could be likened to a Gold Coast. A few towns, like New Rochelle and Rye, along with the more affluent neighborhoods, have many of the problems common to urban areas. The west side of the Hudson River in New York, Rockland County, tends to be more working-class. This isn't to say that there aren't millionaires living in Rockland County, like on the South Shore, but Westchester is the more desirable address.

DEMOGRAPHICS OF
THE SUBURBAN AND NEARBY COUNTIES

Following are some basic statistics, just to give you a general overview of the counties that make up the tri-state area suburbs. Within each county, of course, there are many towns, and within each town are neighborhoods. There is in almost every town in America a right side and a wrong side of the tracks. However, for comparison, these demographic profiles can be a good place to start. Most of these data come from the most recent census, combined with regional updates. For specific suburban communities profiled, I've used all available sources, starting with the census but also relying on news sources and discussions with local residents, community officials, and realtors.

Total Population by County

Connecticut	
Fairfield	846,600
New Haven	823,300
Northern New Jersey	
Bergen	847,600
Essex	777,800
Hudson	567,900
Morris	460,400
Passaic	463,600
Sussex	149,700
Union	502,000
Warren	106,300

(continues on next page)

Total Population by County, continued

Central New Jersey	
Hunterdon	127,300
Mercer	343,500
Middlesex	729,600
Monmouth	601,600
Somerset	288,700
Long Island	
Nassau	1,318,800
Suffolk	1,367,300
Mid-Hudson	
Dutchess	71,000
Sullivan	263,600
Orange	336,900
Ulster	169,200
Lower Hudson	
Putnam	91,800
Rockland	280,000
Westchester	891,000

Population by Ethnicity

County	White	Black	Asian	Hispanic
Connecticut				
Fairfield	78.0%	9.6%	2.8%	9.6%
New Haven	80.8%	10.2%	1.8%	7.2%
Northern New Jersey				
Bergen	79.6%	4.6%	8.6%	7.1%
Essex	42.1%	39.8%	3.6%	14.5%
Hudson	42.8%	11.8%	8.4%	37.0%
Morris	86.3%	2.9%	5.2%	5.6%
Passaic	58.7%	12.5%	3.7%	25.0%
Sussex	95.0%	0.9%	1.4%	2.7%
Union	61.8%	18.5%	3.7%	15.9%
Warren	95.0%	1.5%	1.2%	2.3%
Central New Jersey				
Hunterdon	94.3%	2.0%	1.8%	1.9%
Mercer	69.7%	19.0%	4.1%	7.1%
Middlesex	73.4%	7.4%	8.7%	10.5%
Monmouth	82.8%	8.7%	3.7%	4.9%
Somerset	82.9%	6.3%	5.7%	5.0%
Long Island				
Nassau	80.3%	8.6%	4.0%	7.1%
Suffolk	83.5%	6.2%	2.4%	7.9%
Mid-Hudson				
Sullivan	82.1%	8.5%	1.2%	8.2%
Dutchess	84.1%	8.5%	3.0%	4.5%

(continues on next page)

Population by Ethnicity, continued

County	White	Black	Asian	Hispanic
Orange	82.8%	7.1%	1.7%	8.4%
Ulster	88.7%	4.6%	1.8%	5.0%
Lower Hudson				
Putnam	94.5	1.0%	1.3%	3.2%
Rockland	77.2%	9.6%	5.3%	7.9%
Westchester	70.2%	13.6%	4.7%	11.5%

Population by Age

	Under 5	5–14	15–24	25–64	65 & Over	65–74	75 & Over
Connecticut							
Fairfield	7.0%	13.1%	11.4%	54.7%	13.8%	7.6%	6.2%
New Haven	7.2%	13.3%	12.3%	51.8%	15.4%	8.3%	7.1%
Northern New Jersey							
Bergen	6.1%	11.7%	11.2%	55.3%	15.6%	8.9%	6.8%
Essex	7.7%	13.8%	13.5%	52.3%	12.7%	7.1%	5.6%
Hudson	7.4%	12.4%	13.5%	54.0%	12.8%	7.4%	5.4%
Morris	6.7%	13.1%	12.3%	57.0%	10.9%	6.1%	4.8%
Passaic	8.1%	13.5%	13.6%	51.8%	12.9%	7.1%	5.8%
Sussex	8.5%	16.1%	11.2%	54.9%	9.2%	5.0%	4.3%
Union	7.1%	12.4%	11.9%	53.5%	15.2%	8.7%	6.5%
Warren	7.8%	14.2%	11.3%	52.9%	13.7%	7.6%	6.1%

(continues on next page)

Population by Age, continued

	Under 5	5–14	15–24	25–64	65 & Over	65–74	75 & Over
Central New Jersey							
Hunterdon	7.2%	13.9%	11.0%	58.1%	9.7%	5.5%	4.3%
Mercer	7.1%	13.0%	13.9%	52.7%	13.2%	7.6%	5.6%
Middlesex	7.1%	12.2%	14.1%	54.7%	11.9%	7.4%	4.5%
Monmouth	7.3%	14.1%	11.7%	53.8%	13.1%	7.2%	5.9%
Somerset	7.3%	12.3%	10.9%	58.5%	11.1%	6.5%	4.6%
Long Island							
Nassau	6.6%	12.4%	12.2%	54.5%	14.3%	8.8%	5.5%
Suffolk	7.5%	13.9%	13.4%	54.4%	10.9%	6.2%	4.7%
Mid-Hudson							
Sullivan	7.7%	14.2%	11.6%	51.7%	14.8%	8.4%	6.4%
Dutchess	7.5%	13.5%	13.2%	54.2%	11.6%	6.4%	5.2%
Orange	8.9%	15.7%	13.1%	51.7%	10.6%	5.9%	4.7%
Ulster	7.4%	13.2%	12.4%	53.8%	13.2%	7.2%	6.0%
Lower Hudson							
Putnam	8.1%	14.3%	11.8%	56.7%	9.1%	4.9%	4.2%
Rockland	7.7%	14.8%	12.9%	54.4%	10.2%	5.6%	4.6%
Westchester	7.2%	12.1%	11.8%	54.5%	14.4%	7.8%	6.6%

Types of Households

	Owner-Occupied	Rental	Percentage Owned	Percentage Rented
Connecticut				
Fairfield	212,787	88,946	69.7%	29.1%
New Haven	196,597	102,477	65.0%	33.9%
Northern New Jersey				
Bergen	214,983	89,342	70.0%	29.1%
Essex	133,102	141,402	48.1%	51.1%
Hudson	72,781	133,234	34.9%	63.9%
Morris	111,725	35,459	75.2%	23.9%
Passaic	89,310	63,842	57.7%	41.3%
Sussex/Warren	60,673	16,712	77.3%	21.3%
Union	113,979	63,936	63.5%	35.6%
Central New Jersey				
Hunterdon	31,358	6,576	81.8%	17.2%
Mercer	78,922	36,047	68.0%	31.0%
Middlesex	164,538	73,205	68.7%	30.6%
Monmouth	145,587	48,620	73.8%	24.6%
Somerset	69,046	18,910	77.7%	21.3%
Long Island				
Nassau	351,708	76,266	81.4%	17.7%
Suffolk	346,358	74,532	81.6%	17.6%

(continues on next page)

Types of Households, continued

	Owner-Occupied	Rental	Percentage Owned	Percentage Rented
Mid-Hudson				
Delaware/Sullivan	30,340	10,266	72.1%	24.4%
Orange	69,528	29,290	68.7%	28.9%
Ulster	42,984	15,761	71.4%	26.2%
Lower Hudson				
Dutchess/Putnam	87,090	28,541	74.1%	24.3%
Rockland	61,900	21,311	73.6%	25.3%
Westchester	194,013	118,041	61.2%	37.3%

Crimes Reported Annually (per 100,000 People)

Connecticut	
Fairfield	5,130
New Haven	6,337
Northern New Jersey	
Bergen	2,980
Essex	9,294
Hudson	6,485
Morris	2,310
Passaic	5,187
Sussex	1,917
Union	5,181
Warren	1,870

(continues on next page)

Crimes Reported Annually (per 100,000 People), continued

Central New Jersey	
Hunterdon	1,550
Mercer	5,195
Middlesex	3,910
Monmouth	3,534
Somerset	3,055
Long Island	
Nassau	2,950
Suffolk	3,810
Mid-Hudson	
Dutchess	3,017
Sullivan	4,355
Orange	3,199
Ulster	3,198
Lower Hudson	
Putnam	1,740
Rockland	2,865
Westchester	3,856

THINGS TO CONSIDER WHEN CHOOSING A SUBURB

There are many extremely livable communities outside of New York City, and deciding which one is right for you will take into account a number of different things. Do as much research on your own as you can, and also talk to a realtor. A good realtor should be able to answer most of your questions satisfactorily (and you can also test the extent of that person's knowledge by seeing if the answers mesh with what you learned on your own). The rest (like commute and budget), only you can decide.

The most important factors to consider are (1) distance from your prospective community to the City and (2) what mode of transportation you will use to get back and forth. Driving is largely impractical (and expensive) unless you will be traveling at off hours (avoiding 8:00–9:30 coming into the city and 4:15–7:30 leaving) and parking your car in a very convenient garage (upward of $400 per month). If your community is on a train line, there will be a schedule that is commuter-friendly, as long as you are traveling at peak hours. If you expect to work odd or long hours, find out about the train schedule outside of rush hours so that you don't find yourself stuck planning your life around the train (which to some extent, everyone outside of the City must do). If you are commuting from Long Island (on Long Island Rail Road) or New Jersey (New Jersey Transit or the PATH train), your train will come into Penn Station (34th Street and Seventh Avenue). Is that convenient to where you'll be working? How far is your commute from the station to your office? If you live in Connecticut and Westchester County, you'll be coming into Grand Central Station (42nd Street between Lexington and Vanderbilt Avenues) on Metro North trains. Can you walk to your office from there? Or can you take the 4, 5, 6, 7, or S subway to get where you need to go? It's worthwhile to do some research on your commute to determine both the actual commute time from the prospective community and the add-on time from the station to the office. Although you shouldn't buy a house exclusively based on where you are planning to work (because you're likely to switch jobs before you switch houses), arriving into Penn Station versus Grand Central will make a difference in your commute time.

Some areas, like Rockland County, New York, and parts of northwestern New Jersey (like Teaneck and Englewood) aren't serviced by any trains. In these regions, there are commuter buses, which many people prefer over the trains. One of the big benefits of many of the bus lines is that, rather than pulling into Port Authority (New York's bus station), they make stops and drops within the New York City street grid, which gets you closer to your office and removes an extra step of the commute—you don't have to take the subway or city bus to your office.

Choosing the Right Suburb

- What is my budget?
- How far am I willing to commute each day?
- What are my commuting options?
- Is there a train line that accesses my town? How frequent is the service?
- Is there commuter bus? Which buses have routes near my home? Can I walk to the bus stop?
- Where does the bus let me off in relation to my office?
- How are the schools in the community?
- Are there sidewalks?
- Are there children living in the neighborhood?
- Is the neighborhood safe?
- Do I want to live on a large piece of land and be somewhat isolated?
- How far away are the closest conveniences—grocery store, dry cleaner, video rental?

SUBURBAN COMMUNITIES

The following are condensed portraits of a few communities that represent the major suburban regions in all their diversity. This summary cannot, due to the sheer overwhelming number and variety of suburbs, be a comprehensive list—but it is a good starting point to get you thinking about these areas. Once you start narrowing your choices and regions, you'll want to move on to local sources, experts, and brokers.

Westchester/Rockland

Bronxville (Westchester)
Many adults, having grown up in Bronxville, return there with families of their own. Very similar to Riverdale, though a bit more ritzy and

suburban, Bronxville is only 2¹/₂ miles north of the New York City boundary. Renowned for its excellent public schools (100 percent of recent graduating high school seniors headed off to higher education) and ideal physical location, Bronxville is a community where the housing doesn't come cheap. The average price of a single family home is in the $800,000 range. This is an average, and obviously there are condos that cost less and mansions that cost much, much more. The commute is thirty minutes to Midtown via Metro North.

Chappaqua (Westchester)

Chappaqua, located just nine miles north of White Plains, is in the Town of New Castle, which is the fastest growing community in Westchester County. A community that prides itself on its public education system, Chappaqua public schools continuously rate among the nation's best. A country atmosphere prevails even though this community is less than an hour from Manhattan. Real estate prices and property taxes (to pay for those excellent schools) are high. Condo townhouses range from $225,000 to $575,000 and single family homes range from $500,000 to $900,000 and well beyond. Commuting time on Metro North is approximately fifty minutes to Grand Central.

Mamaroneck (Westchester)

Now a peninsula, but previously an island that was connected to the mainland with rocks drawn from the ground during the time when New York's subway system was being dug, Harbor Island Park is the focal point of Mamaroneck. A waterfront town, Mamaroneck boasts diversity in population, restaurants, housing options, and schools. Residential options include rentals, co-ops, condos, and single family homes. Prices range from around $140,000 for a two-bedroom condo to $4 million and beyond at Edgewater Point, but the mean price of a single family home is around $325,000. Children attend schools in one of two districts, depending on where their residence is situated. Both schools have good programs: The Mamaroneck system counts about 90 percent of its graduating high school seniors going on to higher education, and the Rye Neck District counts approximately 85 percent. The commute to Grand Central is forty minutes on Metro North.

The Nyacks (Rockland)

Diversity is the salient feature of the Nyacks, a community made up of Nyack, South Nyack, West Nyack, and Upper Nyack. People from all walks of life live in this area, and the downtown of Nyack is a bustling village that attracts a host of tourists too. Only twentu-five miles from Midtown, many City transplants have chosen Nyack as their home—which might in part explain the variety. Housing options include rentals, which due to the great shortage of available units are priced high, with an average of $1,200 for a one-bedroom apartment. Homes range from $135,000 in Central Nyack to $800,000 and beyond (approximately the price for which actress Rosie O'Donnell purchased a home from a local resident in 1996). Students in all the Nyacks, except for West Nyack, go to school in the Nyack School District. Students in West Nyack go to school in the Clarkstown Central School District. Both systems boast 95 percent of graduating high school seniors carrying on with continuing education. Approximately eighty minutes to Midtown on a combination of the Red and Tan bus line and the subway to Manhattan.

Long Island

Dix Hills (Suffolk County)

A wealthy neighborhood centrally located between the two major east–west thoroughfares on Long Island (the Long Island Expressway, or LIE, and Northern State Parkway), Dix Hills is highly regarded for its excellent schools, especially those in the Half Hollow Hills Schools District. Once a shrinking community with an aging population, Dix Hills is now home to many young families and has a strong emphasis on community. Real estate is expensive; many homes sit on lots of one acre or more because of local zoning, which in some areas requires lots to be one acre or larger.

Garden City (Nassau County)

From its inception in 1869, Garden City has been one of the most sought-after addresses in Nassau County. Boasting an excellent school district and easy access to Long Island Rail Road (LIRR) train service, this town continues to be a community in which people aspire to live.

Homes range from $350,000 to $3.5 million (and up). Garden City is forty-five minutes from Penn Station on the LIRR.

Glen Cove (Nassau County)
One of the great elements about this community is its ethnic diversity. A melting pot unto itself, Glen Cove welcomed immigrants arriving from Europe starting in the 1860s and now arriving from Puerto Rico, Africa, and elsewhere. One of only two actual cities on Long Island, Glen Cove has affordable homes; they range from the mid-$160,000s to mid-$300,000s but also range up to the multimillions for some of the older estates. The schools are solid, and nearly 60 percent of students continue on to four-year colleges. Glen Cove offers views of Long Island Sound and Hempstead Harbor, three public beaches, and an easy one hour commute to the City on LIRR.

Great Neck Estates (Nassau County)
Once home to F. Scott Fitzgerald and his wife Zelda, Great Neck Estates is an affluent community that has a very highly regarded school system (often sending 95 percent or more of its high school graduates on to higher education) and well-regulated appearance (no tree may be cut down without a permit). Homes range from the high $300,000s to well into the millions.

Oyster Bay (Nassau County)
Public slips at the marina (for town residents only) are only one example of what sets Oyster Bay apart from its neighbors. Somewhat off the beaten path of traffic, this town is a real community, and its downtown, with mom-and-pop businesses like the local hardware store and cafés, drives that point home. By LIRR alone, this commute can be lengthy, but by driving to the Syosset station ten minutes away the train ride is thirty minutes shorter and the trains are more frequent. Co-ops begin at around $110,000, condos around $300,000, and homes range from low $300,000s to $900,000 and well beyond.

West Islip (Suffolk County)

It's not unusual for second-generation West Islipers to settle in the community with their own families, because this town is a real community. A bit far from the city for those keeping long hours in the office, West Islip schools are good (boasting 90 percent and upward of graduating high school students continuing on to some form of higher education), the property is varied, and the people are friendly. Condos range from $150,000s to $250,000s and homes range from mid-$100,000s for a cottage to $400,000 for a house with a dock on a canal to well over $1 million for a larger estate.

Northern New Jersey

Hoboken and Jersey City

These two satellite cities (which would be considered a major urban axis in any other region of the country) are collectively known as "the sixth borough," and for good reason. Like Brooklyn Heights to the east, Hoboken and Jersey City have recently emerged as extremely desirable residential options for New Yorkers (that's right; though they live in New Jersey, many residents of these cities consider themselves New Yorkers—and for all intents and purposes they are). Rents are lower than in the City, but you're right across the river—closer than you'd be in most of the boroughs. Superb and efficient public transportation via PATH train (the New Jersey Transit equivalent of the New York City subways, with Manhattan stations at the World Trade Center and Penn Station) gets you into the City in ten minutes, and there are also extensive bus and ferry options. Directly across from the World Trade Center and Downtown Manhattan, Jersey City and Hoboken offer superior commutes for those who work in the Financial District. Housing is diverse, ranging from large, new apartment complexes with New York skyline views to apartments in subdivided former private homes—and there are still some large loft spaces available. Continued waterfront development promises that these areas will continue to improve. Despite easy access to Manhattan, however, Jersey City and especially Hoboken have developed thriving restaurant and entertainment industries of their own. The local newspapers, the *Hoboken Reporter* and the *Jersey Journal*, are the best sources for housing advertisements.

Fort Lee (Bergen County)
Only six miles to Midtown, the town of Fort Lee is as centrally located outside of the city as you can get. Sitting in the shadow of the picturesque George Washington Bridge (GWB), Fort Lee offers residents options from co-ops and condos to single family homes. Most of the town's residents are without children (mainly because the children have grown up and the parents have relocated to Fort Lee for the convenience), as is indicated by the less than 10 percent of the population in the school system. The smallest co-ops range from $25,000 up to $700,000 for large three-bedrooms. Single family homes can be had for around $180,000 at the low end and escalate to $400,000 or $500,000 depending on the area and the work that needs to be done. New condo communities are also available, with units ranging from $250,000 to upward of $850,000. The commute to Midtown is thirty minutes via New Jersey Transit bus.

Morristown (Morris County)
Whereas less than ten years ago Morristown had vacant stores and a shrinking downtown, now the town that is historically known as Washington's headquarters (twice) during the Revolutionary War is a booming example of an astonishing rebound. With a strong public school program (more than 85 percent of graduating high school seniors continue on to higher education) and Fortune 500 companies in Morris County, the community is diversified with as many as 50 percent of residents renting and the rest owning their homes. Rents range from $700 to $1,850 and homes cost from approximately $150,000 to $850,000.

Mountainside (Union County)
A true suburban community, but without the strip malls, Mountainside is a peaceful, family town that is on the rise. Here you will find no apartments for rent, no condos or co-ops. The preponderance of the homes in Mountainside are single family homes, and

most of those that are now going on the market (just shy of 40 percent) are being sold off by the large percentage of residents who are over sixty-five. With vast parkland, a community pool in the summertime, free concerts, and boating on Echo Lake, it's no wonder that the vast majority of people moving into the community are young couples in their late twenties to early forties with children in tow or on the way. The public schools are highly desirable, with 95 percent of all high school graduates attending institutions of higher education. Homes range in price from $300,000 to $800,000 (and up) but expect to find most somewhere in the middle. About an hour by commuter bus to Midtown.

Scotch Plains (Union County)

There is a real feeling of community in this town, originally settled in 1684 by Scottish immigrants, and it is evidenced by the small but thriving downtown, the influx of new young residents, and the increase in property values. Unlike much of New Jersey, it is possible to find homes here that are more than thirty years old, such as pre-war colonials and Cape-style homes, but they tend to be in high demand. Homes range in price from a modest $175,000 to $1 million and beyond, though there are plenty in the middle. Schools are solid, with 90 percent of graduating high school seniors going on to higher education.

Southern Connecticut

North Stamford (Fairfield County)

Slightly removed from the hustle and bustle of Stamford proper, North Stamford is its antithesis, being completely un-zoned for businesses. Previously a summer retreat for worn-out New Yorkers, North Stamford is now a community unto itself with a highly regarded public school system (over 85 percent of graduating high school seniors go on to higher education), as well as a preparatory school, parochial school, and other education options. A blend of old and new homes, North Stamford property does not come cheap, and homes on one- to three-acre plots range from $400,000 to $600,000 and climb well into the multimillions. Approximately 65 minutes from Grand Central via Metro North.

Greenwich (Fairfield County)

Long known as a very white, very exclusive area, Greenwich has slowly been changing to a more accepting, tolerant community. The highly regarded public school system (close to 90 percent of graduating high school seniors go on to higher education) offers not only the usual cadre of classes in foreign languages and the sciences, but also team sports including fencing, rugby, and water polo. There are also nine private schools in the community in the event that the public schools don't fit the bill. Beaches, ice skating, golf courses, and playing fields are among the facilities that are open to members of the community. Though rare, houses can be found for approximately $300,000 (a real fixer-upper), but you're more likely to find homes ranging from $500,000 or $600,000 to $7 or $8 million. Approximately one hour via Metro North.

Rowayton (Fairfield County)

This traditional New England community, once home to farmers and oystermen, maintains the atmosphere of a village despite its proximity to Norwalk. The small town offers strong schools (with almost 85 percent of graduating high school seniors going on to higher education), which are very diverse and border on artsy, and a strong community spirit. Homes range from $500,000 well up into the millions for the large waterfront estates. Approximately seventy minutes commute via Metro North.

Outside the Area

If your career has forced a move to the New York area but you absolutely, positively can't abide by the urban or hard-core suburban lifestyle, you still have some options within a relatively doable commute to the City. Likewise, special circumstances may force you to commute from farther than you might choose in the best of all possible worlds.

I've known people who commuted to Manhattan from as far north as Vermont, as far south as Virginia, and as far west as Pittsburgh. For example, my husband worked for an attorney whose wife got an important political appointment in Washington, D.C., so this attorney and his wife moved to one of the D.C. suburbs, near the airport. He flew to work in New York City every day for four years (it's only an hour-long flight). I also know a professor who commutes between New York and Vermont. I met an economic consultant a while back who lives on a farm in western Pennsylvania and flies to New York for three days every week (he keeps a small apartment here too). Where there's a will there's a way, and with modern transportation and enough money you can work in New York and live just about anywhere in the Northeastern or Middle Atlantic states.

But most people who choose to live outside the Greater New York Metropolitan Area won't commute so far. The following are brief sketches of the most convenient (relatively speaking) areas outside the traditional urban and suburban corridor. As with the suburbs (even more so here), we'll rely on representative examples to characterize each region. For basic demographic information about these regions, by county, see the demographic profiles in "The Suburbs."

UPSTATE NEW YORK

Stretching north and west from Westchester and Rockland is the vast expanse of New York State, one of the largest in America. Once you leave the urban, southern portion of New York, you're in an area that looks a lot more like New England than like New York City. For example, in Dutchess County, just a couple of hours easy drive from Manhattan on the Taconic Parkway, are the rural towns of Red Hook and Rhinebeck, where farming is still a way of life. Red Hook and Rhinebeck are approximately forty-five minutes north of Poughkeepsie (home of Vassar College), and they offer small-town country living within reasonable grasp of the Big City. This region of Upstate New York is becoming somewhat popular as a weekend and summer destination for Manhattanites, and a few have fallen in love with the area and taken up year-round residence. Noteworthy in Rhinebeck is the Omega Institute, a meditation center on a large parcel of land. Nearby Bard College is a small school especially known for liberal arts and artistic studies. Public schools in these communities are very respectable and offer honors classes for children who are gifted in particular subject areas. Homes can be had for $125,000 up to $600,000, but many homes with large parcels of land can be bought for $200,000 to $300,000. Rhinecliff, approximately a ten- to fifteen-minute drive from Rhinebeck and Red Hook, has train service that takes two hours into Midtown.

CENTRAL AND SOUTHERN NEW JERSEY

As you head south past the major commuter suburbs of New Jersey, you come to Princeton. It doesn't get much more collegiate than this, and the Ivy League town lives up to the Ivy League school's reputation. The thriving downtown area of Princeton, anchored by the university, epitomizes a healthy cross between quaintness and the *Preppy Handbook*. Public schools here are likened to prep schools in other communities, and though just under 90 percent of graduating high school seniors went on to higher education, class averages of SAT scores regularly are nearly 175 points above the national average. To further that point, at least 70 percent of teachers at Princeton (public) High School hold advanced degrees. Homes on the lower end start at around $200,000 and range to $2.5 million or more for estates and mansions on the upper end. Expect to pay in the neighborhood of $300,000 to $600,000 for a single family home. On New Jersey transit, the commute is approximately seventy-five minutes, but if time is of the utmost importance to you, you can jump the Amtrak train to Penn Station (it'll cost you) and shave about thirty minutes off your time.

Beyond Princeton and Trenton is the large mass of coastal land that constitutes Southern New Jersey and the Jersey Shore. Atlantic City is the most notorious town in this area, but all along the shore (and inland) sit interesting towns with a lot of history.

WESTERN AND UPSTATE CONNECTICUT

Those who don't like the Westchester-like atmosphere of the Southern Connecticut suburbs might do well to explore an area like Litchfield County. The picture of New England tranquility and small-town quaintness is what you'll find in this region that is approximately $2^{1}/_{4}$ to $2^{1}/_{2}$ hours from New York City. Towns like Washington, Washington Depot, Litchfield, and Bethlehem are among the upstate towns that typify the area. Old homes and farms dating back to the turn of the century (and before) dot the area, and each town's central downtown is a only a block or two long, with upscale boutiques, perhaps an ice cream parlor, and a handful of restaurants at most. For grocery shopping and shopping malls, you'll have to travel, because these towns guard their community images like a dog guarding sheep. The schools in the area are solid, and there are also many prestigious boarding schools nearby such as the Canterbury School and Hotchkiss, where many children from Manhattan attend on reaching high school age. There is a great range in property costs and, though a small single family home might be had for $250,000 outside of town on a small piece of land, at the other end of the spectrum the great estates and Victorian mansions go for $1 million or more. There is no train service in Litchfield County, and though you could drive thirty or more minutes to the New Milford train depot, the most efficient way to get to New York City from this area is by car. The drive, depending on your point of departure, will range from $2^{1}/4$ to $2^{1}/2$ hours.

THE EAST END OF LONG ISLAND

Long a favorite weekend and summer resort for the beautiful people of Manhattan, the Hamptons, which lie on the South Fork of eastern Long Island, have exploded in popularity in the past decade. This commute isn't for the faint of heart—the drive takes you through all the worst areas of Long Island and Queens traffic congestion (unless you can afford to commute by helicopter)—but there are those who do it. They suffer the indignity of the commute in order to live in what is one of America's most beautiful coastal regions—it is evocative of Brittany and Normandy, with better weather, and there are numerous vineyards in the area (mostly on the nearby North Fork). Plus, because of all the affluent Manhattanites in the area, the dining and nightlife in the Hamptons is simply fabulous (you can't talk about the Hamptons without using the word *fabulous* at least once!). The North Fork is less settled, but is now gaining some popularity as Hamptons prices become more and more prohibitive. Train and bus service is available, but it's slow.

CHAPTER 2

Advice on Finding an Apartment

N ew York is one of the few cities in the world where it is common and accepted practice that people rent for life. Thus, over the years, renting in New York City has evolved, both culturally and legally, into a form of quasi-ownership wherein the apartment you rent can truly be called a home (though now, with the housing market as it is—very tight for renters, very brisk for buyers and sellers—more and more people, including young singles, are buying). And a renter can truly enjoy an excellent lifestyle by renting for an extended period of time. I've been living in the same rental apartment for the past nine years and I have no plans of moving—ever. Moreover, unlike most towns, the quality of housing available to renters and buyers in New York City is essentially the same (except that, once you get into apartments of three bedrooms and larger, purchase becomes the more realistic option).

Renting allows the occupant more freedom than does buying. If you want to move, you can. If you want to save your money for something other than a mortgage, you can. Renting is also, owing to standardized leases and high volume, a very quick and relatively simple process in New York City. When you see the apartment of your dreams, you put your money down (immediately), process the necessary paperwork, and move in—perhaps just a couple of days later. There's no mortgage to secure, no attorneys to hire, and no closing dates to set, postpone, and postpone again.

In most towns, the word *rent* is synonymous with the word *apartment*, and the concept of *ownership* is synonymous with *house*. You rent an apartment; you buy a house. But in New York, for all intents and purposes, *there are no houses*. Other than a very small handful of luxury townhouse dwellings (which are only of concern to the super-rich), every single person in Manhattan lives in a multiple-dwelling apartment building. So, whether you buy or rent in New York City, you're going to be living in an apartment.

When you rent an apartment in New York, it's called "a rental" or just "an apartment." When you buy, it's called "a condo" or "a co-op" (see chapter 3 for more details on condos and co-ops), but it's still an apartment. You can get a rental in a brownstone or buy a condo or co-op in a brownstone. You can rent in a high-rise or buy in a high-rise. The physical options are mostly the same, although they vary from building to building. Some buildings only have rentals and others only have purchase options, but throughout any neighborhood—and even mixed within some buildings—you will have the option to rent or buy an apartment.

Even the services in rental apartment buildings rival those of nice co-ops and condos (dry cleaning pickup and delivery, newspaper

CITY FACT

You'd think everybody would want to have celebrity neighbors, but movie stars, rock stars, and other household names are often rejected by co-op boards and therefore can't purchase apartments in the buildings where they want to live. Many co-ops want to remain exclusive, low-key, and unencumbered by the host of problems (reporters and photographers lingering about, for starters) that celebrities attract.

delivery to your apartment door, rooftop sun deck, common storage areas, laundry rooms—yes, you can have all those things in a New York City apartment building). Still, when you get into the category of the super-large and super-luxurious (apartments valued in excess of $2 million), it becomes more and more likely that the apartments you're looking at will be for sale only. And the more you spend—and the higher up the food chain you move in purchase price—the more exclusive the buildings become. The apartments get larger, there are fewer apartments per building, and there are more extensive services (squash courts, elevator operators). In this city that never sleeps and has everything to offer at the snap of a finger, often it is those extra services (and the corresponding deep pockets of the occupants) that distinguish you from the multimillionaire in the building next door. As a renter, you can still live in the neighborhood, but perhaps not in the building.

If at all possible, newcomers to the City should start with rentals. The commitment of purchasing is just too extreme for the uninitiated. Unless you're especially familiar with the neighborhoods and the culture of New York City, you're taking a rather large risk in buying an apartment in a neighborhood that you don't know and may not like. You can rent for just a year (or less), but buying is a long-term decision. The transaction costs alone (in terms of bank financing and legal fees) make it prohibitive to move any time soon—and there's always the risk of a drop in the market imprisoning you in a particular home. Even if you have kids and you've selected a specific neighborhood based on the public schools, you can nonetheless rent in that neighborhood and your kids will attend the same schools. One exception to this rule would be if you have pets, in which case rental buildings can be more restrictive than co-ops and condos (although this is not always the case—you have to ask either way). Otherwise, I'd advise you to get to know the city first and, possibly, buy later.

When New Yorkers hunt for apartments, they generally select an apartment based the following factors:

- Space or size
- Cost
- Neighborhood
- Safety

- Conveniences
- Location (proximity to work or schools)

Different people will have different priorities, but the most common balance to strike is among cost, size, and neighborhood. The consid-erations of safety, location, and conveniences tend to be sec-ondary. It sounds harsh to say so, but most New Yorkers are willing to live on a slightly less secure block in exchange for a superior apartment—that is, provided we're still in the realm of rela-tively acceptable safety (which should be the case in any major Manhattan residential neighbor-hood). Some people prioritize differently, but usually space, money, and neighborhood are at the top of the list.

The neighborhood guides in chapter 1 give indications of housing costs by neighborhood, but one thing you might have noticed is that, within the more popular residential areas of Manhattan (the places most readers of this book will be set-tling), the variation isn't all that great. Thus, for convenience, and to help get you thinking, here's a rough guide to what you can expect to pay in monthly rent for an apartment in a quality, doorman building in Upper Manhattan (north of 23rd Street, for the purposes of the real estate market):

MOVING TIP

"Many theaters sell Standing Room Only tickets, which means exactly that: You get to see the show for much, much less money—but you have to stand in the back of the theater. After the first inter-mission, though, at all but the hottest, newest, most popular shows, you should be able to find a place to sit where some-one else decided to leave or didn't show up in the first place."

—Karen Marcus, account manager

- Studios: $1,200–$1,500
- 1-bedroom: $1,700–$2,200
- 2-bedrooms: $2,700–$3,500

This is what you should expect to pay in Lower Manhattan (south of 23rd Street):

- Studios: $1,200–$1,800
- 1-bedroom: $1,500–$2,000
- 2-bedrooms: $2,600–$4,000

There are, of course, apartments available that are both below and above the prices indicated. Brownstones, walk-ups, and non-doorman buildings, for example, would have lower rental prices. However, these prices are a good guideline to get you started.

RENTING VERSUS BUYING

Pros of Renting

- Get to know the city before you buy
- Better apartment options if you can't afford to buy
- More freedom—not tied down to your apartment
- More financial freedom
- Better for temporary residence
- More money going into your pocket every month
- Good option for young people
- Less restrictive—condo and co-op buildings have lots of rules
- It's quicker and easier to rent

Cons of Renting

- Rent money goes to landlord, not toward the purchase of your home
- No tax benefits
- Most of the nicest and most exclusive apartments are condos and co-ops
- More and better services in high-end condo and co-op buildings
- A finite number of large (three bedrooms and bigger) apartments for rent
- Limits on renovations—you're making improvements on someone else's property
- More restrictive on pets

RENTAL JARGON

You don't have to be in New York long before you start hearing the phrases "rent controlled" and "rent stabilized" being tossed around. In fact, it is a favorite joke of New Yorkers that there are only three topics of conversation at New York cocktail parties: (1) Co-ops versus condos; (2) someone who knows someone who has a rent-controlled apartment ("Can you believe what they're paying? And wouldn't you just kill for a closet at that price!"); and, in true Woody Allen fashion, (3) who's seeing which therapist. A slight exaggeration (*slight*), but housing is such an important factor in every New Yorker's life that we've all caught ourselves (natives and transplants alike) saying these sorts of things—or at least thinking them.

While it's important to understand these terms, it's also important not to obsess about them. Wherever you rent in New York City, the laws are extremely favorable to tenants. It's just that some sets of laws are more favorable than others.

Rent Stabilization

Rent Stabilization is a body of regulations that apply to any rental building with multiple apartments built between February 1947 and January 1974. The Rent Stabilization guidelines limit the percentage that a landlord can raise the rent with each lease renewal. The percentage varies from year to year and is decided by the Rent Guidelines Board. The increase is put into effect by landlords each year in October. The landlord is also entitled to increase the rent a certain percentage when a tenant vacates an apartment and when renovations and improvements are made. Tenants in rent-stabilized apartments must be offered either a one- or two-year lease and have an automatic right to renew their leases indefinitely.

An apartment is legally allowed to be de-stabilized (removed from the Rent Stabilization Guidelines) when it is vacated and reaches a rent of $2,000. With the annual increases on the lease, the allowable renovation increase, and the vacant apartment increases, many landlords are able to reach the $2,000 rent limit, and these apartments are de-stabilized forever.

Most rental apartments built after January 1974, and all rental apartments in co-op and condo buildings and buildings with five or fewer apartments, are exempt from the rent-stabilization laws.

If you're lucky enough to find a rent-stabilized apartment, grab it. I've heard many a sad tale of newcomers to New York who lost great apartments because they didn't comprehend the absurd urgency with which a renter must put money down in order to secure an apartment (especially now, in this market, where prices have been steadily climbing since 1995 and "deals" are becoming scarcer and scarcer). Of course, all of these people eventually found other apartments and, as fully indoctrinated New Yorkers, will never allow themselves to lose an apartment again.

Rent Control

This much-misused term (people often say "Rent Control" when they really mean "Rent Stabilization") has a very specific legal meaning. Rent Control was started during the early 1940s World War II era when there was a great housing shortage in the city and landlords were raising rents to extreme highs and, at least in some cases, throwing tenants out on the street with little notice. The Rent Control laws were developed to protect tenants from unscrupulous landlords; the rent-controlled apartments that remain are a holdover from residents who have been living in the same apartment since before July 1, 1971. That means rent control applies to many older residents in New York City, but probably not to you.

MOVING TIP

"When you move into a new neighborhood, spend a couple of hours with a pad and pen systematically exploring every street and avenue within reasonable proximity of your home. Walk into all the shops and restaurants, even if they don't immediately strike your fancy. You're certain to find some unusual things on the side streets that you wouldn't have otherwise discovered on your daily walk to the bus or subway, like a small specialty bookstore or an interesting bar or a favorite butcher."

—Andrew Shafran, garment industry executive

If and when these apartments become available (usually because the tenant dies), they are renovated (many haven't been renovated for decades because of the low rent and lack of profits to the landlord), and rents are raised to fair market value—often an increase of many hundreds of dollars, and even thousands if the neighborhood has become very popular (like the Upper West Side, the Village, or Chelsea).

Family members often add themselves to rent-controlled leases so that they can take over the apartment if the opportunity should arise, although theoretically they're supposed to have lived in the apartment all along. If there is no family member to take over the apartment (a terrible tragedy for renters the city over—and every landlord's dream), rent-controlled apartments are switched over to rent-stabilized apartments and the rent is raised to fair market value.

If, somehow, you should find yourself with the opportunity to latch onto one of these rare gems, call me first. But if you must have it for yourself, don't hesitate for a moment. If someone offers you a sublease on one of these apartments, don't wait for even one breath, or the opportunity will be lost. But realistically, you'll probably be like the rest of us. Aim to get a decent deal on a decent space and don't hold your breath for winning the renter's lottery.

For additional information on tenant rights, pick up a copy of *What Every Landlord and Tenant Should Know*, published by the Citizens Housing and Planning Council. The publication details the

CITY FACT

Snug Harbor, opened in 1833 on Staten Island as a home to retired sailors, now functions as a cultural center for the community. Sitting on eighty-three acres of land (some of it waterfront), and protected by the New York City Landmark Preservation Commission, Snug Harbor offers classes, year-round concerts, readings, dance and stage performances.

rights of both landlords and tenants and can be had for $5 from the city council, which is located at:

50 East 42nd Street, Suite 407
New York, NY 10017
(212) 286-9211

APARTMENT JARGON

You're probably familiar with the meaning of the terms "one-bedroom" and "two-bedroom" with reference to apartments—they're self-explanatory. The following are some other key terms you'll hear bandied about in reference to New York City apartments.

- *Studio:* A studio is an apartment that has a combined living and sleeping area. Generally it is one room with a small kitchen in a corner or in a little nook, and the rest of the space is used for living and sleeping (some people have a futon couch that they convert into a bed for sleeping).

- *Alcove Studio:* An alcove studio is a modified version of a studio apartment. Off of the studio it generally has a "room" (the so-called alcove), which can be used for sleeping but will not have a proper door or doorway (otherwise it would be billed as a one-bedroom).

- *Loft:* A loft is a former commercial or industrial building that has been converted into apartments. Generally, these are large open spaces with high ceilings. They are usually found in Greenwich Village, SoHo, TriBeCa, Chelsea, Flatiron, and lower Manhattan and often do not have the services of a doorman. Beware, though, that the term *loft* now has a certain cachet and some unscrupulous brokers and landlords are advertising any large studio apartment as a "loft."

BUILDING JARGON

These are the most common terms used in describing New York City buildings:

- *Walk-up:* A building—often a brownstone or a townhouse—that has no elevator.

- *Brownstone* or *Townhouse:* Previously one-family homes (often "country" homes—before the turn of the century and into the early 1900s—for rich families living downtown) with four or five stories, many brownstones and townhouses are now multiple-unit apartment buildings (many have ten studio or one-bedroom units). The units can be extremely small but also extremely charming with original moldings from the time of construction (from the 1800s through the early 1900s). These buildings will not have a doorman and most likely no elevator.
- *Prewar* and *Postwar:* Buildings built before and after (1940s–1970s) World War II.

THINGS TO ASK AND CONSIDER WHILE LOOKING

Choosing an apartment is a personal decision. Sometimes the decision will be an easy one based on only one thing: the answer to the question, "Can I afford this apartment or can't I?" Most New Yorkers spend one-fourth (or more) of their salary on rent each year. But even at the most basic level, there are still issues to consider and questions to ask when looking for a rental apartment.

First, figure out how much money you can afford to spend on your monthly rent. That will help you determine everything else. Figure out an exact dollar amount. Knowing this will prevent you from wasting your time looking at apartments you can't afford—and you'll avoid the inevitable feeling sorry for yourself when you see an apartment you love that doesn't fit within your budget. This simple (and necessary) exercise will help you narrow down the field and rule out certain options.

Second, decide where you want to live and see if your allotted rent will realistically enable you to live in that neighborhood. For example, if you have $800 to spend and you want to live alone, you'll be hard-pressed to find an apartment on the Upper West Side for that money. But, if you want to live with a roommate (or you're willing to make that compromise in order to get a better apartment in the neighborhood you really want), with the combined rent allowances for each roommate you'll be much more likely to get what you're after for the same outlay of cash.

Third, what is the nearest public transportation? Most every New Yorker commutes to work on the subway, by bus, or on foot. Is it convenient to your office? This is a very important factor because when you compute your commute, you have to account for the walking time back and forth to the bus or subway stop.

Fourth, is the apartment that you're looking at on the fourth floor of a brownstone? That means you have to walk up and down those stairs every day with your groceries, when the deliveryman comes with takeout food, to get the newspaper on Sunday morning. How much do you value your creature comforts and are you willing to trade the strain of the walk-up for the nicer apartment or the better location?

Fifth, how important is it to you have a doorman in the building? Doorman buildings are safer because there is always someone there at the door, admitting people to the building and making sure that people who don't have a reason to be there don't get in. That doorman will also receive your packages for you when you're at work or away on vacation. He'll receive your dry cleaning when it's dropped off. If the mailman has a package and you're not home and you don't have a doorman, you have to make arrangements to pick it up at a time when the post office is open and you're not at work—easier said than done when you factor in commuting time. Then again, perhaps your non-doorman building will have a superintendent who lives on the ground floor and can receive your packages for you. Be sure to ask. Or, maybe you're willing to pick up your dry cleaning yourself and have all of your packages sent to you at the office. You'll have to carry them home, but then you don't have to worry about a doorman. Unless you have an infinite amount of

MOVING TIP

"Being part of a studio audience while a TV show is being taped is a real blast—and it's free! You can plan in advance and send in a postcard requesting tickets for a specific date, or, if spontaneity is more your speed, you can line up for stand-by seats. *The David Letterman Show* tops my list."

—Pablo Vasquez, building superintendent

money, most things about renting (and buying) an apartment are tradeoffs. And only you can decide which things rank high and which ones don't even hit the radar screen.

Sixth, do you have children? There are numerous factors to consider with children: The size of the apartment (especially if you're moving from a house), safety of the neighborhood, nearby public and private schools, and open spaces to run and play such as parks and playgrounds.

These are all issues that will come up when you're looking for your new apartment; you have to know what you value, what is important to you, and what your top priorities are. Each of these issues will rank higher or lower to different people, and some people will be willing to pay a lot of money to have them, whereas others don't care if they have them at all. I like to be close to Central Park so I can run and go for walks. Friends with dogs feel the same. Other friends, who live Downtown, could care less if they're near Central Park or any other park (or at least that's what they say). To them, being near their child's school is most important. Or, for some, being close to the greenmarket so they can buy fresh produce each week ranks high.

Following is a checklist of some important questions to ask yourself and your landlord when you're considering an apartment:

- What can I afford? Figure out a dollar amount.
- Is this the neighborhood in which I want to live?
- Do I want to live alone or with a roommate?
- Is there an elevator in the building? Is this important to me?
- Is there a doorman? Is this important to me? Who will receive my packages when I'm at work?
- Am I allowed to have a pet? A cat? A dog?
- What schools are nearby? What public school district am I in? Are there any private schools nearby?
- Is the apartment big enough to have a roommate if I want one or later decide I need one?
- What is the nearest public transportation? Is it convenient to where I'll be commuting each day—to work or school?
- Are there any services available in the building? Dry cleaning? Health club?

- What are the nearby attractions? Is there a park? A playground?
- What is available in the neighborhood? Lots of restaurants? A grocery store? A bank?
- Is the neighborhood safe?
- Who lives in the neighborhood?
- "Is there anything I should know?" A good catch-all question. You never know what they'll say when you ask this one.

BEFORE YOU RENT: TAKE STEPS AND BE PREPARED

To rent an apartment in New York, there are many steps you'll have to take before you can actually sign the lease. It helps to be prepared, so that when the right apartment comes along, you'll be ready to sign on the spot.

Before you look, you'll need:

- *A Local Bank Account:* Open one as soon as possible. You'll need to have a local bank account in order to get a certified check that will cover the cost of your rental. Landlords won't accept out-of-state checks or, for at least the first month and safety deposit, personal checks either.

- *A Certified Check:* If you can't arrange to open a local account before you begin looking for an apartment, bring enough money in *traveler's checks* (to cash at the bank for a certified check) to cover the first month's rent

CITY FACT

The New York City public schools consistently turn out the most Intel Science Talent Search (called the Westinghouse awards until 1998) semi-finalists in the region.

and the security deposit of one month's rent, plus a little extra for incidentals (the cost of the bank check, perhaps a slightly higher rent than originally planned, the cost of the broker's fee—count on 10–15 percent of your first year's rent if you are planning on using a broker). You can also use one of the check-cashing kiosks, located all over the city, to get a money order, but they'll charge you a fee.

- *A Credit Report*: Your landlord will require a credit report (which may cost you $25–$50) before renting to you.

Next is a checklist of necessary items and information that you must bring along when viewing apartments, before a landlord will even consider renting (and a broker will consider showing) anything to you:

- Official personal identification with photograph—like a passport (and preferably another piece of ID as well)
- A letter of employment, including your salary and start date
- A listing of *all* bank accounts and credit card numbers (list everything)
- A listing of personal and business references, including contact information
- A listing of previous landlords, including contact information
- Tax returns
- Pay stubs
- Any other sources of income with verification

Above and Beyond the Rent

Landlords in New York are a tough bunch, in part because local rental laws are skewed favorably to the renters (it's a democratic city through and through)—ask any local landlord and they'll have plenty of war stories to tell, but that's a whole other story. So, in order to protect themselves from a difficult tenant that they won't be able to evict later, landlords want to check you out while they can, because it may be their last chance before you settle in for life. That's why the following, seemingly unreasonable requirements are essential to most landlords (though some are stricter still and others are slightly more flexible).

- You must earn annually forty to fifty times the amount of the monthly rent. That is to say, your rent will not be more than about a quarter of your salary (which is really more like a third to a half when you factor in taxes).

• If your salary does not make the cut, you will need a co-signer, or guarantor, to guarantee the lease. The best person to ask for this huge favor is a family member, preferably someone who lives in town or at least in the tri-state area (New York, New Jersey, or Connecticut), owns property there, and has a large enough income to satisfy the landlord. Your guarantor will have to provide a lot of financial paperwork and documentation in order to satisfy your landlord, so prepare yourself, and them, psychologically before you begin the process.

CITY FACT

The Edgar Allen Poe Cottage in the Bronx is where, from 1846 to 1849, the poet and his wife resided while he was writing. The cottage is open for tours, and among the items on display are period furniture and changing exhibits.

TO HUNT ALONE OR WITH A BROKER?

Looking for a new apartment is an exciting event. It can also be overwhelming and frustrating. But, armed with the necessary information, finding your first apartment in New York can be a snap.

You must decide whether you want to look with a broker or on your own. Obviously there are pros and cons to both methods and you may decide one thing and, somewhere along the way, change to the other.

Using a broker can be a great asset because, if you get a good one, he or she can save you a lot of time (by showing you only apartments in your price range, only apartments that are known to be respectable and not already rented, and so on). The broker might have exclusives—apartments that no one else is showing—that you couldn't get on your own. The broker will be able to tell you all about the neighborhood and the buildings within the area and help you find an apartment that's a good fit. Your broker will know the history of the buildings that you are viewing: Who is the landlord? Is the landlord responsible and reliable? Is there a lot of noise in the building? Street noise? Is it a good building? Have there been problems here in the past?

A broker who finds you an apartment where you feel happy, safe, and satisfied is well worth the commission—but what about all of the others (and there are *plenty* of others)?

One of the most important things to recognize about looking for an apartment with a broker is that, if and when they find you your new residence, you must pay a hefty commission of one month's rent—minimum (many require 10–15 percent of your first year's rent). Furthermore, the brokers who have these jobs (especially on the lower-priced rentals) tend to be from the bottom of the real estate barrel for one reason or another—either they're new in the business or they're perhaps on the slippery side. So you need to know exactly what you're looking for and make sure you get it (but be realistic, you're not going to get a three-bedroom apartment on Fifth Avenue for $1,000 a month). Set forth clear specifications so the broker doesn't waste your time and you don't find yourself looking at apartments that are in the wrong neighborhood, outside your price range, too big or too small. Don't worry about hurting the broker's feelings, either—I assure you, the broker doesn't much care about yours. It never ceases to amaze me how many broker-related horror stories I hear that could have been prevented if my friends had cared more about themselves than about a broker's feelings.

Brokering is a high-volume business (especially with the lower-rent apartments). That means that your broker will have a limited amount of time to show you each apartment before having to run off to the next appointment. For the same reason, many brokers handle only one neighborhood (so that they can shoot around from one building to another showing apartments to prospective renters all day long); if that neighborhood falls off your list, you might need to find another broker to work with who specializes in your neighborhood of choice.

Most important, *do not let a broker push you into an apartment you don't want.* Do not be afraid to speak up. If you don't like the person with whom you're working, ask for someone else. And do not take what your broker says as the gospel. Some brokers may have hidden agendas, like getting a kickback from a landlord when placing a tenant into one of that landlord's buildings, or a bonus for renting a certain number of apartments in a particular building that year. The more informed you are, the better off and more protected you will be.

Which leads us to the next point—if you're willing to do the research, you can do exactly the same thing for yourself that the broker does, without having to give up a huge chunk of change. If you read the papers religiously and pound the pavement, you can view most of the same apartments that the brokers will show you. In fact, there are some excellent apartment buildings that are broker-free. So unless you read the paper or hear about the apartment via word of mouth, you'll never even see it with your broker. Furthermore, if your broker shows you an

MOVING TIP

"If you have a limited budget, be flexible about where you're willing to live. Chances are, you'll do a lot better than if you limit yourself to one specific neighborhood, especially a trendy one."

—Irene Keating, Director of Relocation Services, Douglas Elliman

apartment that you read about in the paper and you decide to rent it, you still have to pay the commission—it doesn't matter that you could have found it on your own.

How you want to proceed will depend on how much time you have on your hands (if you already have a job that you have to be at, your time will be more limited) and how much time you have before you need to move into your own place. If you're living at home with your parents and commuting into the City, you'll have more time to look than if you're sleeping on a friend's couch or staying in a hotel. Either way, once you decide you want to rent an apartment, you have to go out and pound the pavement until you find something that works for you. Looking at one apartment a week won't get you anywhere, and neither will "just looking around" on a preliminary trip to the City a few months in advance of your actual move. You have to make this your number one priority, and you can't rest until you've found your new home.

Pros of Using a Broker

A good broker will:

- Save you time
- Have exclusives on apartments and relationships with landlords
- Have more information than you could get on your own
- Know the neighborhoods better than you do
- Help you find a good apartment fit
- Know the history of the building (landlord, noise level, quality of building)

Cons of Using a Broker

Unless you find one of the above gems, you may encounter a broker who will:

- Require a minimum of one month's rent and up to 10–15 percent of one year's rent for the service of finding you an apartment
- Be at the bottom of the real estate food chain (read: inexperienced or scum of the earth), especially on lower-priced rentals
- Have a high-volume clientele that is often conversely related to quality of service
- Perhaps have a hidden agenda like getting kickbacks from a landlord or a bonus from a given apartment building
- Be a specialist in only one neighborhood
- Provide you with information that, with research, you could find on your own

RESOURCES FOR FINDING A RENTAL APARTMENT

Newspapers

The *New York Times*

www.nytimes.com

Some would claim that, in addition to word of mouth, this is the only tool you need to rent or buy an apartment in New York City—and they wouldn't be far off. The *Times*'s listings are an excellent resource for any apartment hunter. Widely available all over the city and tri-state area, the *Times* features apartment listings (and listings for houses outside of the City) in the Real Estate section of the Sunday paper ($2.50). Get a jump start on the competition by looking online before the paper comes out and by buying the paper on Saturday night.

The *Village Voice*

www.villagevoice.com

A free weekly publication that is widely available on many street-corners (look for them in the brightly colored, usually red, newspaper boxes). The *Voice* is an especially good resource for downtown (Greenwich Village, East Village, SoHo, TriBeCa, and Chelsea) rentals and sales. It also includes listings for all five boroughs and northern New Jersey. New issues appear on Wednesdays. Also check online for a jump start on the competition.

Government Organizations

NYS Division of Housing and Community Renewal

www.dhcr.state.ny.us/ora/ora.htm

The Office of Rent Administration is responsible for regulating rents in approximately 1.2 million privately owned rental units statewide.

Apartment Brokers

Bellmarc Realty
Rental division
(212) 957-3100

www.bellmarc.com

Brooklyn Properties
213 Seventh Avenue
Brooklyn, NY 11215
(718) 788-3888

www.brooklynproperties.com

Citi Habitats
30 East 33rd Street, 3rd Floor
New York, NY 10016
(212) 685-7777
(877) NYC-HOME

www.citihabitats.com

Douglas Elliman
3 East 54th Street
New York, NY 10022
(212) 350-8500

www.douglaselliman.com

Comprehensive listings throughout Manhattan

Feathered Nest (Brown Harris Stevens)
770 Lexington Avenue, 10th Floor
New York, NY 10021
(212) 317-7800

www.bhsusa.com/home.html

Fenwick-Keats Realty
(888) FEN-WICK

www.fenwick-keats.com

Selling and renting properties
throughout Manhattan

Halstead Rentals
1065 Madison Avenue
New York, NY 10028
(212) 381-2271

www.halstead.com

Comprehensive listings throughout Manhattan

Robert Hill
(917) 738-2206

roberthill.com

Specializing in the rental and
sale of apartments in brownstones, townhouses, prewar, and
luxury doorman buildings in
New York City

William B. May
Main Office
575 Madison Avenue
New York, NY 10022
(212) 872-2200

www.wbmay.com

TO LIVE ON YOUR OWN OR WITH A ROOMMATE?

Some people are roommate people and some people aren't. Whether or not you have a successful roommate experience will depend on the personalities of you and your roommate and on the relationship you establish and develop over time. For some people the years they lived with a roommate were the best times of their lives and for others they were a nightmare they'd rather forget. Though you can't completely control the situation, there are certainly steps you can take. How will it be for you?

Many recent college graduates, students of all ages (graduate, doctoral, art), and newcomers to the City choose to live with roommates (local colleges and universities are a great place to look for roommates; check the bulletin boards all around campus and ask around as to whether the institution has any sort of a matching service). And different people have roommates for different reasons. One of the most common reasons is to save money, but plenty of people live with roommates because they feel safer, because they don't know anyone in the City and having a roommate is an instant friend or acquaintance, because for the same per-person outlay of cash each month they can get more apartment than they could on their own, or because they want to live with friends. What many people don't consider is whether or not they're cut out for the roommate lifestyle and how sharing an apartment with one or more people, possibly strangers, will affect them.

The number one complaint of people with roommates with whom I spoke was lack of privacy. Imagine coming home from a stressful day at the office and all you want to do is put your feet up, watch the news, and order takeout Chinese—but your Chatty Cathy roommate won't leave you alone. Your only option for privacy is to go out (who knows where) or to go to your room and close the door—if you have a door.

The incompatible roommate—one of you is a night owl musician working the club scene, the other is a nine-to-fiver—is an age-old problem. The lack of flexibility that accompanies the benefits of having a roommate can ruin even the best of friendships. What if your roommate decides to move out on a moment's notice? Who is responsible for finding you a new roommate? Living with a roommate and wanting, or needing, a lifestyle change is often not as easy as breaking a lease with a landlord (most landlords don't mind when you break the lease and move out early because that means that they can raise the rent the allowable percentage and get more money from the next tenant for the same apartment). And, only one of you will have the lease—which means that that person holds all the power, responsibility, and rights. Good if you want to stay in the apartment and ask your roomie to leave, but bad if your roommate skips out on the rent and you're stuck holding the bag.

Living with a roommate is an excellent option for many people, but you have to assess your situation (and yourself) to determine if this is the lifestyle for you. Many people love living with roommates and others can't stand it—only you can decide.

For you roommate-seekers out there, take some steps to make life with your roommate a pleasant and cooperative one. Enter into the relationship as you would enter a marriage or a business partnership. In most cases, only one of the renters can be the leaseholder. So you have to decide if you want to move in with someone who has all of the rights and all of the responsibility or whether you want to be the person holding the lease. There are a lot of benefits to being the leaseholder, but there are drawbacks too. The lease is in your name, so you're responsible for the full amount of the rent regardless of what your roommate does. Perhaps your roommate is chronically late with the rent each month, or decides to move out on a moment's notice and doesn't have a replacement. Or, worse still, what if your roommate holds the lease and is moving to Kansas and you're unable to renew the lease so you have to move out? Or what if your roommate wants to kick you out because a newfound love wants to move in? These are all common problems among roommates and the more steps you take to work things out in advance, the better off everyone will be.

Pros of Living with a Roommate

- Save money—rent, utilities, phone, food
- Achieve economies of scale (with pooled resources, for the same amount of money each month you can get a bigger or better apartment)
- Live with a friend (or friends)
- Safety
- An instant friend or at least a companion

Cons of Living with a Roommate

- If you and your roommate are incompatible, you may very well be miserable.
- There's a lack of flexibility if you have a lifestyle change.
- Most landlords insist on having only one person's name on the lease, so one of you will have all of the responsibility, burden, and rights.
- There'll be a lack of privacy.

Deciding on a Roommate

- *Sit down and have a heart-to-heart, get-to-know-you conversation with your potential roommate.* The more you know about this person in advance, the better off you'll both be.

- *Don't be afraid to pry.* You're going to be roommates, so you'll learn all of each other's foibles sooner or later. Better you should know them sooner in case there's anything you want to avoid altogether.

- *Establish a clearly defined legal relationship.* One person will hold the lease and therefore the right and responsibility to the apartment. That person should pay more in rent (you can take the bigger room to justify that). You should also sit down with your roommate before move-in day and set forth in writing what happens if your roommate decides to move out or is late with the rent or the bills.

CITY FACT

The Bronx is the only borough of New York City that is part of the North American mainland. All of the other boroughs are on islands (Manhattan and Staten Island are their own islands, while both Brooklyn and Queens are geographically part of Long Island).

- *Establish a clearly defined, mutually respectful roommate relationship.* After you define the legalities of the relationship, define the issues that will affect you both in the day-to-day living.

Issues to Discuss

- Do you want to split the groceries each week or do you each want to have a shelf in the refrigerator and separate kitchen cabinets so that you can buy your own?
- Should you divide the phone bill each month or get separate phone lines? (I'd vote for separate phones.)
- What if only one of you has an air conditioner—how do you divide the utilities during the summer? Can the one without sit in the room with when the roommate isn't home?
- What is the policy on using each other's belongings? Do you have to ask? Are some things okay to use without asking while others aren't?
- If all of the plates and dishes are yours, what happens when your roommate breaks something? If the VCR is yours and you both use it in common space, who replaces it if one day it doesn't work anymore? To whom does the replacement belong?
- What is the policy on house guests, overnight guests, boyfriends and girlfriends?
- What is the policy on parties, music, and noise?
- On what day each month will the rent money be due, the bills paid, and the apartment cleaned?

Each person is going to have different issues and priorities, but the more you discuss and agree on in advance, the better off you'll be. Some of these things may sound petty or even silly, but I spoke to people who have "broken up" over each and every one of these issues. So before you brush it off as irrelevant, think long and hard about what your priorities are and be sure to discuss the issues before the first box is moved in. I guarantee you, you'll be happier for it in the long run.

Helpful Hints

- It helps to have a roommate of the same gender (unless, of course, you're romantically involved).
- The more roommates you have, the more the issues multiply.
- It helps to have a roommate of a similar age.

The golden rule of happy (and successful) roommates: *If a problem arises, speak up!* Do not let issues fester until they become much bigger than they have to be. If your roommate is doing something that is making you crazy (finishing the milk and not replacing it, taking your newspaper to the office, playing music at full volume), let your feelings be known right away.

MOVING TIP

"Treat each apartment viewing as if it might be The One. Make your appointments for early in the morning—so you're the first person to see the apartment—and bring a deposit so you can put money down on the spot. If you don't, someone else will."

—John Munson, photographer

Roommate Finder Services

The best roommate finder service is your mouth. Open it wide and start talking, because the most likely reason you're going to hook yourself up is that you happened to tell someone who told someone's aunt and she has a friend who has a son-in-law whose sister is looking for a roommate. And then you're sitting pretty. So talk it up and tell *everyone* you encounter that you're on the hunt. A word of caution, however: Just because it happens to be the son-in-law's sister doesn't mean you're going to like her, so treat the meeting with her, your prospective roommate, like a meeting with a perfect stranger—because you can be just as miserable with her as with anyone else (and just as happy too).

Apartment Share
8 West 38th Street, Suite 1205
New York, NY 10018
(212) 302-5929

www.apartmentshare.com

Matching roommates in Brooklyn, Queens, Manhattan, and Hoboken. There is a $150 fee ($50 of which is refundable within the first thirty days) for six months of listings.

Hobokenroommates
(800) 374-6367
(201) 377-7094

www.hobokenroommates.com

Free to list your apartment if you're looking for a roommate and $65 for three months of apartment listings if you're hunting for a place to live. Serving Hoboken, Weehawken, Jersey City, Port Imperial, Edgewater, and Fort Lee (covering the entire region from Hoboken to Fort Lee).

Rainbow Roommates
268 West 22nd Street
New York, NY 10011
(212) 982-6265

www.rainbowroommates.com

RR serves all five boroughs and Northern New Jersey (merger of Roommates NYC and Rainbow Roommates). They offer four-month memberships, which includes not only apartment listings but also counseling on neighborhoods, advice on interviewing with room-mates, and general guidance. The cost of membership is $175.

Roommates Central
89 Fifth Avenue, Suite 1002
New York, NY 10003
(212) 807-7851

www.roommatescentral.com

RC has listings for roommates throughout New York City. The cost is $200 for sixty days of listings. For each additional month, there is a $50 charge.

Roommate Finders

250 West 57th Street (at
Broadway), 16th Floor
New York, NY 10019
(212) 489-6860

Roommate Finders is the oldest in the business by far (they've been in business nineteen years longer than any other roommate service in the City). When matching up prospective roommates, they take into account thirty-five different factors. They cover Manhattan from 95th Street down to Battery Park.

Other Places to Look

National Roommates

nationalroommates.com

National Roommates is a portal, best utilized as a starting point (otherwise regional sites should be better) in your search for a roommate. But it also has other useful areas that I liken to the bulletin board in a college dorm—used furniture for sale, already ticketed passengers with plane tickets for sale.

CITY FACT

As of the most recent count by the Division of Housing and Community Renewal (718-739-6400), there are 70,572 *rent-controlled* apartments in New York City. Of those, there are 9,428 in the Bronx; 19,111 in Brooklyn; 30,939 in Manhattan; 10,497 in Queens; and 597 in Staten Island. There are 877,731 *rent-stabilized* apartments: 178,114 in the Bronx; 22,112 in Brooklyn; 316,280 in Manhattan; 155,896 in Queens; and 5,329 in Staten Island.

The *New York Times*

Check especially online. See Resources, above.

Village Voice

Check especially online. See Resources, above.

Temporary Housing

Although temporary housing is a great option in many cities, my advice regarding temporary housing in New York City is to avoid it altogether if at all possible. The options for mainstream accommodations (hotels, short-term stay corporate furnished apartments, extended stay hotels, hostels) are either extremely overpriced or extremely dingy and dreary—or a combination of both. You will find that apartments in New York are rented at an alarming pace. If you are ready to rent, it can take as little as a day, a week, or, for the extremely slow, a month to find yourself a new home. Because of this, you should take steps to assure yourself that you don't have to shell out a bunch of cash (short-term fully equipped lease apartments *start* at the low, low price of $2,200 per month for a studio—if you're lucky—and easily range up to $12,150 for the low-end two-bedroom leases) or settle into a ratty hostel while you're looking. If you know someone in the City, find out if, while you get your bearings, you can impose for a few nights (and it will be an imposition—unless your friends are extremely wealthy or very lucky, their space will be limited). For New York apartment dwellers, allowing friends to stay over is a favor that lasts a lifetime, but ask anyway because they'd happily ask you too.

If you are being hired in advance by a corporation, try during your initial negotiations to include in your relocation package temporary housing while you are looking for something permanent. Many big law, accounting, and investment firms will offer this to you outright with no negotiations at all. Indeed, many of them have services to help you find a permanent residence.

If you have no choice but to seek temporary housing, go for the less mainstream options. Though they may end up being a little more work to arrange, it will be well worth the effort because the accommodations will be more pleasant and you'll save a bundle of cash. Some decent temporary housing options include:

- College dorm rooms (only if it's summer)
- Subletting an apartment (from a friend, cousin, brother of a friend's cousin)
- YMCA/YMHA
- Un-hosted apartments
- Women's residences
- Servicemen's or -women's residences

COLLEGE DORM ROOMS

Many of the universities and colleges in New York have little housing or no housing at all, even for their students, so the choices are limited.

New York University (NYU)
14 Washington Place
(212) 998-4621

www.nyu.edu/housing/summer

CITY FACT

The Greenbelt, at 2,500 acres, is the pride of Staten Island. More than three times the size of Central Park, this incredible nature preserve offers, among other things, well-marked hiking trails and regularly scheduled talks, walks, and programs. Call (718) 667-2165 for more information.

SUBLETTING

The best way to sublet an apartment is to know someone who is leaving the City for a while and who wants to have someone in the apartment paying the rent. If this seems like a long shot because you don't know a single soul in town, try the second best way to sublet an apartment—go to the nearest college campus and read the walls (see chapter 10 for a lengthy listing). Many students in New York City live "off campus" because the City is their campus and many students don't even have the luxury of living in a campus dorm. So whether they're off for a semester abroad, taking a year off from school, or leaving for the summer, there are tons of apartments that are available on a short-term basis, and many students post notices of availability around campus (try entryways to university buildings), especially in the student union. So read the walls. If that doesn't turn anything up, you may find a few sublets advertised, so get a copy of the *Voice* and pick up a copy of the Sunday *Times*.

YMCA/YMHA

De Hirsch Residence
92nd Street YMHA/YWHA (Young Men's/Women's Hebrew Association)
1395 Lexington Avenue
(212) 415-5650

www.92ndsty.org

Short stays (a minimum of three or more days) are $79 per night in a single, $49 per person per day in a double (the Y will match you up with another single if you want to share a room). Long-term stays (two months up to a year) are $895 for a single, $725 per person per month in a shared room (you can be traveling alone and still get matched up in a double). The accommodations are similar to college dorm rooms. They are fully furnished and have shared bathrooms and kitchens. In order to be eligible, you must apply for a room (you can't just show up, even if it's on a short-stay basis), which takes approximately one week to process, and you must either be a full-time student, have a full-time job, or a combination of the two. It is advisable to file your paperwork for residence at least two months in advance in order to secure a room. There is also a fully equipped health club in the building (including a twenty-five-yard pool—a rarity in NYC), which you can use for an extra fee.

McBurney YMCA
206 West 24th Street
(212) 741-9226

Coed facility. Rates of $64–$66 for singles to $77 for doubles, and the price includes the use of the health club and pool.

The Vanderbilt YMCA

224 East 47th Street

(212) 756-9600

Coed facility. Rates are $72 for a single, $86 for a double (both with shared bath) per night and include the use of the health club and pool.

West Side YMCA

5 West 63rd Street

(212) 875-4273

Rooms are available to men and women at a rate of $70 per single and $82 per double and include the use of the health club and pool.

UN-HOSTED APARTMENTS

Un-hosted apartments are the ideal alternative to corporate apartment rentals. You stay in someone's apartment (they're not there), in a real building (as opposed to corporate glass and steel, ranging from brownstones to high-rises), in a real neighborhood, and you can settle in while you're looking for your permanent residence. I've listed only the oldest and most reputable companies, though many more have sprung up in recent years.

Abode Ltd.

P.O. Box 20022

New York, NY 10021

(212) 472-2000

(800) 835-8880

www.abodenyc.com

MOVING TIP

"To avoid a broker's fee, try renting an apartment in one of the no-fee buildings. There are several books that include listings of all the buildings in a given neighborhood—that's how I found my apartment."

—Daphne Matalene, advertising sales representative

Abode keeps thirty un-hosted apartments ranging from studios (starting at $135) to three-bedroom/three-bath (up to $4,000), all available on a nightly basis with a minimum of four nights. With stays of one month or longer, price adjustments can be negotiated.

MOVING TIP

"Take advantage of New York's public libraries. There are so many of them to choose from (over 1,000) and some, like the branch on 42nd Street and Fifth Avenue, are amongst the biggest and best in the world. It's also a good place to escape."

—Fatima Elmjid, Flushing, Queens

(via Casablanca, Morocco), ice cream scooper

Bed, Breakfast, and Books
35 West 92nd Street, 2C
New York, NY 10025
(212) 865-8740

Studios, one-bedroom, and a few two-bedroom apartments are available for stays of two nights and longer. Prices range from $110 for the studios to $250 and up for the two-bedroom apartments. Book as far in advance as possible.

Oxbridge
1623 Third Avenue
New York, NY 10128
(800) 550-7071
(212) 348-8100

www.oxbridgeny.com

Urban Ventures
38 West 32nd, Suite 1412
New York, NY 10001
(212) 594-5650

www.nyurbanventures.com

Urban Ventures has studio to three-bedroom apartments ranging from $105 for the studios and climbing to $360 for the most expensive three-bedrooms. There is a four-night minimum stay; price adjustments are available for longer stays.

WOMEN'S RESIDENCES

Most of the women's residences require a minimum stay of three months, so they may not be the ideal option, but they are safe, clean, and cheap, and most of them even include a few meals, so you could certainly do worse.

The Markie Residence

123 West 13th Street (between Sixth and Seventh Avenues)
(212) 242-2400

The Markie is run by the Salvation Army and is a safe bet at $225 per week (a one-month minimum). The price includes a single room with a private bath, two meals per day (your choice of B, L, D), and weekly maid service. Guests must apply for a room and there is usually a six-week wait list, so apply early. Rooms are open to women eighteen years of age and older, and guests must either be students or employed.

Parkside Evangeline Residence

18 Gramercy Park South
(212) 677-6200

Parkside is also run by the Salvation Army. There is a three-month minimum stay (though during slow periods, they will allow shorter stays); most rooms are singles with private baths (though there are a few doubles and a few singles with shared bath). The cost is $191–$205 per week for an excellent downtown location (Gramercy Park is peaceful, lovely, and exclusive), and that includes breakfast and dinner. Apply at least one month in advance.

Webster Apartments

419 West 34th Street
(212) 967-9000

Webster has a minimum stay of four weeks with a room rate of $162–$199 per week, based on your salary. Accommodations are single rooms with shared baths, and breakfast and lunch are included daily. My impression of Webster is that it is a very rule-oriented and unbending residence (I was cut off because I asked too many questions) and if you're predisposed to taking umbrage with rules, you'd do better to live elsewhere. Apply in advance.

SERVICEMEN'S AND SERVICEWOMEN'S RESIDENCES

The Navy Lodge

Building 408 North Pass Road
Fort Wadsworth
Staten Island, NY 10305
(800) NAVY-INN

The Navy Lodge is a hotel for military personnel; any active-duty serviceperson, retiree, reservist, or honorable discharge (with a military ID) can book a room at the hotel for $60 a night. These same people can also book a room for relatives at the same rate. Active-duty personnel can reserve sixty days in advance; all others can book thirty days in advance.

Soldiers', Sailors', Marines' & Airmen's Club (operated by the USO)

283 Lexington Avenue (between 36th and 37th streets)
(212) 683-4353

The Soldiers' and Sailors' Club is a tremendous bargain for military, former military, and government personnel. The rates are $25 per night for enlisted parties, $35 for officers and retired, and $40 for government employees and honorable discharge personnel. Stays can range from one to twenty days, at which time you must check out for at least one night before returning to the residence (you can do that three times before they give you the boot). The rooms and baths are shared.

CHAPTER 3

Advice on Buying an Apartment in the City or a House in the Suburbs

As discussed in detail in chapter 2, I strongly advise newcomers to New York City, absent extraordinary circumstances, to rent before buying. But let's assume that you are ready to buy, for whatever reason. Maybe you lived in New York before and you're moving back, so you already know the territory. Or perhaps you have a compelling tax reason that requires you to buy something now. Or you could be a professional real estate investor who objects to renting on principle. Or it's always possible that you just got a really good deal. Or you're stubborn and you won't take my advice—fine, you won't hurt my feelings. Okay, so how should you proceed?

Since, when purchasing an apartment, the universe of apartments is similar to what you'd examine in a prospective rental situation, many of the same rules apply: You have to figure out where you want to live, what your budget will allow, and all your other preferences.

In addition, as a prospective apartment owner in New York, you are faced with the ages-old question of, "Condo or Co-op?" These are your two options for apartment purchases. Physically, they're the same—you can't tell by standing in an apartment whether it's a condo or a co-op. But the processes of buying a condo versus buying a co-op are quite different.

When you buy a condominium, you're buying your unit outright. Either you buy your apartment from the previous owner, or, if it's a new building, you buy it from the investment/development group. Either way, you own the actual, physical apartment. You pay your mortgage to the bank, your taxes to the government, and your common charges (covering care for common areas like the lobby, hallways, laundry room and utilities, costs for insurance, maintenance, salaries for doormen) to the building. You are autonomous in your ownership so you can renovate your apartment as you see fit (though you will be responsible for any damage you do to the building in the process). There is an elected condo board, but the board's control is limited to the common aspects of the building. The board traditionally does not have the right to restrict you from selling your apartment or subletting it if you so choose. By the same token, because there are no restrictions on who can buy into the building, you may find that the demographics of your neighbors is regularly in flux. What may have started out as a family-oriented building may later turn out to be more of a singles building—roommates sharing apartments, a lot of coming and goings—and you may have no say in that matter.

Co-ops have traditionally been an altogether different matter. When you buy into a co-op, you buy the right to live in your apartment by purchasing shares in a corporation. Each apartment has a share value, which is based on the size and desirability of the unit, assigned to it at the co-op's inception. The owners/leaseholders own the building together, and they decide (via the co-op board) who can buy into the building, whether a member can undertake a major renovation (based on how it will affect the building as a whole), what work will be done to maintain and improve the building, and so forth. Co-ops are usually far more exclusive than condos, and owners reserve the right to keep it that way. Someone who buys into a specific co-op building may be buying because he or she likes the outlook and policies of the other tenants. When people buy into the building, they'll want to guard their right to keep those policies from changing. A family-oriented building might keep unattached singles out, and buildings are entitled to do so. Some co-ops are so exclusive that they demand that all apartments be purchased outright for cash—no mortgages of any kind are permitted.

Financially, co-op members are responsible for the building as a whole. Each member is responsible for monthly maintenance charges (which are based on the number of shares assigned to each unit). These payments go toward paying the building's expenses, which include property taxes, repairs, improvements, insurance, operating costs, and perhaps a mortgage or loan payments. *This is not to say that people who own condos don't pay property taxes too, it's just the way the payments are divided—either you pay your taxes to the building, or you pay them directly to the government.* In a condo the property is your own, the same as if you owned a house. Therefore, you pay the taxes directly to the government. In a co-op, because you own shares in the building (and not the actual unit itself), you pay your taxes to the building in your monthly maintenance charges (which, based on the building as a whole, are paid to the government).

There is also more of an element of risk involved in buying into a co-op, because if one of the members defaults on monthly maintenance fees, the other members are ultimately responsible for picking up the slack (another reason why co-op boards can be very strict when reviewing and assessing a potential buyer—they want to be certain that each new member is more than capable of carrying the load).

In either instance, co-op or condo, it is very important to consult with a seasoned real estate attorney who will be able to decipher for you the ins and outs of the building's financial situation. Just as the board will be checking out all of your credentials, so should you check out theirs. If the building just had its roof replaced, you may be buying into an extra $500,000 of debt (which will be divvied up among tenants and added into your monthly service charges each month). Is the apartment worth it to you? Or could you find one that is equally as nice that doesn't have that extra debt attached? Of course, at any time a roof could go or an elevator could have to be replaced. You can't make your decision in fear of the future, but with the help of an expert, you can decide as wisely as facts permit at the time.

According to Irene Keating, director of relocation services at Douglas Elliman (which grossed over $2 billion last year in Manhattan rentals and sales), co-op buildings constitute approximately 85 percent of all occupant-owned apartments, versus only 15 percent for condos, and therefore your selection will be somewhat dictated by supply and demand.

But don't get too bogged down in the formal definitions of co-ops and condos. Gone are the days when co-ops and condos were two completely different animals. The differences are disappearing, formally and informally, as buildings work to make the best financial arrangements possible. For example, where once condos used to be unable legally to take out loans on behalf of the building (for repairs and so on), now they can do so and finance the payments in the form of monthly common charges. And condos are now figuring out ways to guarantee some exclusivity and more control to their boards. The bottom line is, when assessing the costs and investment value of a co-op versus a condo, you have to look at each building as a separate entity.

Condo Basics

- You own your apartment outright.
- Everyone in the building owns the common areas together.
- Monthly maintenance fees tend to be low because each condo owner is only responsible to pay for a share of the common areas.
- You can renovate your apartment as you wish, as long as it does not affect the building.
- Condos are usually less restrictive than co-ops.
- Condos are usually less exclusive than co-ops.
- Condos usually have no one protecting the best interest of the building as a whole.
- You can sell your apartment to whomever you choose.
- Typically, you can sublet your apartment to whomever you want and for as long as you want.
- Condos usually require 15–20 percent of the cost of the apartment down.

Co-op Basics

- A co-op is a corporation. You own your apartment in the form of shares in the corporation (rather than the apartment itself). Your shares are based on the value of your apartment (which is based on the square footage and desirability).
- When you buy into a co-op, you are buying exclusivity.
- Co-ops can be very restrictive because the members are acting to protect the interest of the building (which has long been established before you arrived).
- Co-op members have the right to deny you the sale of *your* apartment if they don't approve of the prospective buyer (so long as the refusal is not discriminatory in nature).
- Monthly co-op payments tend to be higher than those of condos (but payments include property taxes).

CITY FACT

The Bronx Zoo and Wildlife Conservation Society Park is the largest metropolitan zoo in the United States. It contains 6,445 animals (665 species) living in natural habitats.

- You must seek board approval before any major renovations are planned.
- There is greater financial risk in a co-op.
- Co-ops generally require 20–25 percent of your payment down (sometimes more).

THE FINANCIAL FACTORS

Work out the finances of what each apartment will cost, including:

- Money down
- Monthly common charges or maintenance fees
- Monthly mortgage payment (and the percentage of the payment that represents interest)

- Property taxes
- Closing costs
- Costs of needed renovations or repairs

Only after you have added up all of the numbers (having calculated mortgage interest payments as tax deductions) and assessed *all* of the financial factors can you make an informed decision.

RESOURCES FOR BUYING AN APARTMENT

See "Resources for Finding a Rental Apartment" in chapter 2.

Realtors

New York City is unlike most other places in that realtors do not have access to multiple listings. Many apartment showings in New York are exclusives (though there are brokered splits; for example Halstead has a listing that you want to see with your broker from Bellmarc, and, if you buy, the brokers from Halstead and Bellmarc split the commission). Select your firm carefully, based on size and listings, because to some extent that will determine what properties you see.

There are also buildings that, because they are so large, have brokers who specialize in just that specific building or complex, in which case you'd do well to go through those building specialists. For example, there are brokers who specialize in sales and rentals in Battery Park City, whose population is larger than that of many small towns, with hundreds upon hundreds of apartments. The same would apply to Lincoln Towers on the Upper West Side, which is one of the largest condo communities in Manhattan. There are also co-op and condo buildings that don't use brokers, especially new buildings that might have their own salespeople, whom you must go through in order to buy into the building. That's why, when selecting your realtor, you must have a clear idea where you want to live, which will in turn help determine which firm (or building realtor) you use.

The following are the most noteworthy brokers in New York:

Bellmarc Realty

Westside Office
424 Columbus Avenue
(212) 874-0100

Lincoln Center Office
1776 Broadway
(212) 957-3100

Eastside Office
1015 Madison Avenue
(212) 517-9100

Midtown Office
681 Lexington Avenue
(212) 688-8530

Gramercy/Chelsea Office
352 Park Avenue South
(212) 252-1900

Downtown Office
16 East 12th Street
(212) 627-3000

Brooklyn Properties

213 Seventh Avenue (between 3rd and 4th Streets)
(718) 788-3888

www.brooklynproperties.com

Sales throughout Brooklyn

Brown Harris Stevens

www.bhsusa.com/home.html

Residential Sales East Side
655 Madison Avenue, 3rd Floor
New York, NY 10021
(212) 593-8300

MOVING TIP

"Keep something to read or do—a book, a magazine, some homework—with you at all times. I live in Queens, so I spend extra time commuting to my job every day. The train may get delayed, but if I have reading material or a little chore to do, I don't mind the wait because I'm using my time productively."

—Tafima Awwad, City University student

Residential Sales West Side
2112 Broadway, Mezzanine
New York, NY 10023
(212) 588-5600

Residential Sales Downtown
2 Fifth Avenue
New York, NY 10011
(212) 906-0500

770 Lexington Avenue, 4th Floor
New York, NY 10021
(212) 508-7200

CITY FACT

Shea Stadium, in Queens, is home to the New York Mets. It is also famous for the legendary Beatles concert, which was held on August 23rd, 1966, and the visit of Pope John Paul II, which occurred on October 3rd, 1979.

Coldwell Banker
www.coldwellbanker.com

Hunt Kennedy West
238 West 78th Street
New York, NY 10024
(212) 877-1300

Hunt Kennedy East
1200 Lexington Avenue
New York, NY 10028
(212) 327-1200

Hunt Kennedy Downtown
401 Avenue of the Americas
New York, NY 10014
(212) 255-4000

Beautiful Homes, Inc.
733 Allerton Avenue
Bronx, NY 10467
(718) 654-4000

Corcoran
660 Madison Avenue
New York, NY 10021
(212) 355-3550

www.corcoran.com

Douglas Elliman
Relocating Office
(212) 891-7640

www.douglaselliman.com

City and suburbs. The largest brokerage by far, with branches in the following locations:

Manhattan—Eastside
575 Madison Avenue
New York, NY 10022
(212) 891-7277

980 Madison Avenue
New York, NY 10022
(212) 650-4800

60 East 56th Street
New York, NY 10022
(212) 702-4000

3 East 54th Street
New York, NY 10022
(212) 350-8500

Manhattan—Westside
2112 Broadway
New York, NY 10023
(212) 362-9600

Manhattan—Downtown
103 Fifth Avenue
New York, NY 10003
(212) 645-4040

Tribeca Gallery
90 Hudson
New York, NY 10013
(212) 965-6000

Wall Street
99 Battery Place
New York, NY 10280
(212) 898-4700

137 Waverly Place
New York, NY 10014
(212) 675-6980

248 Mercer Street
New York, NY 10012
(212) 475-8888

Fenwick-Keats Realty
401 West End Avenue
New York, NY 10024
(212) 787-0707

www.fenwick-keats.com
(888) FEN-WICK

Selling and renting properties
throughout Manhattan

Fenwick-Keats East
1185 Lexington Avenue
New York, NY 10028
(212) 772-0707

Fenwick-Keats North
463 Fort Washington Avenue
New York, NY 10033
(212) 795-0707

Goodstein Realty
The Goodstein Organization
Manhattan
242 East 51st Street
New York, NY 10022
(212) 750-5550

www.goodsteinrealty.com

Halstead East
1065 Madison Avenue
New York, NY 10028
(212) 734-0010

Halstead West
408 Columbus Avenue
New York, NY 10024
(212) 769-3000

Halstead SoHo
451 West Broadway
New York, NY 10012
(212) 475-4200

Halstead Village
784 Broadway
New York, NY 10003
(212) 253-9300

Sotheby's International Realty
www.sothebysrealty.com

Manhattan
980 Madison Avenue, 2nd Floor
New York, NY 10021
(212) 606-7660

Downtown
379 West Broadway
New York, NY 10012
(212) 431-2440

Stribling & Associates
924 Madison Avenue
New York, NY 10021
(212) 570-2440

www.striblingny.com

Stribling-Wells & Gay
340 West 23rd Street
New York, NY 10011
(212) 243-4000

William B. May
www.wbmay.com

Apparently, realtors at William B. May can sell you a house in several different languages, including Russian, Turkish,

MOVING TIP

"There are all sorts of free events all over the City throughout the year, but the best time to take advantage of free events is during the summer. In Central Park, for example, there are concerts (rock, country, classical, and even opera), fireworks displays, and dramatic productions. For some events, like the Shakespeare in the Park performances, you'll have to line up to get tickets, but for others, like the concerts, you just show up."

—Karen Poznansky, television producer

Chinese, and Hebrew. You can contact them at the following branches:

Main Office
575 Madison Avenue
New York, NY 10022
(212) 872-2200

Beekman/Sutton
900 First Avenue
New York, NY 10022
(212) 829-8000

Greenwich Village
529 Hudson Street
New York, NY 10014
(212) 691-1400

TriBeCa
51A Hudson Street
New York, NY 10013
(212) 962-6293

Brooklyn Heights
150 Montague Street
Brooklyn, NY 11201
(718) 875-1289

Park Slope
100 7th Avenue (at Union Street)
Brooklyn, NY 11215
(718) 230-5500

Buying a House in the Suburbs

Finally, if you choose to live in the suburbs, you will most likely purchase a house. Buying a house in the tri-state area isn't really any different than buying a house anywhere else in America—it's just a little more expensive.

TO HUNT ALONE, OR WITH A REALTOR?

Whereas many people in the City buy, sell, and rent apartments without realtors, it's almost unheard of for people in the tri-state area to buy houses without realtors (though, if you do decide to buy from an unlisted seller, you can save some money—the seller will be more likely to negotiate because of the lack of a sales commission). However, assuming that you are not familiar with the region and you'd like to find something fairly quickly, you'd be best served to work with one of the area realtors.

As a specialist in the field, your realtor should know the neighborhoods and the schools and should be able to connect you with exactly what you're looking for better than you could yourself. They'll also be happy to do it in a hurry because the faster they sell you a house, the faster they make their commission and go on to the next client. Furthermore, community realtors are more likely than brokers to take the time necessary to sell you what you want, because there is the great likelihood of repeat and referral business and building a solid clientele depends upon good service. This is very different from the rental business, because brokers who find rental units for tenants anticipate never hearing from or seeing those tenants again (moving out requires no broker, and buying requires a sales broker), so why should they care how you feel about them in the end?

RESOURCES FOR FINDING YOUR NEW HOME

To hunt alone (and educate yourself on the market), check the town's local paper for listings by regional real estate agencies and independent sellers, and check grocery stores—most have racks of real estate fliers with independent listings by the exit.

See "Resources for Finding a Rental Apartment" in chapter 2.

Area Realtors

Coach Realtors
35 Laurel Road
East Northport, NY 11731
(516) 757-7272

www.coach.com

805 East Jericho Turnpike
Dix Hills, NY 11746
(516) 427-9100

255 West Main Street
Smithtown, NY 11787
(516) 360-1900

66 Gilbert Street
Northport, NY 11768
(516) 757-4000

147 East Main Street
Huntington, NY 11743
(516) 427-1200

212 Commack Road
Commack, NY 11725
(516) 499-1000

2 Muttontown Road
Syosset, NY 11791
(516) 364-1900

15 Bennetts Road, Suite 3
Setauket, NY 11733
(516) 689-2654

791 Route 25A
Miller Place, NY 11764
(516) 821-4900

321 Plandome Road
Manhasset, NY 11030
(516) 627-0120

415 East Main Street
Port Jefferson Village, NY 11777
(516) 642-9000

Coldwell Banker
32 Field Point Road
Greenwich, CT 06830
(203) 622-1100

www.coldwellbanker.com

Coldwell Banker has offices all
over the tri-state area. Check out
the Web site for comprehensive
listings.

Dayton-Halstead
78 Main Street
East Hampton, NY 11937
(516) 324-0421

**Dayton-Halstead
(Bridgehampton Office)**
2450 Main Street
Bridgehampton, NY 11932
(516) 324-6900

City
Fact

The New York City Landmarks Preservation Commission was created in 1965 as a result of the tremendous public outcry in the wake of the demolition of the magnificent old Penn Station. Now, more than three decades later, plans are finally under-way to replace the undistinguished new Penn Station with a more stately and dignified version, similar to the grand railroad stations of old. And, until that's done, you can visit the newly renovated Grand Central Station—one of the grandest in the world.

MOVING TIP

"Make time for adventures—why bother living here if you're not going to explore? For a virtual trip to an exotic foreign land, instead of getting on an airplane, grab the #7 train to Little India in Jackson Heights or Chinatown in Flushing. The sights, sounds and smells will be like a trip to the East—but you'll still be back in time to sleep in your own bed."

—Diane Burrowes, marketing director

Douglas Elliman

www.douglaselliman.com

Port Washington
551 Port Washington Boulevard
Port Washington, NY 11030
(516) 883-5200

Locust Valley
71 Forest Avenue
Locust Valley, NY 11560
(516) 759-0400

Manhasset
154 Plandome Road
Manhasset, NY 11030
(516) 627-2800

Connecticut
30 Milbank Avenue
Greenwich, CT 06830
(203) 869-7800

New Jersey
19 Morristown Road
Bernardsville, NJ 07920-1617
(908) 221-1244

Goodstein Real Estate

www.goodsteinrealty.com

Long Island towns including Great Neck and Roslyn

10 Bond Street
Great Neck, NY 11021
(516) 466-2100

1314 Old Northern Boulevard
Roslyn, NY 11021
(516) 621-3555

Prudential Ragette Realtors
277 White Plains Road
Eastchester, NY 10707
(914) 793-0800

Bronxville Office
2 Park Place
Bronxville, NY 10708
(914) 337-2950

Eastchester Office
277 White Plains Road
Eastchester, NY 10707
(914) 337-7000

Irvington Office
79 Main Street
Irvington, NY 10533
(914) 591-3040

Executive/Relocation
Insurance/Commercial

**Sotheby's International
Realty—Tri-State Region**
980 Madison Avenue, 4th Floor
New York, NY 10021
(212) 606-4160

www.sothebysrealty.com

Covering New York (outside of
Manhattan), New Jersey, and
Southern Connecticut

William B. May (Westchester)
123 Main Street
Irvington, NY 10533
(914) 591-8984

www.wbmay.com

All of the big realty companies have branch offices throughout Long
Island, New Jersey, and Connecticut; so if there is one company that
you are partial to or that you may have had good luck with at home,
check the phone book. Chances are good that there will be a branch
in the area in which you are looking to buy.

Packing Up and Moving Out

By Monstermoving.com

CHAPTER 4

Getting Organized and Planning Your Move

Written for both the beginner and the veteran, this chapter contains information and resources that will help you get ready for your move. If money is foremost on your mind, you'll find a section on budgeting for the move and tips on how to save money throughout the move—as well as a move budget-planning guide. If time is also precious, you'll find time-saving tips and even suggestions for how to get out of town in a hurry. You'll find help with preliminary decisions, the planning process, and packing, as well as tips and advice on uprooting and resettling your family (and your animal companions). A budget worksheet, a set of helpful checklists, and a moving task time line complete the chapter.

Paying for Your Move

Moving can certainly tap your bank account. How much depends on a number of factors: whether your employer is helping with the cost, how much stuff you have, and how far you are moving.

To get an idea of how much your move will cost, start calling service providers for estimates and begin listing these expenses on the move budget-planning guide provided at the end of this chapter.

If you don't have the money saved, start saving as soon as you can. You should also check out other potential sources of money:

- Income from the sale of your spare car, furniture, or other belongings (hold a garage or yard sale).

- The cleaning and damage deposit on your current rental and any utility deposits. You probably won't be reimbursed until *after* your move, though, so you'll need to pay moving expenses up front in some other way.

- Your employer, who may owe you a payout for vacation time not taken.

Taxes and Your Move

Did you know that your move may affect your taxes? As you prepare to move, here are some things to consider:

- Next year's taxes. Some of your moving expenses may be tax-deductible. Save your receipts and contact your accountant and the IRS for more information. Visit *www.irs.gov* or call the IRS at (800) 829-3676 for information and to obtain the publication and forms you need.

- State income tax. If your new state collects income tax, you'll want to figure that into your salary and overall cost-of-living calculations. Of course, if your old state collects income tax and your new one doesn't, that's a factor, too, but a happier one—but remember to find out how much, if any, of the current year's income will be taxable in the old state.

- Other income sources. You'll want to consider any other sources of income and whether your new state will tax you on this income. For example, if you are paying federal income tax on an IRA that you rolled over into a Roth IRA, if you move into a state that collects income tax, you may also have to pay state income tax on your rollover IRA.

- After you move or when filing time draws near, consider collecting your receipts and visiting an accountant.

The Budget Move (Money-Saving Tips)

Here you'll find some suggestions for saving money on your move.

Saving on Moving Supplies

- Obtain boxes in the cheapest way possible.

  Ask a friend or colleague who has recently moved to give or sell you their boxes.

  Check the classified ads; people sometimes sell all their moving boxes for a flat rate.

  Ask your local grocery or department store for their empty boxes.

- Borrow a tape dispenser instead of buying one.

- Instead of buying bubble wrap, crumple newspaper, plain unused newsprint, or tissue paper to pad breakables.

MOVING TIP

Before buying anything for your new apartment or home, stop and consider what you'll need immediately and what you might be able to do without for a while. You'll spend a lot less if you can afford to wait and look for it on sale or secondhand.

- Shop around for the cheapest deal on packing tape and other supplies.

- Instead of renting padding blankets from the truck rental company, use your own blankets, linens, and area rugs for padding. (But bear in mind that you may have to launder them when you arrive, which is an expense in itself.)

Saving on Labor

- If you use professional movers, consider a "you pack, we drive" arrangement, in which you pack boxes, and the moving company loads, moves, and unloads your belongings.

- Call around and compare estimates.

- If you move yourself, round up volunteers to help you load and clean on moving day. It's still customary to reward them with moving-day food and beverages (and maybe a small cash gift). You may also have to volunteer to help them move some day. But you may still save some money compared to hiring professionals.
- Save on child and pet care. Ask family or friends to watch your young children and pets on moving day.

Saving on Trip Expenses

Overnight the Night Before You Depart

- Where will you stay the night before you depart? A hotel or motel might be most comfortable and convenient, but you could save a little money if you stay the night with a friend or relative.
- If you have the gear, maybe you'd enjoy unrolling your sleeping bag and "roughing it" on your own floor the night before you leave town. If you do this, try to get hold of a camping sleeping pad or air mattress, which will help you get a good night's sleep and start your move rested and refreshed.

Overnight on the Road

- Look into hotel and motel discounts along your route. Your automobile club membership may qualify you for a better rate. Check out other possibilities, too—associations such as AARP often line up discounts for their members, as do some credit cards.
- When you call about rates, ask if the hotel or motel includes a light breakfast with your stay.
- If your move travel involves an overnight stay and you're game for camping, check into campgrounds and RV parks along your route. Be sure to ask whether a moving truck is allowed. Some parks have size restrictions; some RV parks may not welcome moving trucks; and some limit the number of vehicles allowed in a campsite.

Food While Traveling

Food is one of those comfort factors that can help make the upsetting aspects of moving and traveling more acceptable. Eating also gives you a reason to stop and rest, which may be exactly what you or your family needs if you're rushing to get there. Here are a few pointers to consider:

- Try to balance your need to save money with your (and your family's) health and comfort needs.

- Try to have at least one solid, nutritious sit-down meal each day.

- Breakfast can be a budget- and schedule-friendly meal purchased at a grocery or convenience store and eaten on the road: fruit, muffins, and juice, for example.

- Lunch prices at sit-down restaurants are typically cheaper than dinner prices. Consider having a hot lunch and then picnicking in your hotel or motel on supplies from a grocery store.

Scheduling Your Move

Try to allow yourself at least three months to plan and prepare. This long lead time is especially important if you plan to sell or buy a home or if you are moving during peak moving season (May through September). If you plan to move during peak season, it's vital to reserve two to three months in advance with a professional moving company or truck rental company. The earlier you reserve, the more likely you are to get the dates you want. This is especially important if you're timing your move with a job start date or a house closing date, or are moving yourself and want to load and move on a weekend when your volunteers are off work.

WHEN IS THE RIGHT TIME TO MOVE?

If your circumstances allow you to decide your move date, you'll want to make it as easy as possible on everyone who is moving:

- Children adjust better if they move between school terms (entering an established class in the middle of a school year can be very difficult).

- Elders have special needs you'll want to consider.
- Pets fare best when temperatures aren't too extreme, hot *or* cold.

THE "GET-OUT-OF-TOWN-IN-A-HURRY" PLAN

First the bad news: Very little about the move process can be shortened. Now the good news: The choices you make might make it possible to move in less time. The three primary resources in a successful move are time, money, and planning. If you're short on time, be prepared to spend more money or become more organized.

Immediately check into the availability of a rental truck or professional moving service. Next, give your landlord notice or arrange for an agent to sell your home. (If you own your home, you may find it harder to leave town in a hurry.) If your employer is paying for your move, ask if it offers corporate-sponsored financing options that will let you buy a new home before you sell your old one. Then consider the following potentially timesaving choices:

- Move less stuff. Of all the moving tasks, packing and unpacking consume the most time. The less you have to deal with, the quicker your move will go. Consider drastically lightening the load by selling or giving away most of your belongings and starting over in your new location. Although buying replacement stuff may drain your pocketbook, you can save some money by picking up some items secondhand at thrift stores and garage sales. (And after all, everything you have *now* is used, isn't it?)

- Make a quick-move plan. Quickly scan through chapters 4 and 5, highlighting helpful information. Use the checklists and the task time line at the end of this chapter to help you.

- Get someone else to do the cleaning. Before you vacate, you'll need to clean. You can be out the door sooner if you hire a professional cleaning company to come and clean everything, top to bottom, including the carpets. Again, the time you save will cost you money—but it may well be worth trading money for time.

Planning and Organizing

Start a move notebook. This could be as simple as a spiral-bound notepad or as elaborate as a categorized, tabbed binder. Keep track of this notebook. You'll find it invaluable later when the chaos hits. In your notebook, write notes and tape receipts. Of course, keep *this* book with your notebook! You may find the checklists and moving task time lines at the end of this chapter helpful. You may also find it helpful to assign a "do-by" date to each task on the checklist. To help you gauge what you face in the coming weeks, perhaps you will find it useful at this point to scan through the task time lines before reading further.

The section of the Moving Task Time Line that will help you the most at this point is "Decision Making: Weeks 12 to 9," which you'll find at the end of this chapter.

Preliminary Decisions

Before you even begin to plan your move, there are a number of decisions you'll need to make regarding your current residence, how you will move (do it yourself or hire a professional), and your new area.

LEAVING YOUR CURRENT HOME (RENTED PROPERTY)

Leaving a rental unit involves notifying your landlord and fulfilling your contractual obligations. This won't be a problem unless you have a lease agreement that lasts beyond your desired move date.

Your rights and options are dictated by state and local landlord/tenant laws and by your lease agreement. Exit fees can be expensive, depending on the terms of your lease. Here are some tips that may help you get out of a lease gracefully and save a few bucks at the same time.

- Know your rights. Laws governing landlord/tenant agreements and rights vary by state and municipality. Consult state and local law and call and obtain a pamphlet on renter's rights for your state and municipality.

- Review your lease agreement. There's no point in worrying until you know whether you have anything to worry about—and no use finding out too late that there were things you could have done.

- Look for a way out. Ask your landlord to consider letting you find a replacement tenant to fulfill your lease term (in some areas, this is a right dictated by law). If your move is due to a corporate relocation, your landlord or the property management company *may* be more willing to be flexible with exit fees—especially if you provide a letter from your employer. (And you may be able to get your employer to pick up the cost if you can't get the fees waived.)

- Adjust the timing. If you need to stay a month or two longer than your current lease allows and you don't want to sign for another six months or longer, ask your landlord for a month-to-month agreement lasting until your move date.

LEAVING YOUR CURRENT HOME (OWNED PROPERTY)

If you own your home, you'll either sell it or rent it out. If you sell, you'll either hire a real estate agent or sell it yourself. If you rent it out, you'll either serve as your own landlord or hire a property management agency to manage the property for you. Here are a few quick pros and cons to help you with the decisions you face.

Hiring a Selling Agent: Pros

- Your home gets exposure to a wide market audience, especially if the agent you choose participates in a multiple listing service.
- Homes listed with a real estate agent typically sell more quickly.
- Your agent will market your home (prepare and place ads and so on), and will also schedule and manage open houses and showings.
- Your agent will advise you and represent your interest in the business deal of selling, including offers, negotiation, and closing, guiding you through the stacks of paperwork.

Hiring a Selling Agent: Cons

- Hiring an agent requires signing a contract. If, for whatever reason, you want out, you may find it difficult to break the contract (it's wise to read carefully and sign only a short-term contract. Typical real estate agent contracts are ninety to 120 days in length).
- You pay your agent a fee for the service, typically a percentage of the selling price.

Selling Your Home Yourself: Pros

- You don't pay an agent's fee.
- You retain more control over showings, open houses, walkthroughs, and so on.

Selling Your Home Yourself: Cons

- Selling a home takes time. You must arrange your own showings and schedule and conduct your own open houses. Combined with everything else that happens during move preparation

CITY FACT

In 1698, the population of New York City was 4,937. Today, that many people work in an average-sized Midtown office building.

(working, interviewing for jobs, finding a new home, planning your move, packing, and so on), you will probably be swamped already. Add home showings (which are based around the buyer's schedule, not yours), and you may find yourself looking for an agent to help you after all.

- You pay for marketing costs, which can add up. Consider the cost of flyers, newspaper ads, or listing your home on a "homes for sale by owner" Web site.
- Since you don't have a real estate agent to represent you in the sale, you may need to hire an attorney at that point, which could take up some of the savings.

RENTING OUT YOUR PROPERTY

If you prefer to rent out your home, you can turn it over to a property management agency or be your own landlord. The services an agency will perform depend on the agency and your agreement with them. The following table details some of the rental issues you'll need to consider. As you review these, ask yourself how far away you're moving and whether or not you can handle these issues from your new home. Remember that every piece of work you must hire out cuts into the money in your pocket at the end of the month.

Rental Issue	You As Landlord	Hired Property Manager
Vacancy	You interview candidates, show the property, and choose tenants	The agency finds and selects tenants
Cleaning	You clean or arrange for cleaning services between tenants	The agency arranges for cleaning services between tenants
Late Rent	You collect rent and pursue late rent	The agency collects rent and pursues late rent
Rental Income	The rent you collect is all yours	The agency charges a fee, usually a percentage of the monthly rent
Repairs	You handle repairs and emergencies or find and hire a contractor to do the work	The agency handles repairs and emergencies

Strategic Financial Issues
Related to Renting Out Your Old Home

If your property is located in a desirable neighborhood that is appreciating in value 3 percent or more annually, keeping it may in the long run defray or overcome the cost of management fees. If you rent out your property, it ceases being your primary residence. Find out from your accountant if this will affect your federal or state income taxes or local property taxes (some counties/municipalities give owner-occupied credits that reduce the tax burden). If there is an impact, you'll want to figure the difference into your decision of whether or not to sell and into the total you charge for rent.

Deciding How to Move:
Hiring Professionals or Moving Yourself

At first, you may be inclined to handle your own move to save money. But there are other factors to consider, and, depending on your situation, you may actually *save* money if you use professional services. Consider the range of service options some professional companies offer. The right combination could save you some of the headache but still compete with the cost of a do-it-yourself move. For example, some professional moving companies offer a "you pack, we drive" arrangement, in which you pack boxes and the moving company loads, moves, and unloads your belongings. Call around and inquire about rates. Also consider the following list of pros and cons to help you decide what's best for you.

The section of the Moving Task Time Line that will help you the most at this point is "Decision Making: Weeks 12 to 9," which you'll find at the end of this chapter.

The Pros of Using Pros

- *Time.* You may not have the hours it will take to pack, move, and unpack, but professional movers do—that's their day job.
- *Materials.* The moving company provides boxes and packing materials.*
- *Packing.* The movers pack all boxes (unless your contract states that you will pack).*
- *Loading and Unloading.* The movers load your belongings onto the moving van and unload your belongings at your destination.*
- *Unpacking.* The movers remove packed items from boxes and place items on flat surfaces.*
- *Debris.* The movers dispose of packing debris such as boxes, used tape, and padding.*
- *Experience.* The movers will know just what to do to transport your precious belongings in good condition.
- *Safety.* The movers do the lifting, which could save you a real injury.

Professional moving contracts typically include the services marked with an asterisk (*). Don't count on something unless you know for sure that the contract covers it, though—it's a good idea to ask your mover a lot of questions and read the contract carefully.

The Cons of Using Pros

- *Administrative chores.* Using professionals requires you to do some up-front work: obtaining estimates, comparing and negotiating prices and move dates, reviewing contracts, and comparing insurance options.
- *Loss of control.* The movers typically take charge of much of the packing and loading process, and you need to adapt to their schedule and procedures.

The Pros of a Self-Move

- *Control.* You pack, so you decide what items get packed together, how they get packed, and in which box they reside.
- *Cost-cutting.* You may save some money. But as you compare costs, be sure to factor in *all* self-move-related moving and travel costs. These include fuel, tolls, mileage charge on the rented truck, food, and lodging. All these costs increase the longer your trip is.

The Cons of a Self-Move

- *Risk to your belongings.* Because of inexperience with packing, loading, and padding heavy and unwieldy boxes and furniture, you or your volunteers may inadvertently damage your property.
- *Risk to yourself and your friends.* You or your volunteers may injure yourselves or someone else.
- *Responsibility.* Loading and moving day are especially hectic, and you're in charge.
- *Reciprocal obligations.* If you use volunteers, you may be in debt to return the favor.

OTHER THINGS TO KNOW
ABOUT PROFESSIONAL MOVING SERVICES

Your moving company may or may not provide the following services, or may charge extra for performing them. Be sure to ask.

- Disassembling beds or other furniture
- Removing window covering hardware (drapery rods, mini-blinds) or other items from the walls or ceiling
- Disconnecting and installing appliances (dryer, washer, automatic ice maker)
- Disconnecting and installing outside fixtures such as a satellite dish, a hose reel, and so on
- Moving furniture or boxes from one room to another

MOVING INSURANCE IN A PROFESSIONAL MOVE

By U.S. law, the mover must cover your possessions at $0.60 per pound. This coverage is free. Consider taking out additional coverage, though, because under this minimal coverage, your three-pound antique Tiffany lamp worth hundreds of dollars at auction fetches exactly $1.80 if the moving company breaks it.

MOVING TIP

If you are renting a truck, you'll need to know what size to rent. Here is a general guideline. Because equipment varies, though, ask for advice from the company renting the truck to you.

10-foot truck:

　　one to two furnished rooms

14- to 15-foot truck:

　　two to three furnished rooms

18- to 20-foot truck:

　　four to five furnished rooms

22- to 24-foot truck:

　　six to eight furnished rooms

Your homeowner's or renter's insurance provider may be willing to advise you on moving insurance options, and the moving company will offer you a number of insurance options. Be sure you understand each option—what it covers and what it costs you. Ask a lot of questions and read everything carefully. No one wishes for mishaps, but it's best to be prepared and well informed should something break or show up missing.

STORAGE

If you want your moving company to store some or all of your possessions temporarily, inquire about cost and the quality of their facilities:

- Are the facilities heated (or air-conditioned, depending on the time of year that matters to you)?
- Does the moving company own the storage facility or subcontract storage to someone else? If they subcontract, does your contract with the moving company extend to the storage facility company?

New York Storage Companies

Chelsea Mini-Storage
(212) 564-7735

www.chelsea-mini-storage.com

Keepers
(212) 674-2166

www.keepers.storage.com

Eleven locations throughout the five boroughs, New Jersey, and Long Island.

Manhattan Mini Storage
(212) STO-RAGE; (212) 786-7243

www.800storage.com

Moishe's

(800) 536-6564

www.moishes.com

Facilities in Manhattan, Queens, Brooklyn, and New Jersey.

StorageUSA

(800) STOR-USA

www.sus.com

Locations throughout the five boroughs, New Jersey, Connecticut and Long Island.

CHOOSING A MOVER

- Start by asking around. Chances are your friends, family, or colleagues will have a personal recommendation.

CITY FACT

There are 12,187 medallion-licensed taxis in New York City. In order to drive a yellow cab in the City, a driver must purchase (or lease) a medallion from the owner, usually at auction. Medallions are currently bringing in more than $150,000 at auction.

- Take their recommendations and list them in a notebook, each on a separate sheet. Call these companies to request a no-obligation, free written estimate—and take notes on your conversation.

- Find out if the company you're talking to offers the services you need. For example, if you want to ship your car, boat, or powered recreational craft in the van along with your household goods, ask if this service is available.

- Do a little investigating. Ask the company to show you its operating license, and call the Better Business Bureau to ask about complaints and outstanding claims.

GETTING AN ESTIMATE

You need to know what kind of estimate the moving company is giving you. The two most common are "non-binding" and "binding." A *non-binding estimate* (usually free, but potentially less accurate) is one in which the moving company charges you by the hour per worker per truck and quotes you an approximate figure to use in your planning. Depending on circumstances, your final cost could be significantly greater than what shows up in the estimate.

The second type is a *binding estimate,* which you typically pay for. In this type, the professional mover performs a detailed on-site inspection of your belongings and quotes a flat price based on the following:

- The amount of stuff you're moving, whether it is fragile or bulky, and how complicated it is to pack
- Final weight
- Services provided
- Total length of travel

Once you choose a mover, it's a good idea to have a representative visit your home, look at your belongings, and give you a written (binding) estimate. Getting a written estimate may cost you money, but it helps prevent surprises when it comes to pay the final bill.

You play a big role in making sure that the estimate you receive is accurate. Be sure you show the moving company representative everything you plan to move.

- Remember to take the representative through every closet, out to the garage, into the shed, down to the basement, up into the attic, and to your rented storage facility if you have one.
- Tell the representative about any item you *don't* plan to move (because you plan to get rid of it before you move). Then be sure to follow through and get rid of it so there are no surprises on moving day.
- Point out any vehicles you want to ship in the van along with your household goods, and ask your representative to include the cost in your estimate.

WHAT MIGHT INCREASE YOUR FINAL BILL

It is reasonable to expect that certain circumstances will unexpectedly increase your final bill, including:

- You do the packing and it's incomplete or done improperly.

- Circumstances unexpectedly increase the time and labor involved in your move. For example:

    You're moving out of or into a high-rise and movers don't have access to an elevator (perhaps it's broken).

    Access at either location is restricted (for example, there is no truck parking close by or the movers have to wait for someone to unlock).

- You change your move destination after you receive your written estimate.

- You require delivery of your belongings to more than one destination.

Researching Your New Area

The section of the Moving Task Time Line that will help you the most at this point is "Decision Making: Weeks 12 to 9," which you'll find at the end of this chapter. Other chapters of this book discuss the details of your destination city. Here are some additional move-related tips and resources.

MOVING TIP

Start packing as soon as you get boxes. Some things you can pack long before the move. For example, off-season holiday decorations and off-season clothes can be boxed right away. The more you do early on, the less there is to do closer to move day, when things are hectic anyway.

GENERAL CITY INFORMATION

- Visit your local library and read up on New York City.
- Go online and read the *New York Times* (*www.nytimes.com*).
- Have a friend or family member mail you a week's worth of newspapers or have a subscription delivered via postal mail.
- Visit *www.monstermoving.com* for easy-to-find city information and links to local services, information, and Web sites.

JOBS, HOUSING, AND COST OF LIVING

Visit *www.monster.com* for career assistance, and visit *www.monster-moving.com* for links to apartments for rent, and real estate and other services, as well as free cost-of-living information.

CHOOSING SCHOOLS

Selecting schools is of supreme importance for family members who will attend public or private schools.

Do Your Homework

- Ask your real estate agent to help you find school information and statistics or a list of contacts for home school associations.
- Search the Web.

>   Visit *www.2001beyond.com*. There you can compare up to four districts at once. Information on both public and private schools is provided. The extensive twelve-page report provides information on class size, curriculum, interscholastic sports, extracurricular activities, awards, merits, and SAT scores. It also provides the principal's name and phone number for each school in the district. You may need to pay a nominal fee for the twelve-page report (or the cost may be covered by a sponsoring real estate professional, if you don't mind receiving a phone call from an agent).

>   Visit *www.monstermoving.com*, which provides links to school information.

Visit Schools

Arrange to visit schools your children might attend, and bring them along. Your children will pick up on subtleties that you will miss. As you talk with your children about changing schools, try to help them differentiate between their feelings about moving to a new school and area and their feelings about that particular school by asking direct but open-ended questions. (An *open-ended* question is one that invites dialogue because it can't be answered with a simple "yes" or "no"— "What was the best or worst thing you saw there?" for example, or "Which electives looked the most interesting?")

PLANNING AND TAKING A
HOUSE- OR APARTMENT-HUNTING TRIP

Preparing and planning in advance will help you make the most of your trip. Ideally, by this point, you will have narrowed your search to two or three neighborhoods or areas.

- Gather documents and information required for completing a rental application (see list on page 112).

- Consider compiling all this information into a "Rental Résumé." Even though most landlords won't accept a rental résumé in lieu of a completed application, spending the time up front could be helpful in a market where rentals are scarce. Handing the landlord a rental résumé lets them know you're serious about finding the right place and are professional and organized in how you conduct your affairs.

- Go prepared to pay an application fee and deposits. Typically, landlords require first and last month's rent and a flat damage and cleaning deposit (usually equal to a month's rent). Landlords require a certified check for these payments, so you'll nee a local bank account or enough traveler's checks to exchange for a certified check at a local bank.

- Take your Move Planning Notebook. List properties you want to visit, one per notebook page. Clip the classified ad and tape it onto the page. Write notes about the property, rent rate, deposit amount, and terms you discuss with the landlord or property manager.

Planning

Now that you've made pre-move decisions, it's time to plan for the physical move. First, you'll need to organize your moving day. Next, you'll need to prepare to pack.

These are the sections of the Moving Task Time Line that will help you the most at this point:

- "Organizing, Sorting, and Notifying: Weeks 9 to 8"
- "Finalizing Housing Arrangements and Establishing Yourself in Your New Community: Weeks 8 to 6"

- "Making and Confirming Transportation and Travel Plans: Week 6"
- "Uprooting: Weeks 5 to 4"
- "Making and Confirming Moving-Day Plans: Week 3"

You'll find the Moving Task Time Line at the end of this chapter.

PLANNING FOR MOVING DAY

The Professional Move: Some Planning Considerations

- Confirm your move dates and finalize any last contract issues.
- Ask what form of payment movers will accept (check, money order, certified check, traveler's checks) and make necessary arrangements.

The Self-Move: Organizing Volunteers

- Ask friends and relatives to "volunteer" to help you load the truck on moving day.
- Set up shifts, and tactfully let your volunteers know that you are counting on them to arrive on time and stay through their "shift."
- A week or two before moving day, call everyone to remind them.
- Plan on supplying soft drinks and munchies to keep your crew going.

PLANNING CARE FOR YOUR CHILDREN AND PETS

Moving day will be hectic for you and everyone, and possibly dangerous for your young children. Make plans to take younger children and your pets to someone's home or to a care facility.

PLANNING YOUR MOVING-DAY TRAVEL

Driving

- If you will be renting a truck, be prepared to put down a sizable deposit the day you pick up the truck. Some truck rental companies only accept a credit card for this deposit, so go prepared.

- If you belong to an automobile club such as AAA, contact them to obtain maps, suggested routes, alternate routes, rest-stop information, and a trip packet, if they provide this service.
- Visit an online map site such as *www.mapblast.com*, where you'll find not only a map but also door-to-door driving directions and estimated travel times.
- Find out in advance where you should turn in the truck in your new hometown.

Traveling by Air, Train, or Bus

- Arrange for tickets and boarding passes.
- Speak with the airline to request meals that match dietary restrictions.
- Speak with the airline or the train or bus company to make any special arrangements such as wheelchair accessibility and assistance.
- Plan to dress comfortably.
- If you will be traveling with young children, plan to dress them in bright, distinctive clothing so you can easily identify them in a crowded airport, train station, or bus terminal.

MOVING TIP

Save the TV, VCR, kids' videos, and a box of toys to be loaded on the truck last. On arriving at your destination, if you can't find someone to baby-sit, set aside a room in your home where your young children can safely play. Set up the TV and VCR and unpack the kids' videos along with some toys and snacks.

PREPARING TO PACK: WHAT TO DO WITH THE STUFF YOU HAVE

Moves are complicated, time-consuming, and exhausting. But the process has at least one benefit. A move forces us to consider simplifying our lives by reducing the amount of our personal belongings. If we plan to keep it, we also must pack it, load it, move it, unload it, and unpack it. Here are some suggestions for sifting through your belongings as you prepare for packing.

- Start in one area of your home and go through everything before moving to the next area.

- Ask yourself three questions about each item (sentimental value aside):

  Have we used this in the last year?

  Will we use it in the coming year? For example, if you're moving to a more temperate climate, you might not need all your wool socks and sweaters.

  Is there a place for it in the new home? For instance, if your new home has a smaller living room, you might not have room for your big couch or need all your wall decorations.

If you answer "no" to any or all of these questions, you might want to consider selling the item, giving it away, or throwing it out.

Packing

Here are some tips to help you with one of the most difficult stages of your move—packing.

- Follow a plan. Pack one room at a time. You may find yourself leaving one or two boxes in each room open to receive those items you use right up until the last minute.

- On the outside of each box, describe the contents and room destination. Be as specific as you can, to make unpacking easier. However, if you are using a professional moving service but doing the packing yourself, consider numbering boxes and creating a separate list of box contents and destinations.

- Put heavy items such as books in small boxes to make them easier to carry.

- Don't put tape on furniture because it may pull off some finish when you remove it.

- As you pack, mark and set aside the items that should go in the truck last (see checklist at the end of this chapter). Mark and set aside your "necessary box" (for a list of items to include in this box, see the checklist at the end of this chapter).

PACKING FRAGILE ITEMS

- When packing breakable dishes and glasses, use boxes and padding made for these items. You may have to pay a little to buy these boxes, but you're apt to save money in the long run because your dishes are more likely to arrive unbroken. Dishes and plates are best packed on edge (not stacked flat atop each other).
- Pad mirrors, pictures, and larger delicate pieces with sheets and blankets.
- Computers fare best if they are packed in their original boxes. If you don't have these, pack your hardware in a large, sturdy box and surround it with plenty of padding such as plastic bubble pack.
- Use plenty of padding around fragile items.
- Mark "FRAGILE" *on the top and all sides* of boxes of breakables so it's easily seen no matter how a box is stacked.

CITY FACT

New Yorkers have a language all their own. "The City" means Manhattan—even to residents of the other four boroughs. Although Manhattan is an Island, "The Island" always means Long Island. Real New Yorkers stand "on line," not "in line." Visitors and commuters from New Jersey and Long Island are the "B&T" (bridge and tunnel) crowd. And in New York it never hurts to know a little Yiddish, especially when ordering a bagel with "a schmear" (a little cream cheese).

WHAT *NOT* TO PACK

- Don't pack hazardous, flammable, combustible, or explosive materials. Empty your gas grill tank and any kerosene heater fuel as well as gasoline in your power yard tools. These materials are not safe in transit.
- Don't pack valuables such as jewelry, collections, important financial and legal documents, and records for the moving van. Keep these with you in your car trunk or your suitcase.

PACKING AND UNPACKING SAFELY WITH YOUNG CHILDREN

No matter how well you've kid-proofed your home, that only lasts until the moment you start packing. Then things are in disarray and within reach of youngsters. Here are some tips to keep your toddlers and children safe.

- Items your youngsters have seldom or never seen will pique their curiosity, presenting a potential hazard, so consider what you are packing or unpacking. If you stop packing or unpacking and leave the room even for a moment, take your youngsters with you and close the door or put up a child gate.
- Keep box knives and other tools out of a child's reach.
- As you disassemble or reassemble furniture, keep track of screws, bolts, nuts, and small parts.
- Beware of how and where you temporarily place furniture and other items. (That heavy mirror you just took down off the wall—do you lean it up against the wall until you go get the padding material, inviting a curious youngster to pull or climb on it?) For the same reason, consider how high you stack boxes.
- On arriving at your destination, if you can't find someone to baby-sit, set aside a room in your home where your young children can safely play. Set up the TV and VCR and unpack the kids' videos, books, coloring books and crayons or markers, and some toys and snacks.
- Walk through your new home with children and talk about any potential dangers such as a swimming pool or stairs, establishing your safety rules and boundaries.

- If you have young children who are unaccustomed to having stairs in the home, place a gate at the top and one at the bottom. If your child is walking and over toddler age, walk up and down the stairs together a few times holding the railing until they become accustomed to using the stairs.

Handle with Special Care: Uprooting and Settling the People and Pets in Your Life

The most important advice you can hear is this: Involving children as much as possible will help transform this anxiety-causing, uncertain experience into an exciting adventure. It would take a book to cover this topic comprehensively, but here are some suggestions for making the transition easier:

- *Involve children early.* Ask for their input on decisions and give them age-appropriate tasks such as packing their own belongings and assembling an activity bag to keep them busy while traveling.

- *Don't make empty promises.* Kids can hear the hollow ring when you say, "It'll be just like here. Just give it time," or "You can stay friends with your friends here." That's true, but you know it's not true in the same way, if you're moving a long distance.

MOVING TIP

Take a tape measure and your notebook with you. Measure rooms; sketch your new home and write room measurements on your sketch. Before you move, you'll know whether your current furniture will fit and will have a good idea of how it should be arranged.

- *Deal with fear of the unknown.* If possible, take children with you to look at potential neighborhoods, homes or apartments, and schools. It may be more expensive and require extra effort, but it will ease the transition and help children begin to make the adjustment.

- *Provide as much information as you can.* If it's not possible to take children with you when you visit new neighborhoods, homes or apartments, and schools, take a camera or video recorder. Your children will appreciate the pictures, and the preview will help them begin the transition. You can also use a map to help them understand the new area and the route you will take to get there.
- *Make time to talk with your children about the move.* Especially listen for—and talk about—the anxieties your children feel. By doing so, you will help them through the move (your primary goal)—and you'll deepen your relationship at the same time, which may be more important in the long run.
- *Share your own anxieties with your children—but be sure to keep an overall positive outlook about the move.* Because most aspects of a move are downers, a negative outlook on your part may shed gloom over the whole experience—including its good aspects. On the other hand, a positive outlook on your part may counteract some of your child's emotional turmoil, uncertainty, and fear.
- *Make it fun.* Give older children a disposable camera and ask them to photograph your move. Once you arrive and are settled in, make time together to create the "moving" chapter of your family photo album.

HELPING FAMILY MEMBERS MAINTAIN FRIENDSHIPS

Moving doesn't have to end a friendship.

- Give each child a personal address book and have them write the e-mail address, phone number, and postal mail address for each of their friends.
- Stay in touch. E-mail is an easy way. Establish an e-mail address for every family member (if they don't already have one) before you move so they can give it out to friends. Many Web mail services are free and can be accessed from anywhere you can access the Internet. Examples include *www.msn.com, www.usa.net,* and *www.yahoo.com.*
- Make (and follow through with) plans to visit your old hometown within the first year following your move. Visit friends and drive by your old home, through neighborhoods, and past land-

marks. This reconnection with dear friends and fond memories will help your family bring finality to the move.

TRAVELING WITH YOUR PET

- Keep a picture of your pet on your person or in your wallet just in case you get separated from Fido or Fluffy during the move.
- Place identification tags on your pet's collar and pet carrier.
- Take your pet to the vet for an examination just before you move. Ask for advice on moving your particular pet. Specifically ask for advice on how you can help your pet through the move—what you can do before, during, and after the move to help your pet make the transition smoothly.
- Find out if you will need any health certificates for your pet to comply with local regulations in your new home, and obtain them when you visit the vet.
- If your pet is prone to motion sickness or tends to become nervous in reaction to excitement and unfamiliar surroundings, tell your veterinarian, who may prescribe medication for your pet.
- Ask for your pet's health records so you can take them to your new vet.
- If your pet is unusual—say, a ferret or a snake or other reptile—there are specific laws in New York regarding the transportation

CITY FACT

The neighborhood of Marble Hill used to sit at the northernmost point in Manhattan. In 1895, in order to accommodate large ships, the City channeled the Harlem River to run south of Marble Hill and filled in the canal that had formerly separated Marble Hill from the Bronx. Today, geographically, Marble Hill is in the Bronx—but politically it remains part of the borough of Manhattan.

or housing of such an animal. Contact the department of agriculture or a local veterinarian to find out.

- Cats: It's wise to keep your cat indoors for the first two weeks until it recognizes its new surroundings as home, and few New Yorkers ever let their cats outdoors.

- Dogs: If appropriate, walk your dog on a leash around your neighborhood to help it become familiar with its new surroundings and learn its way back home (though you'll never unleash your dog in New York City, except in fenced-in, designated dog-runs).

- If your pet will travel by plane, check with your airline regarding fees and any specific rules and regulations regarding pet transport.

- Your pet will need to travel in an approved carrier (check with your airline regarding acceptable types and sizes).

- Your airline may require a signed certificate of health dated within a certain number of days of the flight. Only your vet can produce this document.

Move Budget-Planning Guide

Housing

Home repairs	$ _____
Cleaning supplies and services	$ _____

Rental expenses in new city

Application fees (varies—figure $15 to $35 per application)	$ _____
First and last month's rent	$ _____
Damage and security deposit	$ _____
Pet deposit	$ _____
Utility deposits	$ _____
Storage unit rental	$ _____

Total . . . . **$** _____

Moving

Professional moving services or truck rental	$ _____
Moving supplies	$ _____
Food and beverage for volunteers	$ _____
Tips for professional movers; gifts for volunteers	$ _____

Moving travel:

Airline tickets	$ _____
Fuel	$ _____
Tolls	$ _____
Meals: per meal $_____ × _____ meals	$ _____
Hotels: per night $_____ × _____ nights	$ _____

Total . . . . **$** _____

(continues on next page)

(continued from previous page)

Other Expenses

_____	$ _____
_____	$ _____
_____	$ _____
_____	$ _____
_____	$ _____
_____	$ _____
_____	$ _____

Total. . . . . $ _____

GRAND TOTAL. . . . . $ _____

Utilities to Cancel

Utility	Provider name and phone	Cancel date[1]
Water and sewer		
Electricity		
Gas		
Phone		
Garbage		
Cable		
Alarm service		

1. If you are selling your home, the shutoff of essential services (water, electricity, gas) will depend on the final closing and walk-through. Coordinate with your real estate agent.

Utilities to Connect

Utility	Provider name and phone	Service start date	Deposit amount required
Water and sewer			
Electricity			
Gas			
Phone			
Garbage			
Cable			
Alarm service			

Other Services to Cancel, Transfer, or Restart

Service	Provider name and phone	Service end date[1]	Service start date[1]
Subscriptions and Memberships			
Newspaper			
Memberships (health club and so on)			
Internet Service Provider			

1. If applicable

(continues on next page)

(continued from previous page)

Other Services to Cancel, Transfer, or Restart			
Service	**Provider name and phone**	**Service end date**[1]	**Service start date**[1]
Government and School			
Postal mail change of address			
School records			
Voter registration			
Vehicle registration			
Financial			
Bank account[2]			
Direct deposits and withdrawals			
Safe deposit box			
Professional			
Health care (transfer doctors' and dentists' records for each family member)			
Veterinarian (transfer records)			
Cleaners (pick up your clothes)			

1. If applicable; 2. Open an account in your new town before closing your existing account.

Checklists

MOVING SUPPLIES

Packing and Unpacking

_____ Tape and tape dispenser. (The slightly more expensive gun-style dispenser is a worthwhile investment because its one-handed operation means you don't need a second person to help you hold the box closed while you do the taping.)

_____ Boxes. (It's worth it to obtain specialty boxes for your dinnerware, china set, and glasses. Specialty wardrobe boxes that allow your hanging clothes to hang during transport are another big help.)

_____ Padding such as bubble wrap.

_____ Markers.

_____ Scissors or a knife.

_____ Big plastic bags.

_____ Inventory list and clipboard.

_____ Box knife with retractable blade. (Get one for each adult.)

Loading and Moving

_____ Rope. (If nothing else, you'll need it to secure heavy items to the inside wall of the truck.)

_____ Padding blankets. (If you use your own, they may get dirty and you'll need bedding when you arrive. Padding is available for rent at most truck rental agencies.)

_____ Hand truck or appliance dolly. (Most truck rental agencies have them available for rent.)

_____ Padlock for the cargo door.

THE "NECESSARY BOX"

Eating

_____ Snacks or food. (Pack enough durable items for right before you depart, your travel, and the first day in your new home—and disposable utensils, plates, cups.)

_____ Instant coffee, tea bags, and so on.

_____ Roll of paper towels and moistened towelettes.

_____ Garbage bags.

Bathing

_____ A towel for each person.

_____ Soap, shampoo, toothpaste, and any other toiletries.

_____ Toilet paper.

Health Items

_____ First aid kit including pain relievers.

_____ Prescription medicines.

Handy to Have

_____ List of contact information. (Make sure you can reach relatives, the moving company, the truck driver's cell phone, and so on.)

_____ Small tool kit. (You need to be able to take apart and reassemble items that can't be moved whole.)

_____ Reclosable plastic bags to hold small parts, screws, bolts.

_____ Spare lightbulbs. (Some bulbs in your new home might be burned out or missing.)

_____ Nightlight and flashlight.

OVERNIGHT BAG

_____ Enough clothes for the journey plus the first day or two in your new home.

_____ Personal toiletries.

ITEMS FOR KIDS

_____ Activities for the trip.

_____ Favorite toys and anything else that will help children feel immediately at home in their new room.

Pet Checklist

_____ Food.

_____ A bottle of the water your pet is used to drinking.

_____ Dishes for food and water.

_____ Leash, collar, identification tags.

_____ Favorite toy.

_____ Medicines.

_____ Bed or blanket.

_____ Carrier.

_____ Paper towels in case of accidents.

_____ Plastic bags and a scooper.

_____ Litter and litter box for your cat or rabbit.

Last Items on the Truck

CLEANING

_____ Vacuum cleaner.

_____ Cleaning supplies.

GENERAL

_____ Necessary box.

_____ Setup for kids' temporary playroom.

_____ Other items you'll need the moment you arrive.

New Home Safety Checklist

GENERAL

_____ Watch out for tripping hazards. They will be plentiful until
you get everything unpacked and put away, so be careful, and
keep a path clear at all times.

HEAT, FIRE, ELECTRICAL

_____ Be sure nothing gets placed too close to heaters.

_____ Test smoke, heat, and carbon monoxide detectors. Find out
your fire department's recommendations regarding how
many of these devices you should have and where you should
place them. If you need more, go buy them (remember to
buy batteries) and install them.

_____ Find the fuse or breaker box before you need to shut off or
reset a circuit.

WATER

____ Check the temperature setting on your water heater. For child safety and fuel conservation, experts recommend 120 degrees Fahrenheit.

____ Locate the water shutoff valve in case of a plumbing problem.

Moving Task Time Line

DECISION MAKING: WEEKS 12 TO 9

____ Consider your moving options (professional versus self-move) and get quotes.

____ If you are being relocated by your company, find out what your company covers and what you will be responsible for doing and paying.

____ Set a move date.

____ Choose your moving company or truck rental agency and reserve the dates.

____ You should already be applying to local schools for young children.

If You Own Your Home

____ Decide whether you want to sell or rent it out.

____ If you decide to sell, choose a real estate agent and put your home on the market or look into, and begin planning for, selling it yourself

____ If you decide to rent out your home, decide whether you want to hire a property management agency or manage the property yourself.

____ Perform (or hire contractors to perform) home repairs.

If You Currently Rent

_____ Notify your landlord of your plans to vacate.

_____ Check into cleaning obligations and options.

Tour Your New City or Town

_____ Research your new area at the library or online at *www.monstermoving.com.*

_____ Contact a real estate agent or property management agency to help you in your search for new lodgings.

_____ Go on a school-hunting and house- or apartment-hunting trip to your new town or city.

Additional items:

_____

_____

_____

_____

_____

_____

_____

_____

_____

_____

_____

_____

_____

_____

_____

_____

_____

_____

_____

ORGANIZING, SORTING, AND NOTIFYING:
WEEKS 9 TO 8

_____ Obtain the post office's change of address kit by calling 1-800-ASK-USPS or visiting your local post office or *www.usps.gov/moversnet/* (where you'll find the form and helpful lists of questions and answers).

_____ Complete and send the form.

_____ List and notify people, businesses, and organizations who need to know about your move. You may not think of everyone at once, but keep a running list and add people to your list and notify them as you remember them. As you notify them, check them off your list.

_____ Start sorting through your belongings to decide what to keep. Make plans to rid yourself of what you don't want: pick a date for a garage sale; call your favorite charity and set a date for them to come pick up donations; call your recycling company to find out what they will accept.

_____ For moving insurance purposes, make an inventory of your possessions with their estimated replacement value.

_____ If you have high-value items (such as antiques) that you expect to send with the moving company or ship separately, obtain an appraisal.

Additional items:

_____

_____

_____

_____

_____

_____

_____

_____

FINALIZING HOUSING ARRANGEMENTS
AND ESTABLISHING YOURSELF
IN YOUR NEW COMMUNITY: WEEKS 8 TO 6

_____ **Home.** Select your new home and arrange financing; establish a tentative closing date or finalize rental housing arrangements.

_____ **Insurance.** Contact an agent regarding coverage on your new home and its contents as well as on your automobile.

_____ **Finances.** Select a bank, open accounts, and obtain a safe deposit box.

_____ **New Home Layout.** Sketch a floor plan of your new home and include room measurements. Determine how your present furniture, appliances, and decor will fit.

_____ **Mail.** If you haven't found a new home, rent a post office box for mail forwarding.

_____ **Services.** Find out the names and phone numbers of utility providers and what they require from you before they will start service (for example, a deposit, a local reference). (You can list your providers and service start dates on the checklist provided in this chapter.) Schedule service to start a few days before you arrive.

Additional items:

_____

_____

_____

_____

_____

_____

_____

_____

_____

MAKING AND CONFIRMING TRANSPORTATION AND TRAVEL PLANS: WEEK 6

_____ Schedule pick-up and delivery dates with your mover.

_____ Make arrangements with your professional car mover.

_____ If you need storage, make the arrangements.

_____ Confirm your departure date with your real estate agent or landlord.

_____ Make your travel arrangements. If you will be flying, book early for cheaper fares.

_____ Map your driving trip using _www.mapblast.com_ or ask your automobile club for assistance with route and accommodation information.

Additional items:

_____

_____

_____

_____

_____

_____

_____

_____

_____

_____

_____

_____

_____

_____

_____

_____

_____

UPROOTING: WEEKS 5 TO 4

_____ Hold your garage sale, or donate items to charity.

_____ Gather personal records from all health care providers, your veterinarian, lawyers, accountants, and schools.

_____ Notify current utility providers of your disconnect dates and your forwarding address. (You can list your providers and service end dates on the checklist provided in this chapter.)

Additional items:

_____

_____

_____

_____

_____

_____

_____

_____

_____

_____

_____

_____

_____

_____

_____

_____

_____

_____

_____

_____

_____

_____

_____

MAKING AND CONFIRMING MOVING-DAY PLANS: WEEK 3

_____ Make arrangements for a sitter for kids and pets on moving day.

_____ Call moving-day volunteers to confirm move date and their arrival time.

_____ Obtain travelers checks for trip expenses and cashiers or certified check for payment to mover.

_____ Have your car serviced if you are driving a long distance.

Additional items:

_____

_____

_____

_____

_____

_____

_____

_____

_____

_____

_____

_____

_____

_____

_____

_____

_____

_____

WEEK 2

_____ If you have a pet, take it to the vet for a checkup. For more pet-moving tips, see the section earlier in this chapter on moving with pets.

_____ Arrange for transportation of your pet.

_____ If you are moving into or out of a high-rise building, contact the property manager and reserve the elevator for moving day.

_____ Drain oil and gas from all your power equipment and kerosene from portable heaters.

Additional items:

_____

_____

_____

_____

_____

_____

_____

_____

_____

_____

_____

_____

_____

_____

_____

_____

_____

_____

_____

_____

MOVING WEEK

_____ Defrost the freezer.

_____ Give away any plants you can't take with you.

_____ Pack your luggage and your necessary box for the trip (see the list provided in this chapter).

_____ Get everything but the day-to-day essentials packed and ready to go.

Additional items:

_____

_____

_____

_____

_____

_____

_____

_____

_____

_____

_____

_____

_____

_____

_____

_____

_____

MOVING DAY

_____ Mark off parking space for the moving van using cones or chairs.

_____ See "Moving Day" section of chapter 5 for further to-do items.

Getting from Here to There: Moving Day and Beyond

This chapter guides you through the next stage in your move: moving day, arriving, unpacking, and settling in. Here you'll find important travel tips for both the self-move and the professional move, information related to a professional car move, and pointers for your first days and weeks in your new home.

The Professional Move

Early on moving day, reserve a large place for the moving truck to park. Mark off an area with cones or chairs. If you need to obtain parking permission from your apartment complex manager or the local government, do so in advance.

GUIDE THE MOVERS

Before work starts, walk through the house with the movers and describe the loading order. Show them the items you plan to transport yourself. (It's best if these are piled in one area and clearly marked, maybe even covered with a sheet or blanket until you're ready to pack them in your car.)

Remain on-site to answer the movers' questions and to provide special instructions.

BEFORE YOU DEPART

Before you hit the road, you will need to take care of some last-minute details:

- Walk through your home to make sure everything was loaded.
- Sign the bill of lading. But first, read it carefully and ask any questions. The bill of lading is a document the government requires movers to complete for the transportation of supplies, materials, and personal property. The mover is required to have a signed copy on hand, and you should keep your copy until the move is complete and any claims are settled.
- Follow the movers to the weigh station. Your bill will be partly based on the weight of your property moved.

UNLOADING AND MOVING IN

Be sure to take care of these details once the movers arrive at your new home:

- Have your money ready. (Professional movers expect payment in full before your goods are unloaded.)
- Check for damage as items are unpacked and report it right away.
- Unless the company's policy prohibits the acceptance of gratuities, it is customary to tip each mover. $20 is a good amount; you may want to tip more or less based on the service you receive (especially if your move requires excessive stair climbing).

The Self-Move

The following tips should help you organize and guide your help, as well as make the moving day run more smoothly:

- The day before your move, create a task list. Besides the obvious (loading the truck), this list will include tasks such as disconnecting the washer and dryer and taking apart furniture that can't be moved whole.

- Plan to provide beverages and food for your volunteers. Make it easy on yourself and provide popular options such as pizza or sub sandwiches (delivered), chilled soda pop and bottled water (in an ice chest, especially if you're defrosting and cleaning the refrigerator).

- On moving day, remember, you are only one person. So if you need to defrost the freezer or pack last-minute items, choose and appoint someone who knows your plan to oversee the volunteers and answer questions.

- Be sure you have almost everything packed before your help arrives. Last-minute packing creates even more chaos and it's likely that hastily packed items will be damaged during loading or transit.

MOVING TIP

A few weeks before you move, start eating the food in your freezer. Also use up canned food, which is bulky and heavy to move.

- If you end up with an even number of people, it's natural for people to work in pairs because they can carry the items that require two people. If you have an odd number of people, the extra person can rotate in to provide for breaks, carry light items alone, or work on tasks you assign.

- Be sure to match a person's physical ability and health with the tasks you assign.

- Appoint the early shift to start on tasks such as disconnecting the washer and dryer and taking apart furniture (such as bed frames) that can't be moved whole.

- Before work starts, walk through the house with your volunteers and describe your loading plan.

- Know your moving truck and how it should be packed for safe handling on the road (ask the truck rental company for directions).

- Load the truck according to the directions your truck rental agency gave you. Tie furniture items (especially tall ones) to the inside wall of the truck. Pack everything together as tightly as possible, realizing that items will still shift somewhat as you travel.

Move Travel

Arriving by Plane

There are three major international airports that service the New York metropolitan area. In New York City, they are La Guardia Airport and JFK International Airport (both are in Queens), and, in New Jersey, Newark International Airport (in Newark).

From each airport you'll have many transportation options to get into the City: Taxi, bus, shuttle, car service, helicopter, ferry, and even a bus-subway combo. See chapter 6 for specifics.

Arriving by Car

It could take you a decade and a Ph.D. to learn all of the different ways to drive into Manhattan—which are the best routes is a frequent source of discussion and debate, particularly among suburban commuters. What you need to know, at the most basic level, is that I-95 from the north and south and I-80 from the west will all lead you to Manhattan. If you are a member of AAA, get a trip-tik tailored to your exact itinerary; if not, use a map or get online and check out one of the following (or a few to cross-reference) Web sites for directions that are best suited to your travel plans.

Yahoo

www.yahoo.com

Go to the MAPS section

Excite

www.excite.com

Go to MAPS and DIRECTIONS section

Mapblast

www.mapblast.com

Arriving by Bus

Long-distance buses (Greyhound, Trailways, Peter Pan, Vermont Transit, and others) arrive into the City at the Port Authority Bus Terminal, which is located between 40th and 42nd Streets between and 8th and 9th Avenues.

MOVING TIP

Reserve a large place for the moving truck to park on the day you move out. Mark off an area with cones or chairs. If you need to obtain parking permission from your apartment complex manager or the city, do so in advance.

Arriving by Train

Amtrak trains arrive at Penn Station (31st to 33rd Streets, between 7th and 8th Avenues).

SELF-MOVE—DRIVING A TRUCK

- A loaded moving truck handles far differently from the typical car. Allow extra space between you and the vehicle you're following. Drive more slowly and decelerate and brake sooner—there's a lot of weight sitting behind you.

- Realize that no one likes to follow a truck. Other drivers may make risky moves to get ahead of you, so watch out for people passing when it's not safe.

- Know your truck's height and look out for low overhangs and tree branches. Especially be aware of filling station overhang height.

- Most accidents in large vehicles occur when backing. Before you back, get out, walk around, and check for obstacles. Allow plenty of maneuvering room and ask someone to help you back. Ask them to stay within sight of your sideview mirror—and talk over the hand signals they should use as they guide you.
- Stop and rest at least every two hours.
- At every stop, do a walk-around inspection of the truck. Check tires, lights, and the cargo door. (If you're towing a trailer, check trailer tires, door, hitch, and hitch security chain.) Ask your truck rental representative how often you should check the engine oil level.
- At overnight stops, park in a well-lighted area and lock the truck cab. Lock the cargo door with a padlock.

IF YOU'RE FLYING OR TRAVELING BY TRAIN OR BUS

- Coordinate with the moving van driver so that you arrive at about the same time.
- Plan for the unexpected such as delays, cancellations, or missed connections.
- Keep in touch with the truck driver (by cell phone, if possible), who may also experience delays for any number of reasons: mechanical problems, road construction, storms, or illness.
- Dress comfortably.
- If you are traveling with young children, dress them in bright, distinctive clothing so you can easily identify them in a crowded airport, train station, or bus terminal.

PROFESSIONAL MOVERS MAY NEED HELP, TOO

Make sure the movers have directions to your new home. Plan your travel so that you will be there to greet them and unlock. Have a backup plan in case one of you gets delayed. It is also a good idea to exchange cell phone numbers with the driver so you can stay in touch in case one of you is delayed.

TIPS FOR A PROFESSIONAL CAR MOVE

A professional car carrier company can ship your car. Alternatively, your moving company may be able to ship it in the van along with your household goods. Ask around and compare prices.

- Be sure that the gas tanks are no more than one-quarter full.
- It's not wise to pack personal belongings in your transported auto, because insurance typically won't cover those items.
- If your car is damaged in transport, report the damage to the driver or move manager and note it on the inventory sheet. If you don't, the damage won't be eligible for insurance coverage.

MOVING TIP

In New York City, you can't just show up with your truck and move into an apartment building. You'll need an appointment to use the elevator, and many buildings restrict move-ins to certain days of the week.

Be sure to make your move-in appointment for the earliest possible time of day; it will make parking the truck much easier.

Unpacking and Getting Settled

You made it. Welcome home! With all the boxes and bare walls, it may not feel like home just yet, but it soon will. You're well on your way to getting settled and having life return to normal. As you unpack boxes, arrange the furniture, and hang the pictures, here are a few things to keep in mind:

- Approach unpacking realistically. It's not necessary (and probably not possible) to unpack and arrange everything on the first day.
- Find your cleaning supplies and do any necessary cleaning.

- Consider your family's basic needs (food, rest, bathing) and
  unpack accordingly:
  Kitchen: Start with the basics; keep less frequently used
    items in boxes until you decide your room and storage
    arrangements.
  Bedrooms: Unpack bedding and set up and make beds.
  Bathroom: Because this tends to be a small room with little
    space for boxes, unpack the basics early and find a place
    to store the still-packed boxes until you have a chance to
    finish.

MAINTAINING NORMALCY . . . STARTING FRESH

During the move and the days following, it's good to keep things feeling as normal as possible. But this can also be a fresh starting point: a time to establish (or reestablish) family rituals and traditions. Beyond the family, this is a time to meet and connect with new neighbors, schoolmates, and your religious or other community.

- Keep regular bedtimes and wake-up times (naps for kids if
  appropriate).
- If you typically eat dinner together, continue to do this, despite
  the chaos.
- If you typically have a regular family time—an activity or outing—don't feel bad if you must skip it one week due to move-
  related chores, but restart this ritual as soon as you can. In fact,
  your family may appreciate this special time even more in the
  midst of the upheaval and change.

Rome wasn't built in a day, and neither are friendships. If your move means you have to start over, take heart: persistence and work will pay off over time. Here are a few suggestions for making your first connections with people—individuals and communities of people—in your new area.

- Encourage family members who need encouragement in making
  new friends.
- Provide opportunities for building friendships from day one.
  Take a break from unpacking and knock on doors to meet neighbors. (It's not a good idea to start a friendship by asking for help
  unloading, though!)

- Get involved in activities your family enjoys and make time in your schedule for people, even though moving and resettling is a hectic and busy time.
- Meet and connect with your religious or other community.

DISCOVERING YOUR COMMUNITY

Here you'll find suggestions for getting settled in your new surroundings:

- Be sure every family member gets a feel for the neighborhood and main streets; memorizes your new address; learns (or carries) new home, office, and mobile phone numbers; and knows how to contact local emergency personnel including police, fire, and ambulance.
- Go exploring on foot, bike, mass transit, or by car (turn it into a fun outing) and start learning your way around.
- Locate your local post office and police and fire stations, as well as hospitals and gas stations near your home.
- Scout your new neighborhood for shopping areas.
- Register to vote.
- If you have moved to a new state, visit the Department of Motor Vehicles to obtain your driver's license and register your vehicle (see below).
- If you haven't already done so, transfer insurance policies to an agent in your new community.

MOVING TIP

Draw up a detailed plan of your new home, including scale drawings of each room that show each piece of furniture you plan to take with you. Label furniture and boxes as to where they go in the new home, and have copies of the plan to put in each room there. This will give you at least a chance that most of the work of moving in will only need to be done once.

Important Local Telephone Numbers

Twenty-Four-Hour Locksmith

Presto
(212) 831-9667

Local Telephone Service

Bell Atlantic Telephone
(212) 890-1550

For long-distance service, your choices are the same as anywhere else in the country: Sprint, AT&T, MCI, etc.

Cable TV

Time Warner Cable
(212) 567-3833
www.twcnyc.com
Servicing all five boroughs

City Sanitation
(212) 219-8090

Electricity and Gas

Con Edison
(212) 338-3000

Exterminators

Broadway Exterminating
(212) 663-2100

Orkin
(800) 800-ORKIN,
(800) 800-6754
(212) 964-4114 in Manhattan
(203) 324-3758 in Greenwich, CT
www.orkin.com

Terminix
(212) 772-0780 in Manhattan
(718) 652-1040 in the Bronx
(718) 782-0191 in Brooklyn
(718) 352-0111 in Queens
(718) 948-2002 in Staten Island
www.terminix.com

Services also available in Long Island, Westchester County, and New Jersey.

Housing Authority
(212) 306 3000

Passport Information
(212) 399-5290

Police and Fire Departments

Dial 911 (Note: For non-emergency police calls, dial 212-374-5000 to learn the number of your local precinct.)

Traffic Information
(212) 442-7080

See chapter 9 for additional, more extensive listings.

Vehicle Registration

If you're moving to New York with a car, you must have the following information to register your vehicle:

- Proof of ownership
- Completed *Vehicle Registration/Title Application* form
- New York State insurance card
- Proof of inspection
- Sales tax clearance (available at motor vehicle office)
- Proof of name and birth date
- Odometer Disclosure Statement, if the car is less than ten years old
- Bill of sale
- Registration fee

To change your out-of-state license to a New York State license (and to avoid the written and practical tests), you must have a valid (or expired within the last twelve months) license from another state.

MOVING TIP

Unless company policy prohibits acceptance of gratuities, it is customary to tip each professional mover. $20 is a good amount; you may want to tip more or less based on the service you receive (especially where stair climbing is involved). If you move yourself, you might also want to give each of your volunteers a gift. Cash or a gift certificate is a nice gesture. Perhaps one of your volunteers is a plant-lover and will cheerfully accept your houseplants as a thank-you gift. It's also a good idea to supply plenty of soft drinks or water and snacks for them!

TAKING CARE OF THE FINANCIAL IMPLICATIONS OF YOUR MOVE

Now that you have arrived, you can take care of some of the financial and tax implications of your move. Here are some things to think about (it's also wise to consult an accountant):

- Some of your moving expenses may be tax-deductible. Prepare for tax filing by collecting receipts from your move. Also contact the Internal Revenue Service to obtain the publication and form you need. Visit *www.irs.gov* or call (800) 829-3676.

- State income tax. In New York, you'll need to file a state income tax form. For help with your relocation-related taxes, visit *www.monstermoving.com* and check out "Relocation Tax Advisor."

- Other income sources may have tax implications. As you prepare to file, you'll want to consider any other sources of income and whether your new state will tax you on this income. For example, if you are paying federal income tax on an IRA that you rolled over into a Roth IRA and your new state collects income tax, you may also have to pay state income tax on your rollover IRA.

MOVING TIP

Before you leave, measure your current home and draw a sketch plan, showing room measurements and furniture placement. Take the plan with you, along with a tape measure and notebook, and draw up similar plans for the house or rental unit you're thinking of choosing. Sketches needn't be very detailed at this stage to help you avoid unpleasant surprises—no point in dragging that California King bed across country if it won't fit in the bedroom.

Home at Last

Once the truck is unloaded, the boxes are unpacked, and the pictures are hung, once you're sleeping in a *bed*—instead of on a loose mattress—you'll dream sweet dreams. Tomorrow, with the stress of this move slipping away behind you and the next move not even a faint glimmer on the horizon of your mind, you'll begin to discover the opportunities and savor the possibilities of your new city, new job, new school—your new home.

Getting to Know Your Town

CHAPTER 6

What's Around Town

Welcome to New York! This is what you've been waiting for. . . . This is why you came here. . . . This is what makes all the headaches, heartaches, and hassles of living in the City worth it: the restaurants, museums, theater, music, dance, culture, education, and stimulation. But wait—there's more! In New York City, not only is something always going on, but typically there are at least fifty different events happening on any given day in any one of the five boroughs. Your problem will not be *what* to do but *which thing* to do. Should you go to the Second Avenue Street Fair or the Sixth Avenue antique market? Should you eat at a Thai restaurant on the Upper West Side, Upper East Side, or in Chinatown? Go for a hike in Staten Island's Greenbelt, stroll through Central Park, check out Brooklyn's Prospect Park, or play chess in Washington Square Park?

You'll be faced with more choices than this each and every day you live in New York, and it's good to know what's out there so you can spend your time wisely. That means you'll need some tools to help you along. To fully cover the scene in New York—music, arts, theater, dance—each area has special magazines, books, newspapers, Web sites, and other resources. Arm yourself with a subscription to a weekly City magazine, and, if you're on a tight budget, at least be sure to pick up one of the free weekly publications that list all that's going on around town. The best magazines to subscribe to are *New York Magazine* and *Time Out New York* (most New Yorkers live by one or the other), although *The New Yorker* also has good listings. For freebies grab *New*

York Press or the *Village Voice* (and if you should happen to stay in a New York hotel—or walk by one—grab a copy of *Where New York*—an excellent up-to-date resource, and it's free). Each of these publications will help you be a hip City citizen. Also, check your daily newspaper of choice (most helpful on Fridays when the weekend listings get published) because there are weekly listings and events there too. If you flip through one of these publications each week, you'll be on top of the New York Scene—and, dahling, that's all that really matters, isn't it?

Finally, don't forget about the extensive, free resources at the NYCVB:

New York Convention and Visitors Bureau
810 Seventh Avenue
New York, NY 10019
(212) 484-1200

www.nycvb.com

New York City Visitors Information Center
810 Seventh Avenue (at 53rd Street)
(212) 397-1222

www.nycvisit.com

Performing Arts

There are many hundreds of playhouses, opera houses, museums, galleries, music clubs, dance clubs, and dance theaters all around the City. Following is a listing to get you started, but don't stop there—use your tools to educate yourself.

THEATER

A big draw for locals and tourists alike, Theatre Development Fund (TDF) operates the two TKTS half-price booths, one in Duffy Square and the other at Two World Trade Center. You can't decide what you're going to see in advance—you just have to go to one of the two TKTS booths, read what's on the board for the day, and wing it. This is a great way to get discounted Broadway and off-Broadway tickets for half-price (plus a service charge of $2.50 per ticket).

Theatre Development Fund (TDF)
1501 Broadway
New York, NY 10036
(212) 221-0885
www.tdf.org

Broadway Theaters

Ambassador Theater
215 West 49th Street
(212) 239-6200

American Place Theater
11 West 46th Street
(212) 840-2960

Belasco Theater
111 West 44th Street
(212) 239-6200

Biltmore Theater
261 West 47th Street
(212) 239-6200

Booth Theater
222 West 45th Street
(212) 239-6200

Broadhurst Theater
235 West 44th Street
(212) 239-6200

Broadway Theater
1681 Broadway
(212) 239-6200

Brooks Atkinson Theater
256 West 47th Street
(212) 719-4099

Circle in the Square Theater
1633 Broadway
(212) 307-2700

Cort Theater
138 West 48th Street
(212) 239-6200

Criterion Center Theater
1530 Broadway
(212) 239-6200

Douglas Fairbanks Theater
432 West 42nd Street
(212) 239-4321

Edison Theater
240 West 47th Street
(212) 302-2302

Ensemble Studio Theater
549 West 52nd Street
(212) 247-3405

Ethel Barrymore Theater
243 West 47th Street
(212) 239-6200

Eugene O'Neill
230 West 49th Street
(212) 246-0220

45th Street Theater
234 West 45th Street
(212) 333-7421

Gershwin Theater
222 West 51st Street
(212) 586-6510

MOVING
TIP

"Take advantage of the city during bad weather. When most people are running for cover, you can waltz into almost any restaurant in town (they get tons of cancellations when it snows), have the museums all to yourself, and get last-minute tickets to a sold out show."

—Emerson DaSilveira, waiter

Golden Theater
252 West 45th Street
(212) 239-6200

Harold Clurman Theater
412 West 42nd Street
(212) 695-3401

Helen Hayes Theater
240 West 44th Street
(212) 944-9450

Imperial Theater
249 West 45th Street
(212) 239-6200

John Houseman Theater
450 West 42nd Street
(212) 564-8038

Kaufman Theater
534 West 42nd Street
(212) 554-8038

Lamb's Theater
130 West 44th Street
(212) 997-1780

Longacre Theater
220 West 48th Street
(212) 307-2700

Lunt Fontanne Theater
205 West 46th Street
(212) 575-9200

Lyceum Theater
149 West 45th Street
(212) 239-6200

Majestic Theater
247 West 44th Street
(212) 239-6200

Manhattan Theater Club
131 West 55th Street
(212) 246-8989

Mark Hellinger Theater
237 West 51st Street
(212) 757-7064

Marquis Theater
1700 Broadway
(212) 382-0100

Martin Beck Theater
302 West 45th Street
(212) 974-9736

Minskoff Theater
Broadway and 45th Street
(212) 869-0550

Music Box Theater
239 West 45th Street
(212) 239-6200

Nat Horne Theater
9th Avenue at 42nd Street
(212) 279-4200

Nederlander Theater
208 West 41st Street
(212) 921-8000

Neil Simon Theater
250 West 52nd Street
(212) 757-8646

Palace Theater
Broadway at 47th Street
(212) 730-8200

Plymouth Theater
236 West 45th Street
(212) 239-6200

Richard Rogers Theater
226 West 45th Street
(212) 239-6200

Royal Theater
242 West 45th Street
(212) 239-6200

St. James Theater
246 West 44th Street
(212) 398-0280

Samuel Beckett Theater
410 West 42nd Street
(212) 594-2828

Shubert Theater
225 West 44th Street
(212) 398-0280

Virginia Theater
245 West 52nd Street
(212) 977-9370

Walter Kerr Theater
219 West 48th Street
(212) 582-4022

Winter Garden Theater
1634 Broadway
(212) 239-6200

Off-Broadway and Off-Off-Broadway Theaters

Actors Playhouse
100 Seventh Avenue
(212) 691-6226

Astor Place
434 Lafayette Street
(212) 254-4370

Cherry Lane
38 Commerce Street
(212) 989-2020

Circle in the Square Downtown
159 Bleecker Street
(212) 254-6330

Circle Repertory Company
99 Seventh Avenue
(212) 924-7100

Delacorte Theater
81st (in Central Park)
(212) 598-7100

Gramercy Arts Theater
138 East 27th Street
(212) 889-2850

Hudson Guild
441 West 26th Street
(212) 760-9810

Minetta Lane
18 Minetta Lane
(212) 420-8000

Mitzi Newhouse Theater
64th Street and Broadway
(Lincoln Center)
(212) 362-7600

Pearl Theater Company
125 West 22nd Street
(212) 645-7708

Players
115 MacDougal Street
(212) 254-5076

Playhouse 91
361 East 91st Street
(212) 831-2000

Public Theater
425 Lafayette Street
(212) 598-7150

Roundabout Theater
100 East 17th Street
(212) 460-1883

SoHo Repertory Theater
27 Barrow Street
(212) 925-2588

Sullivan Street Playhouse
181 Sullivan Street
(212) 674-3838

Top of the Gate
160 Bleecker Street
(212) 475-5120

Vivian Beaumont Theatre
64th Street and Broadway
(Lincoln Center)
(212) 787-6868

DANCE

Alvin Ailey American Dance Theater
211 West 61st Street, 3rd Floor
(212) 767-0590

Dance Theatre of Harlem
466 West 152nd Street
(212) 690-2800

New York City Ballet
Lincoln Center
(212) 870-5660

www.nycballet.com

MUSIC

Alice Tully Hall
1941 Broadway
(212) 875-5000

www.lincolncenter.org

Mostly classical music

Avery Fisher Hall
10 Lincoln Center Plaza
(212) 875-5030

Mostly classical music

The New York City Marathon was first run in Central Park by 127 runners who completed the 26.2 mile race by looping around and around Park Drive in Central Park. In 1999, the marathon's thirtieth running, 32,503 runners participated and ran through all five of the City's boroughs, making it one of the most celebrated days in the City. 31,785 runners finished the race.

MOVING TIP

"Don't be afraid to go out on a limb or try something new—join the weekly folk dance party at the 92nd Street Y, or register for that acting class you're secretly dying to take (but are afraid to try). There's something wonderful about NYC, because you're completely anonymous, even when everyone is looking."

—Andrew Gordon, litigation attorney

Brooklyn Academy of Music
30 Lafayette Avenue
Brooklyn, NY 11217
(718) 636-4111
www.bam.org

Dance, film, music, theater, and opera seven days a week

Carnegie Hall
156 West 57th Street (between Broadway & 7th Avenue)
(212) 247-7800

Classical, jazz, and more

92nd Street Y
1395 Lexington Avenue
New York, NY 10128
(212) 415-5607

www.92ndsty.org

Lectures and interviews, readings by award-winning authors. Dance performances and concerts including classical, cabaret, jazz, and popular music.

Town Hall
123 West 43rd Street
(212) 997-1003

www.the-townhall-nyc.org

Lectures, films, and music at affordable prices

Nightlife

ROCK, JAZZ, BLUES, ALTERNATIVE

Birdland

315 West 44th Street
(212) 581-3080

Southern cuisine and good old jazz make this a top-rated choice for jazz lovers. Don't forget about the famous Duke Ellington Orchestra.

Blue Note

131 West 3rd Street
(212) 475-8592

You'll be hard-pressed to go wrong at the Blue Note. Some fine blues, but more likely jazz, a great Sunday jazz brunch, and a fun scene to check out.

Bottom Line

15 West 4th Street
(212) 228-7880

Music, stand-up comedy, you name it, all at this famous destination

CBGB & OMFUG

315 Bowery (at Bleecker)
(212) 982-4052

Contemporary music

Chicago B.L.U.E.S.

73 Eighth Avenue (between 13th & 14th Streets)
(212) 924-9755

City Hall

131 Duane Street
(212) 227-7777

Jazz

Cornelia Street Café

29 Cornelia Street
(212) 989-9319

Jazz

Deanna's

107 Rivington Street
(212) 420-2258

Run by Deanna Kirk (a singer), who hits the stage most nights. Open Tuesday through Sunday.

Detour

349 East 13th Street
(212) 533-6212

Jazz, no cover and packed every night of the week

Dharma

174 Orchard Street
(212) 780-0313

Another one of the diamonds popping up on the Lower East Side scene.

Fez

At Time Café
380 Lafayette Street
(212) 533-2680

A variety with alternative and rock in the mix. Full menu, good burgers, and decent wine (if that's your scene).

Hammerstein Ballroom

311 West 34th Street
(212) 564-4882

Iridium

44 West 63rd Street (across from Lincoln Center)
(212) 582-2121

Jazz scene downstairs. Dark and swanky, upscale crowd and a full menu covers your cover.

Irving Plaza

17 Irving Plaza (at 15th Street)
(212) 777-6817

The Jazz Standard

116 East 27th Street
(212) 576-2232

Jazz mix of old greats and aspiring newcomers.

Knitting Factory

Leonard Street
(212) 219-3055

Very popular. Variety, call for schedule of concerts.

Mercury Lounge

17 East Houston Street
(212) 260-4700

The whole nine yards, call for the lineup.

Museum of Modern Art

11 West 53rd Street
(212) 708-0480

Friday night jazz at 5:30 (also "pay what you wish" night), and Thursday and Saturday night jazz starting at 6:00

Small's

183 West 10th Street
(212) 929-7565

Open all night, jazz until 8 in the morn

Sweet Basil

88 Seventh Avenue South
(212) 242-1785

Restaurant with big name jazz players. Saturday jazz brunch.

Tonic

107 Norfolk Street
(212) 358-7503

A variety from Klezmer music to brass and reeds

Village Vanguard

178 Seventh Avenue South
(212) 255-4037

A legend the world over, the Village Vanguard is a history lesson in itself. Miles Davis hit this joint hard!

Wetlands

161 Hudson Street
(212) 386-3600

Everything from the "Bob Marley birthday tribute" to groove (the Groove Collective on Thursdays) and soul. Call for the lineup.

CLUBS

Alphabet Lounge

104 Avenue C
(212) 780-0202

House music, dance

Baktun

418 West 14th Street
(212) 206-1590
www.baktun.com

Down-to-earth house parties, "alternative Fridays," Saturdays are "drum 'n' base."

Black Betty

366 Metropolitan Avenue
Brooklyn (Williamsburg)
(718) 599-0243

Anything goes, from hip hop to Afro-Cuban jazz to reggae.

Centro-Fly

45 West 21st Street
(212) 803-7859

Trip-hop, house music, big beat

Cheetah

12 West 21st Street
(212) 206-7770

Popular dance and music nightspot

Culture Club

179 Varick Street
(212) 243-1999

'80s music

Izzy Bar

166 First Avenue
(212) 228-0444

Hang out and take in the tunes.

Limelight

660 Sixth Avenue (at 20th Street)
(212) 807-7780

Long past its prime, the Limelight is still a scene, just not the hippest one.

The Roxy

515 West 18th Street
(212) 627-0404

Still hanging on, the Roxy maintains a steady crowd with roller skating parties during the week and a mix of folk on the weekends. You won't feel out of place in this joint if you're straight.

Soundfactory

618 West 46th Street
(212) 489-0001

Not the trendy destination it once was, the Soundfactory is starting to draw the crowds back.

CITY FACT

On February 19, 2000, the Museum of Natural History opened its completely renovated planetarium in the new Rose Center for Earth and Space, which is the most expensive ($210 million) and technically advanced planetarium in the world.

Tunnel

220 Twelfth Avenue (at 27th Street)
(212) 695-4682

Everything goes in this place, and, drag queens aside, there's different music in each room and something for everyone— but I was able to (more than) satisfy my curiosity with just one visit . . . years ago.

Vinyl

6 Hubert Street
(212) 343-1379

A dance maven's heaven, some argue that Vinyl is the best dance club in town.

The Warehouse

141 West 140th Street (between Grand Concourse & Walton Avenues)
The Bronx
(718) 992-5974

Good house music dance club in da Bronx!

Museums

Abigail Adams Smith Museum
421 East 61st Street
(212) 838-6878

Eighteenth-century coach house
was the home of Abigail Adams,
daughter of second president,
John Adams.

American Craft Museum
40 West 53rd Street
(212) 956-6047

American Museum of the Moving Image
36–01 35th Avenue
Astoria, Queens
(718) 784-0077

American Museum of Natural History
79th Street & Central Park West
(212) 769-5100

Asia Society Gallery
775 Park Avenue
(212) 288-6400

Center for African Art
54 East 68th Street
(212) 861-1200

Children's Museum of Manhattan
212 West 83rd Street
(212) 721-1234

China Institute Gallery
125 East 65th Street
(212) 744-8181

The Cloisters
Fort Tryon Park
(212) 923-3700

Cooper-Hewitt National Design Museum
2 East 91st Street
(212) 860-6898

Specializing in decorative arts,
the building (the Carnegie
Mansion) is as magnificent (or
more so) than the art.

El Museo del Barrio
1230 Fifth Avenue (at 105th Street)
(212) 831-7272

Cultural center for Spanish
Harlem

The Frick Collection
1 East 70th Street
(212) 288-0700

A fabulous, manageable art museum—my favorites are the impressionist paintings.

Guggenheim Museum
1071 Fifth Avenue
(212) 360-3500

Modern art is on display in this famous Frank Lloyd Wright building.

Intrepid Sea-Air-Space Museum
Pier 86 (46th Street & 12th Avenue)
(212) 245-0072

The International Center of Photography (ICP)
1130 Fifth Avenue (94th Street)
(212) 860-1777

A museum devoted to photography and photojournalism

The Jewish Museum
1109 Fifth Avenue (entrance on 92nd Street)
(212) 860-1888

The Metropolitan Museum of Art
1000 Fifth Avenue (from 81st to 84th Streets)
(212) 535-7710

Art treasures, ancient and modern, from around the world

Morris-Jumel Mansion
1765 Jumel Terrace
(212) 923-8008

Morgan Library
29 East 36th Street
(212) 685-0008

www.morganlibrary.org

Museum of American Folk Art
2 Lincoln Square
(212) 977-7170

Museum of the City of New York
1220 Fifth Avenue (at 103rd Street)
(212) 534-1672

Local-history museum including exhibits of the original Dutch settlement, toys, and theatrical memorabilia

Museum of Jewish Heritage
A Living Memorial to the Holocaust
18 First Place
Battery Park City
(212) 509-6130

www.mjhnyc.org

Museum of Modern Art
11 West 53rd Street
(212) 708-9480

Museum of Television and Radio
25 West 52nd Street
(212) 621-6800

National Academy of Design
1083 Fifth Avenue (89th Street)
(212) 369-4880

Specializing in American art

National Museum of the American Indian
U.S. Customs House
1 Bowling Green (near Battery Park)
(212) 668-6624

New York Historical Society
170 Central Park West
(212) 873-3400

Nicholas Roerich Museum
319 West 107th Street
(212) 864-7752

Pierpont Morgan Library
29 East 36th Street
(212) 685-0610

South Street Seaport Museum
Pier 17
Fulton & South Streets
(212) 669-9424

Theodore Roosevelt Birthplace
28 East 20th Street
(212) 260-1616

Whitney Museum Downtown
33 Maiden Lane
(212) 943-5655

Whitney Museum of American Art
945 Madison Avenue
(212) 570-3676

Galleries

There are many more galleries in New York than there are museums (that means we have a whole lot of them), and the best way to figure out which ones will have shows that interest you is to pick up the appropriate tools. In this arena, aside from the general tools that you already have (which may be enough for you), you might want to pick up a copy of one of the following: *Artnews, Art in America, Modern Painters,* or *Art Forum International.* These will give you more insight specifically into the art world. Invaluable for keeping up to date on the gallery scene is the *Art Now Gallery Guide,* complete with a gallery map to help you find those sometimes elusive locations.

UPTOWN GALLERIES

ACA Galleries
41 East 57th Street (at Madison Avenue)
(212) 644-8300

André Emmerich
41 East 57th Street (between Madison & Fifth Avenues)
(212) 752-0124

Blum-Helman
20 West 57th Street (between Fifth & Sixth Avenues)
(212) 245-2888

Gagosian
980 Madison Avenue (at 76th Street)
(212) 744-2313

Hirschl & Adler Galleries
21 East 70th Street (at Madison Avenue)
(212) 535-8810

M Knoedler & Company
19 East 70th Street (between Madison & Fifth Avenues)
(212) 794-0550

Marian Goodman Gallery
24 West 57th Street (between Fifth & Sixth Avenues)
(212) 977-7160

Marlborough
40 West 57th Street (between Fifth & Sixth Avenues)
(212) 541-4900

MOVING TIP

"Talk to everyone, because the person sitting next to you on that park bench could end up being your new best friend, your roommate, your employer, or even your spouse."

—Susan Barash, author

PaceWildenstein
32 East 57th Street (between Park
& Madison Avenues)
(212) 421-3292

Robert Miller
41 East 57th Street (at Madison)
(212) 980-5454

Sidney Janis Gallery
110 West 57th Street (between
Sixth & Seventh Avenues)
(212) 586-0110

Tatistcheff and Company
50 West 57th Street (between
Fifth & Sixth Avenues), 8th Floor
(212) 664-0907

Terry Dintenfass
20 East 79th Street (at Fifth
Avenue)
(212) 581-2268

DOWNTOWN GALLERIES

Barbara Gladstone
99 Greene Street (between Prince
& Spring Streets)
(212) 431-3334

Charles Cowles
420 West Broadway (between
Prince & Spring Streets)
(212) 925-3500

Curt Marcus Gallery
578 Broadway (between Houston
& Prince Streets)
(212) 226-3200

Gagosian
136 Wooster Street (between
Houston & Prince Streets)
(212) 228-2828

John Weber
142 Greene Street (between
Houston & Prince Streets),
3rd Floor
(212) 966-6115

Leo Castelli
420 West Broadway (between
Spring & Prince Streets)
(212) 431-5160

Mary Boone Gallery
417 West Broadway (between
Spring & Prince Streets)
(212) 431-1818

Max Protetch Gallery
560 Broadway (at Prince Street)
(212) 966-5454

Metro Pictures
150 Greene Street (between
Houston & Prince Streets)
(212) 925-8335

Paula Cooper
155 Wooster Street (between
Houston & Prince Streets)
(212) 674-0766

Postmasters
80 Greene Street (at Spring),
2nd Floor
(212) 941-5711

PPOW
532 Broadway (at Spring Street),
3rd Floor
(212) 941-8642

Sonnabend Gallery
420 West Broadway (between
Spring & Prince Streets)
(212) 966-6160

Sperone Westwater
142 Greene Street (between
Houston & Prince Streets)
(212) 431-3685

Restaurants

Some towns have high school football; New York has restaurants. To say that New Yorkers are passionate about restaurants is a major understatement—when it comes to dining out, we're possessed, obsessed, and crazed. We eat enough to support more than 20,000 establishments, ranging from Gray's Papaya (where two frankfurters and a tropical fruit drink cost $1.95) to Lespinasse (where an eight-course chef's tasting menu with wine accompanying each course can be had for $250 per person, plus tax and tip). And that's not to mention the thousands of street vendors and gourmet (and not-so-gourmet) markets that function as take-out food sources for busy residents.

If you want to stay on top of what's going on in the restaurant universe, start with the weekly *New York Times* "Dining In, Dining Out" section, which in and of itself is larger than many small-town newspapers. Then move on to the weekly restaurant reviews in *New York* magazine and the monthly New York restaurant coverage in

Gourmet magazine. Even at the cheap-eats end of the spectrum, there's plenty of press: The *Village Voice* and *New York Press* have weekly reviews of economical, ethnic, and eclectic eateries. And then of course there's the Internet, which offers an embarrassment of restaurant-review sources, both professional and amateur: *www.newyork.citysearch.com*, *www.fat-guy.com*, *www.edificerex.com*, *www.chowhound.com*, *www.worldtable.com*, and more.

Everybody has heard of a few of New York's most famous restaurants, such as Windows on the World, Tavern on the Green, and the Russian Tea Room. But you won't see any real New Yorkers at those places, unless they're entertaining clients or family from out-of-town. Likewise, remember that the very popular Zagat Survey is, to the real New Yorker, nothing more than a handy address book—no serious restaurant consumer relies on a public opinion poll for dining advice. Instead, a true food-obsessed New Yorker will read the reviews (preferably several of them), talk to friends, and interrogate the management before settling on a place for dinner.

The following are just a few of the most important restaurants in New York, plus my favorites in several essential categories. Most of these are "destination" restaurants, meaning you have to plan to go to them because you don't live or work near them. But dining is often a neighborhood affair, so when it comes to finding the best places within walking distance of your home or office, you're on your own. Good luck!

The stars indicate the price of food only, at dinnertime (most restaurants have lunch and off-hours specials—a great opportunity for budget-conscious diners). Expect tax, tip (16.5 percent is standard in New York—just double the tax—or more in a very exclusive restaurant), and drinks, if any, to add considerably to your bill.

★ = cheap; less than $10 per person

★★ = moderate; $10–$25 per person

★★★ = expensive; $25–$50 per person

★★★★ = luxury; $50 and up per person

NEW YORK'S TOP RESTAURANTS

Aquavit ★★★★
13 West 54th Street (between Fifth & Sixth Avenues)
(212) 307-7311

Chef Marcus Samuelsson's contemporary take on Scandinavian cuisine. It's fabulous—I promise—and the restaurant is serene and beautiful.

Bouley Bakery ★★★★
120 West Broadway (at Duane Street)
(212) 964-2525

One of America's top chefs, David Bouley, presents intense, modern, French-American cuisine in a newly renovated dining room. Great bread, of course!

Cello ★★★★
53 East 77th Street (between Madison & Park Avenues)
(212) 517-1200

Tiny seafood powerhouse in a historic Upper East Side townhouse.

Daniel ★★★★
60 East 65th Street (between Madison & Park Avenues)
(212) 288-0033

Daniel Boulud is one of the foremost French chefs in the world. His menu is inspired by the bounty of the marketplace, and the brand-new dining room is one of the finest in the City.

Gramercy Tavern ★★★★
42 East 20th Street (between Broadway & Park Avenue South)
(212) 477-0777

Perhaps the best American restaurant in America, and therefore the world.

Il Mulino ★★★★
86 West 3rd Street
(212) 673-3783

Incredible Italian restaurant, with lusty, spicy cuisine and a ridiculous wait for tables.

Jean Georges ★★★★
One Central Park West (at Columbus Circle)
(212) 299-3900

The flagship restaurant of legendary French chef and restaurateur Jean-Georges Vongerichten.

Le Bernardin ★★★★
155 West 51st Street (between Sixth & Seventh Avenues)
(212) 489-1515

The reigning champion of French seafood restaurants in America.

Le Cirque 2000 ★★★★
455 Madison Avenue (between 50th & 51st Streets, in the New York Palace Hotel)
(212) 794-9292

One of New York's most perennially popular fine-dining establishments. A favorite of the rich and famous.

Lespinasse ★★★★
2 East 55th Street (between Fifth & Madison, in the St. Regis Hotel)
(212) 339-6739

One of America's finest restaurants. Chef Christian Delouvrier's "cuisine of the earth" is a modern take on French classic haute-cuisine.

March ★★★★
405 East 58th Street (between First Avenue & Sutton Place)
(212) 754-6272

An innovative, Asian-influenced multicourse dining experience from renowned chef Wayne Nish.

Montrachet ★★★★
239 West Broadway (between Walker & White)
(212) 219-2777

The restaurant that put TriBeCa on the map. Hearty French food and an amazing wine list.

Nobu ★★★★
105 Hudson Street (at Franklin)
(212) 219-0500

An unusual twist on Japanese cuisine, this is one of New York's most sought-after restaurants. It's extremely busy, but Next Door Nobu (next door, of course) offers tables on a first-come, first-served basis and serves exactly the same food.

Picholine ★★★★
35 West 64th Street (between Central Park West & Broadway)
(212) 724-8585

Outstanding Mediterranean-inspired cuisine in the shadow of Lincoln Center.

Union Pacific ★★★★
111 East 22nd Street (between Park & Lexington)
(212) 995-8500

Chef Rocco DiSpirito, formerly a sous-chef at Lespinasse, has spread his wings here with one of New York's most interesting and unusual fusion menus.

BEST PIZZA

Patsy's ★★
2287–2291 First Avenue (between 117th & 118th Streets)
(212) 534-9783

This is the only Patsy's location that serves truly outstanding pizza—the others are not managed by the family. It's in a touch-and-go neighborhood, so plan your travel during daytime or with a group.

Sally's Apizza ★★

237 Wooster Street
New Haven, CT
(203) 624-5271

Real New Yorkers aren't afraid to admit it when the best of something is outside the City. We know, for example, that California has great Mexican food and we don't. And we know that the best pizza in America can be found not in New York City but, rather, in nearby New Haven, Connecticut. A great night out for die-hard pizza lovers.

BEST GREEK

Elias Corner ★★★

2401–2402 31st Street (31st Street at 24th Avenue)
Astoria, Queens
(718) 932-1510

Astoria is New York's major Greek neighborhood, and Elias Corner is the best restaurant in the area. Emphasis on fresh seafood.

BEST MODERATELY PRICED CHINESE

Wu Liang Ye ★★★

215 East 86th Street (between
Third & Second Avenues)
(212) 534-8899

36 West 48th Street (between 5th
& 6th Avenues)
(212) 398-2308

338 Lexington Avenue (between
39th & 40th Streets)
(212) 370-9647

CITY FACT

Located on West 70th Street, Congregation Shearith Israel is the oldest Jewish congregation in the country.

Excellent, authentic, spicy Chinese. Really stands out against the competition.

BEST STEAKHOUSE

Christos Hasapo-Taverna ★★★
41–08 23rd Avenue (corner of 41st Street)
Astoria, Queens
(718) 726-5195

A Greek steakhouse and butcher shop in Astoria. Great dry-aged steaks at lower prices than you'd pay in Manhattan.

Flames ★★★
533 North State Road
Briarcliff Manor, NY
(914) 923-3100

Another fantastic out-of-town steakhouse, run by Peter Luger alumni.

Peter Luger ★★★
178 Broadway (just over the Williamsburg Bridge)
Williamsburg, Brooklyn
(718) 387-7400

Without question, the best in New York. Well worth the trip to Brooklyn.

Sparks ★★★
210 East 46th Street (between Second & Third Avenues)
(212) 687-4855

An eminently respectable alternative for those who just won't leave Manhattan. World-class wine list.

BEST KOREAN

Woo Chon ★★
8 West 36th Street (between Fifth & Sixth Avenues)
(212) 695-0676

Twenty-four-hour Korean restaurant with tabletop barbecue.

BEST JEWISH DELI

Katz's Deli ★
205 Houston Street (near Ludlow Street)
(212) 254-2246

The site of the classic scene in *When Harry Met Sally.*

BEST ITALIAN DELI

Italian Food Center ★
186 Grand Street (corner of Mulberry)
(212) 925-2954

Old-world Italian sandwiches in the heart of Little Italy.

BEST BURGER

McHale's ★
Northeast Corner of 46th Street & Eighth Avenue
(212) 246-8948

Gigantic, excellent burgers and fries at an authentic Irish bar in the heart of the theater district.

BEST HOT DOG

Gray's Papaya ★
2090 Broadway (corner of 72nd Street)

Papaya King
179 East 86th Street (corner of Third Avenue)

These competing establishments (Mr. Gray used to work at Papaya King) both serve great frankfurters. New Yorkers eat them with papaya juice—try it, you'll love it.

BEST DINER

Junior's ★★
386 Flatbush Avenue (corner of DeKalb Avenue)
Brooklyn
(718) 852-5257

The definitive Brooklyn diner, with orange vinyl banquettes and some of the world's best cheesecake.

BEST DIVE

Chat 'n Chew ★★
10 East 16th Street (between Fifth Avenue & Union Square West)
(212) 243-1616

You can't help but love the BLTs and pink-frosted chocolate cake at this contemporary take on the greasy spoon.

BEST PASTA

Becco ★★
355 West 46th Street (between 8th & 9th Avenues)
(212) 397-7597

Three varieties of amazing homemade pasta daily, and the price is right.

BEST BURRITOS

Benny's Burritos ★
93 Avenue A (corner of 6th Street)
(212) 254-2054

113 Greenwich Avenue (corner of Jane Street)
(212) 727-3560

Cheap, filling burritos in a great downtown setting.

BEST SOUL FOOD

Charles' Southern-Style Kitchen ★

2841 Frederick Douglass Boulevard (between 151st & 152nd Streets)
(212) 926-4313

The genuine article, Charles started by selling his food out of a truck.
Now he's a neighborhood legend. Fried chicken highly recommended.

BEST ROTISSERIE CHICKEN

El Pollo ★

1746 First Avenue (between 90th & 91st Streets)
(212) 996-7810

482 Broome Street (corner of
Wooster Street)
(212) 431-5666

Slow-cooked Peruvian-style
marinated chicken.

William's Bar-B-Que ★

2350 Broadway (between 85th &
86th Streets)
(212) 877-5384

One of the best rotisserie chick-
ens on the planet.

BEST MODERATELY
PRICED THAI

Thai Mint ★

23 Pell Street (near Mott Street)
(212) 406-4259

Great home-style Thai food with friendly and enthusiastic service.

MOVING TIP

"When selecting a gym, visit a few that
are near to work or home, because different gyms attract different clientele. What
might work for the aerobics queen next
door might not work for you."

—Norman Stewart, lifeguard

BEST MARGARITAS

El Teddy's ★★
219 West Broadway (between Franklin & White Streets)
(212) 941-7070

Order "Teddy's margaritas, up, salt, not too sweet."

BEST BATHROOM

"44" ★★★
44 West 44th Street (between Fifth & Sixth Avenues, in the Royalton Hotel)
(212) 944-8844

See for yourself.

CITY FACT

Opened in 1854, the Astor Library was the first privately endowed, independent, free public reference library in the United States.

BEST BRAZILIAN RODIZIO

Churrascaria Plataforma ★★
316 West 49th Street (between Eighth & Ninth Avenues)
(212) 245-0505

All-you-can-eat roasted meat feast.

BEST LATE NIGHT

Blue Ribbon ★★
97 Sullivan Street (between Prince & Spring Streets)
(212) 274-0404

Outstanding fried chicken.

BEST ALL-NIGHT

Yaffa Cafe ★

97 Street Marks Place (between First & Avenue A)
(212) 674-9302

Eclectic menu with great salads served twenty-four hours a day, seven days a week.

BEST BARBECUE

Pearson's ★

71–04 35th Avenue (between Vernon Boulevard and East River)
Jackson Heights, Queens
(718) 779-7715

Well worth the trip to this out-of-the-way Queens location, this is New York's only true pit barbecue.

BEST MCDONALD'S

McDonald's ★

160 Broadway
(212) 227-3828

They're all the same, right? Wrong! This flagship McDonald's has live music on a grand piano, a doorman in topcoat and tails, hostesses, marble tables, a digital stock ticker, a gift shop, flowers, and a dessert menu (including cappuccino and espresso).

Sports

PROFESSIONAL SPORTS

All tickets for events at Madison Square Garden are sold through Ticketmaster:

(212) 307-7171

Baseball

Yankees
Yankee Stadium
The Bronx
(718) 293-4300

www.yankees.com

Mets
Shea Stadium
Flushing, Queens
(718) 565-4305

www.mets.com

Basketball

New York Knickerbockers (known locally as the Knicks)
Madison Square Garden Center
Seventh Avenue from 31st to 33rd
Streets
(212) 465-6741 (or 465-MSG1)
for information

www.nba.com knicks

www.thegarden.com

The New York Liberty (WNBA)
Madison Square Garden
(212) 465-6741 (or 465-MSG1)
for information

www.wnba.com liberty

www.thegarden.com

Hockey

New York Rangers
Madison Square Garden
(212) 465-6741 (or 465-MSG1)
for information

www.newyorkrangers.com

www.thegarden.com

New York Islanders
Nassau Coliseum
(800) 882-ISLES

www.newyorkislanders.com

Football

Giants
Giants Stadium
East Rutherford, NJ
(201) 935-8111

www.giants.com

Jets
Meadowlands Arena
East Rutherford, NJ
(516) 560-8200

www.newyorkjets.com

Soccer

Metrostars
Giants Stadium
East Rutherford, NJ
(201) 935-8111

www.metrostars.com

Tennis

U.S. Open

USTA National Tennis Center
Flushing Meadows-Corona Park
Flushing, NY

U.S. Open Ticket Information: (212) 239-6250

Tickets through Telecharge at (888) OPEN-TIX (or 888-673-6849)

LEAGUES

There are many different ways to join sports leagues in and around the City. The easiest and most typical way is through your job. Many large corporations and professional associations sponsor team sports each season. For example, the Lawyers Basketball League is taken very seriously by participants and followers alike, so much so that league games and standings are reported daily in the *New York Law Journal.* To join your company's team (whatever the sport), a sign-up sheet is generally circulated or posted in a prominent place so that everyone has the opportunity to get involved. If you don't see a sign-up sheet, ask around or call the HR department. If it should turn out that your company doesn't participate in the corporate leagues, you have a few choices: You can volunteer to start your company's first team yourself or, if that's too ambitious, you can instead join a league through a professional association with which you are already affiliated or one you wish to join (see chapter 11 for a list of professional associations). If none of these options suit you, you can walk by a few of the City's many ball fields, watch for a while and ask team players how to get involved.

For people living outside of the City, there are also neighborhood leagues. Ask your realtor when you're house hunting. Ask at the neighborhood schools, check the local papers and the freebie papers in the grocery store, and, again, ask around at the playing fields because the people who hang out at ball fields are likely to have the most information.

FITNESS

There are hundreds of health clubs throughout the five boroughs. Some are international chains like Bally's, others are local chains like Crunch, and still others are independents like the 92nd Street Y. Most people select their gyms based on a combination of location (proximity to home or office), facilities, and cost. You'll have no problem finding a health club that works for you. Your biggest issue will likely be deciding which one you like best. Following is an extensive (though not complete) list, so that you can become familiar with the scene and get started, if not settled, into your routine. Note: Many employers offer a discounted membership to a nearby health club, but, as with group life and disability insurance, these aren't always the best deals— you may do better (and find a place more to your liking) if you shop around.

American Fitness Center
128 Eighth Avenue (between 17th & 18th Streets)
(212) 627-0065

Bally Total Fitness
www.ballyfitness.com

More than fifteen locations throughout the five boroughs

Chelsea Gym
262 West 17th Street
(212) 255-1150

Mostly gay membership

Crunch Fitness
404 Lafayette Street (between Astor & Fourth Avenue)
(212) 614-0120

54 East 13th Street (between University & Broadway)
(212) 475-2018

162 West 83rd Street (between Columbus & Amsterdam)
(212) 875-1902

1109 Second Avenue (at 59th Street)
(212) 366-3725

152 Christopher Street (at Greenwich Street)
(212) 366-3725

www.crunchfitness.com

A very popular gym with the die-hard, devoted, "never miss a day" gym crowd. A handful of locations and expanding.

David Barton's Gym
623 Broadway
(212) 420-0507

30 East 85th Street
(212) 517-7577

552 6th Avenue (at 15th Street)
(212) 727-0004

An upscale gym with focus on personal training and fitness

Dolphin Fitness Clubs
700 Columbus Avenue (between 94th & 95th Streets)
(212) 865-5454

155 East 3rd Street (between Avenues A & B)
(212) 533-0090

22 West 19th Street (between 5th & 6th Avenues)
(212) 929-6789

201 East 23rd Street (at Second Avenue)
(212) 679-7300

156 William Street
(212) 385-2134

330 East 59th Street (between 1st & 2nd Avenues)
(212) 486-6966

Budget, affordable gym, often with limited equipment and facilities

Downtown Athletic Club
19 West Street
(212) 425-7000
www.dacnyc.org

Equinox Fitness Clubs
344 Amsterdam Avenue
(212) 721-4200

2465 Broadway (between 92nd & 93rd Streets)
(212) 799-1818

140 East 63rd Street (on Lexington Avenue)
(212) 750-4900

897 Broadway (between 19th & 20th Streets)
(212) 780-9300

Yuppie fitness crowd

Excelsior Athletic Club
301 East 57th Street
(212) 688-5280

Manhattan Plaza Health Club
482 West 43rd Street
(212) 563-7001

New York Health and Racquet Club

www.hrcbest.com

Nine locations throughout Manhattan

NYSC (New York Sports Club)

www.nysc.com

New York Sports Clubs blanket the City, including locations throughout Manhattan, Cobble Hill, and Bay Ridge in Brooklyn, Forest Hills and Whitestone in Queens and Staten Island. For the location nearest your home and/or office (they offer one plan that enables you to use all of the NYSC facilities) pick up a phone book, walk in off the street, or try their Web site.

Pumping Iron Gym

403 East 91st Street
(212) 996-5444

Just like it sounds, not for the faint of heart or the aerobics groupie

Reebok Sports Club

160 Columbus Avenue
(212) 362-6800

www.(212).net reebok

This is the NYC celebrity gym (I've seen Seinfeld here working out with a trainer, and Wayne

Gretsky—you get the idea). Beautiful people abound. Facilities are extensive and the cost, well, let's say it's rather expensive. A Reebok Club is scheduled for the East Side too.

Serge Gym

451 West Street
(212) 675-1179

Mostly gay membership

Vertical Club

350 West 50th Street
(212) 265-9400

335 Madison Avenue (at 43rd Street)
(212) 983-5320

139 West 32nd Street (between 6th & 7th Avenues)
(212) 465-1750

330 East 61st Street (between First & Second Avenues)
(212) 355-5100

World Gym

1926 Broadway
(212) 927-6883

232 Mercer
(212) 780-7407

92nd Street YMHA/YWHA

*1395 Lexington Avenue (between
91st & 92nd Streets)
(212) 415-5607*

www.92ndsty.org

Not for those who want to see
and be seen. A very friendly
facility that has lifelong members (I've met *many* who have
been members for more than
thirty years), a twenty-five-yard
swimming pool (rare in this
city), fitness classes, weights, basketball, and more. Nothing here
is exactly cutting edge, but it's a
great deal for NYC and a nice
place to work out. Also an extensive cultural center with all kinds
of programs and classes to get
involved with.

YWCA

Located throughout the five boroughs, the Y's are straightforward neighborhood facilities
attracting all kinds—families,
singles, ethnics, and locals.
Check the phone book for your
nearest location.

Outdoors

PARKS

The best place to start if you're trying to get information on a particular City park is to contact the Department of Parks and Recreation.
The City's park system has more than 28,000 acres of land and
includes 854 playgrounds, 700 playing fields, 500 tennis courts, thirty-
three outdoor swimming pools, ten indoor swimming pools, thirty-
three recreation and senior centers, fifteen miles of beaches, thirteen
golf courses, six ice rinks, four major stadiums, and four zoos.

City of New York Parks and Recreation

*The Arsenal, Central Park
830 Fifth Avenue
(212) 360-8111
Twenty-four-Hour Hotline: (800) 201-PARK*

www.nycparks.org

Battery Park

Located from New York Harbor to Battery Place and Pier A to State Street. Utilized primarily by downtown residents and weekend strollers, Battery Park is an especially lively destination in the summer and is almost twenty-three acres in size.

Bryant Park

On 6th Avenue from West 40th to West 42nd Streets, Bryant Park is a favorite destination for workweek picnic lunches, summer music, and outdoor movies.

Central Park

Bordered by Central Park South (59th Street), Fifth Avenue, Central Park West, and 110th Street. The gem of the city, Central Park is an 843-acre park with a zoo, skating rinks, swimming pool, playgrounds, ball fields, theater, running track (1.6 miles around the reservoir), and lots more. It is *the* refuge for New Yorkers year-round.

City Hall Park

Bordered by Broadway, Park Row, and Chambers Streets, City Hall Park is at the foot of the Brooklyn Bridge and affords great views of the bridge, courthouses, and City Hall.

Fort Tryon Park

Running from Riverside Drive to Broadway and West 192nd Street to Dyckman Park, Fort Tryon Park in Northern Manhattan is almost sixty-seven acres large and includes the Anne Loftus Playground (Broadway and Riverside Drive), the Bennett Rest sitting area (West 191 Street and Bennett Avenue), and the Jacob Javits Playground (Margaret Corbin Circle).

The Greenbelt

Located in central Staten Island, the Greenbelt is a flagship park of the City (like Central Park, Riverside, Fort Tryon, and Prospect Parks —and a handful of others) and measures almost 3,000 acres, comprised of forest, wetlands, lakes, ponds, and streams. Not only can you hike, explore, and chill out here, you can also play golf at La Tourette and play tennis or a game of softball at Willowbrook.

Prospect Park

Located between Prospect Park West, Flatbush, Parkside, and Ocean Avenues, Prospect Park is Brooklyn's crown jewel and measures in at 526 (and a quarter) acres.

Riverside Park

Located on the Hudson River from 72nd Street up to 158th, Riverside Park is 296 (and three-quarters) acres and is utilized by residents from all of the boroughs.

Union Square Park

Between Broadway and four Avenues (Fourth Avenue is the continuation of Park Avenue South) from East 14th to 17th Streets, Union Square Park is most notable for its greenmarket on Mondays, Wednesdays, Fridays, and Saturdays.

Van Cortlandt Park

Located in the Bronx (at Broadway, Jerome Avenue, City Line, and Van Cortlandt Park South), Van Cortlandt Park is a whopping 1,146 (and a half) acres in size and includes multiple playgrounds, a mansion, a golf course, and plenty of room to run, roam, and play.

Washington Square Park

Bordered by Fifth Avenue, Waverly Place, MacDougal, and West 4th Street, Washington Square Park has long been a favorite hangout of teenagers, punk rockers, chess players, jugglers, and dog owners (on account of the dog run). A striking entry will remind visitors of the Arc de Triomphe in Paris (which it's modeled after).

ZOOS

Aquarium for Wildlife Conservation
West 8th Street and Surf Avenue
Brooklyn
(718) 265-FISH

www.wcs.org

The Bronx Zoo
Bronx River Parkway and
Fordham Road
(718) 367-1010

www.wcs.org

The nation's largest urban zoo has long been a favorite destination of children and adults alike. Wednesdays are free.

Central Park Wildlife Center and Wildlife Gallery
Fifth Avenue (at 64th Street)
(212) 861-6030

www.wcs.org

Prospect Park Wildlife Conservation Center
450 Flatbush Avenue
Prospect Park, Brooklyn
(718) 399-7339

www.wcs.org

Staten Island Zoo
Clarence T. Barrett Park
614 Broadway (at Colonial
Court)
Staten Island
(718) 442-3100

www.wcs.org

Noteworthy snake collection. Children's zoo.

GARDENS

Brooklyn Botanic Garden
1000 Washington Avenue
Brooklyn
(718) 622-4433

www.bbg.org

The New York Botanical Garden
200th Street and Kazimiroff
Boulevard
The Bronx
(718) 817-8700

www.nybg.org

Queens Botanical Garden

43–50 Main Street
Flushing, Queens
(718) 886-3800

Free

Staten Island Botanical Garden

Snug Harbor Cultural Center
1000 Richmond Terrace
Staten Island
(718) 273-8200

Free

Conservancy Garden

Central Park between 104th &
105th Streets, near Fifth Avenue

A beautiful, and underutilized, Manhattan garden. Free.

MOVING TIP

"As a New Yorker, there are certain things you should do at least once while you're living in the City, like go to the Halloween Parade in Greenwich Village and to the Feast of San Gennaro in Little Italy."

—Carol Rossi, assistant district attorney

OUTDOOR ACTIVITIES

In June 1997, when *Outside* magazine chose New York as one of the top ten cities in the world for outdoors enthusiasts, there were more than a few raised eyebrows. But why? As *Outside* put it, "New Yorkers approach sport with the same in-your-face moxie they bring to every other pursuit." And, in addition to having a parks system unparalleled for its diversity, New York lies at the crossroads of some of the most beautiful regions in America: the Hudson Valley, the Jersey Shore, the Connecticut Shore, the Catskills, the Poconos, and Long Island. In addition to all that was previously listed, there are numerous other ways to take advantage of New York outside: in-line skating in any of the parks (free clinics in Central Park on weekends); running along the streets, rivers, or parks (once again, Central Park tops the list with the six-mile park-drive loop and the 1.6 mile dirt reservoir track); riding your bike up the West Side along the Hudson River and over the George Washington Bridge . . . you name it, you've got it—just walk (or run, or skate, or bike) out your door.

Ice Skating

There are many outdoor rinks within the City. Wollman (between 62nd and 63rd, enter at 65th) and Lasker (at 106th, most easily accessible from 110th Street) rinks in Central Park rank high with locals. But a special favorite of New Yorkers and tourists alike is ice skating at Rockefeller Center ("Rock Center" to everybody around here).

Rockefeller Center

Fifth Avenue (between 49th & 50th Streets)
(212) 332-7654

Skate rentals available

Running

New York Road Runners Club (NYRRC)

9 East 89th Street
(212) 860-4455

www.nyrrc.org

NYRRC is a great place for meeting other people, getting matched up with running partners for safe running, and expanding your running horizons. Offering free group runs, among other things, from the kiosk in Central Park (at Fifth Avenue and 90th Street, Engineers Gate) at 6:30 A.M. and P.M. on weekdays and at 10 A.M. on weekends. The NYRRC is a cornerstone in many New Yorkers' lives.

Boating and Sightseeing Tours

Big Onion Walking Tours

Cherokee Station
P.O. Box 20561
(212) 439-1090

www.bigonion.com

All guides hold advanced degrees in American History and are licensed by the City of New York. Tours feature New York's historic districts and ethnic neighborhoods.

Circle Line Sightseeing Cruises
Pier 83
West 42nd Street and 12th Avenue
(212) 563-3200

www.circleline.com

Cruise the waters around Manhattan with trips lasting thirty minutes to three hours. Live music is offered seasonally on many cruises. Easily accessible via M42 and M50 busses to Pier 83 or the M15 bus to Pier 16.

Express Navigation
Pier 11, two blocks south of South Street Seaport
(800) 262-8743

Hydroliner boat tour of Manhattan

Gray Line New York Tours
1740 Broadway, 2nd Floor
(212) 397-2620

www.graylinenewyork.com

Double-decker sightseeing tours feature outside seating on the top deck. Narration is available in different languages—just ask.

Helicopter Flight Services
One Penn Plaza, Suite 3600
250 West 34th Street
(212) 849-6847

Sightseeing tours and charters

Liberty Helicopters, Inc.
35 Airport Road, Suite 120
Morristown, NJ 07960
(212) 967-6464

www.libertyhelicopters.com

Flight-seeing tours

CITY
FACT

La Guardia Airport currently sits on a plot of land that, before the airport opened, housed the Gala Amusement Park. At the time that it opened in 1939, the airport was named North Beach Airport and was renamed La Guardia (for the mayor, Fiorello La Guardia) shortly thereafter.

New York Waterway
1040 6th Avenue, 24th Floor
(201) 902-8700, (800) 533-3779

www.nywaterway.com

New York harbor sightseeing cruises. Free bus service between terminals and many Manhattan locations.

Pioneer
Pier 16, South Street Seaport
(212) 748-8786

Historical cruises around New York harbor. Cruising daily, May through September.

Seaport Liberty Cruises
Pier 16, South Street Seaport
(212) 630-8888

New York Harbor and Lower Manhattan sightseeing tours. Cruising March through December.

Short Line Tours
1740 Broadway, 2nd Floor
(212) 397-2620

Sightseeing bus tours

The Spirit of New York
Pier 62 (at West 23rd Street & 12th Avenue)
(212) 742-7278

Lunch, dinner, and "moonlight cocktail" cruises around Manhattan. Cruising throughout the year.

World Yacht Cruises
Pier 81, West 41st Street at the Hudson River
(212) 630-8100

Dinner and Sunday brunch on year-round cruises

Free Events

New York is a town that offers opportunities for the rich, and the not-so-rich, to enjoy events ranging from theater and classical music to movies, street fairs, and antique markets. You can do virtually *anything* for free here, but sometimes you have to be savvy about it. It's always easier to pay for something than to get it for free, but if you're smart, you read the local publications (see previous sections), and you keep on top of the events in the City,

you can get away with spending not a dime, or close to it. Even the things that usually cost money, like the museums and theaters, offer free hours each week, or free productions or dress rehearsals. Pick up a copy of the free *New York Press* or *Village Voice* for weekly happenings and events.

Of course, if you know "someone," and virtually everyone in New York does, doors can be opened for you left, right, and center. That someone can be a struggling artist who gets a break and is having an opening in a posh gallery . . . and you get an invite to the viewing (not to mention the free wine and snacks). It could be a backwaiter

MOVING TIP

"Keep a running list of things you want to do in and around the City so that when you get that free evening or weekend, you don't have to spend your time figuring out what to do—you can just go ahead and do it."

—Renato Bardini, restaurant manager

at a fancy restaurant that is booked solid, but, because you know him, he can get you a reservation when no one else can. Or that someone could be a celebrity you meet (perhaps a parent in your child's school), and you get to attend the opening of her latest film, concert, or fashion show. All of these things are practical realities in New York City; everyone knows someone, and it's just a matter of time until you do, too. But until you do, stay on top of each week's publications. There are always events in NYC that are free, and it's not hard to live like a cultural king without laying out too much dough. And remember, the best way to get to know the City is to walk it, so set out on some adventures of your own, and wander around the neighborhoods, avenues, and streets of New York—you're literally bound to walk into all sorts of events and, more likely than not, they'll be free.

Summer Concerts, Theater, and Events
Central Park, Prospect Park, and others
(212) 360-3444

The New York Philharmonic, City Opera, and Shakespeare in the Park are just a few of the special summer cultural highlights featured at parks throughout the boroughs.

St. John the Divine Cathedral
Amsterdam Avenue (at 112th Street)
(212) 316-7540

The world's largest cathedral (when the building is completed). Visit the biblical garden and children's sculpture garden.

Big Apple Greeters
One Centre Street
New York, NY 10007
(212) 669-2896

Tour New York City with a local.

New York Stock Exchange
(212) 656-5167

World Financial Center Winter Garden
(212) 945-0505

The palm trees are somewhat out of place but soothing and beautiful. There's an open-air feeling to the space, which looks out on the Hudson River. Call for a schedule of free concerts and dance performances.

Grand Tour of Midtown
(212) 986-9317

Fridays at 12:30 P.M.

Penn Station
Eighth Avenue (at 34th Street)
(212) 868-0521

Call for dates on the monthly tour of Penn Station.

New York Public Library
Fifth Avenue (between 40th & 42nd)
(212) 869-8084

Bryant Park
Sixth Avenue (between 40th & 42nd, behind the library)
(212) 983-4142

CITY FACT

Mayor Fiorello H. La Guardia was the first mayor to move into residence at Gracie Mansion (at the East River at 88th Street), which, during his third term in office, became the official mayoral residence.

Enjoy free concerts, summertime Monday night outdoor movies, and other events. Call for a schedule.

Coney Island Boardwalk, Brooklyn

Take a stroll back in time on the boardwalk, every bit worth the trip. Or, enjoy the beach.

Rockefeller Center
30 Rockefeller Center
(212) 698-2950

Enjoy the self-guided tour—pick up maps in the main lobby at building number 30. Also look for special events and exhibits at Rock Center like the Easter Flower Show, winter ice skating at the rink, Christmas windows, and stop by the regular weekday morning filming of the *Today Show* (which also hosts dozens of outdoor early morning events each year).

Heritage Trails

Heritage Trails Visitor and Information Center
(212) 767-0637

Choose from four self-guided walking tours in the downtown area—
or do them all. Tours start from the Federal Hall National Memorial.

Columbus Avenue Market Fair

Columbus Avenue (between 77th & 76th Streets)

Browse through antiques, fresh produce, crafts, and bric-a-brac, on
Sundays.

Schomberg Center for Research in Black Culture

(212) 491-2200

African American culture

Queens Country Farm Museum

(718) 347-3276

A historic homestead

Battery Park Esplanade

Perfect for a breezy walk on the waterfront (Hudson River). Affords
views of New York Harbor and the Statue of Liberty.

Union Square Greenmarket

Broadway to Park Avenues (between 14th & 16th Streets)
(212) 477-3220

Local produce—fruits, veggies, seafood, baked goods—abound at
this favorite New York outdoor market. Year-round on Monday,
Wednesday, Friday, and Saturdays.

Antiques and Stuff Market

Houston Street (between Sullivan & Thompson)

Weekends

Sony Wonder Technology Lab
Madison Avenue (between 55th & 56th)
(212) 833-8100

Municipal Arts Society
(212) 439-1049

A free tour of New York's historic neighborhoods.

Staten Island Ferry
(718) 390-5253

Ride the free Staten Island ferry for great views of Manhattan and the Statue of Liberty—and don't forget about New Jersey.

The Brooklyn Botanic Garden
(718) 622-4433

Tour the gardens, enjoy special events and lectures.

Sixth Avenue Antiques Market
Sixth Avenue (between 24th & 27th Streets)

Find treasures and trinkets, on weekends.

Wave Hill
The Bronx
(718) 549-3200

Overlooking the Hudson River, you can walk around this twenty-eight-acre property that used to be a private estate. Free during the week and Saturdays before noon ($4 for adults, $2 for seniors and students at all other times).

Hudson River Park
(212) 416-5328

"Sounds at Sunset," a summer series hosted by the Battery Park City Authority, features poetry reading, cabaret, and classical music.

MUSEUMS

Virtually all the museums in New York have designated days or hours during which you can gain access to the museum for free or for a minimal donation. Contact each of the museums for specifics (see "Museums," earlier), check their Web sites, a guide book, the NYCVB, or just stop by. A few examples include:

Whitney Museum of American Art (Friday nights free, 212-570-3676)

The Solomon R. Guggenheim (Fridays 5–8, pay what you wish, 212-423-3500)

The Museum of American Folk Art (free, (212-977-7170)

The Cooper-Hewitt National Museum of Design (Tuesday evenings free, 212-860-6868)

The Steuben Gallery (free, 212-752-1441)

The Jewish Museum (pay what you wish, Tuesdays 5–8)

New York Convention and Visitors Bureau
810 Seventh Avenue (at 53rd Street)
(800) NYC-VISIT
(212) 397-8222 (outside the United States and Canada)

www.nycvisit.com

Call or stop by to get a free Visitors' Guide with coupons for discounts and a decent city map. There is also plenty of other helpful free information available at the Bureau if you decide to stop by.

Bargains at Any Price—But All Under $10

Brooklyn Museum of Art
200 Eastern Parkway
(718) 638-5000

$4 for adults, less for children, seniors, and students.

Chinatown

Wander through the heart of Chinatown along Canal, Mott, and Pell Streets. Business lunch, Monday through Friday, is a real bargain, usually ranging from $4.50 to $7.00 (if you splurge).

The Cloisters (a satellite of the Metropolitan Museum of Art)

Fort Tryon Park
(212) 923-3700

$8 for adults, less for children, seniors, and students.

Empire State Building

Fifth Avenue (between 33rd & 34th Streets)
(212) 736-3100

$6 for adults, less for children and seniors

New York Transit Museum

Boerum Place and Schermerhorn Street
(718) 243-3060

The museum itself is set in a 1930s station. Highlighting the history of the City's public transportation system. $3 for adults, less for children, seniors, and students.

Statue of Liberty Ellis Island Immigration Museum

(212) 363-3200
Whitehall Street Ferry

The $7 admission includes entry to the Statue of Liberty, Ellis Island, and the famous and favorite ferry ride.

United Nations

1st Avenue (at 46th Street)
(212) 963-8687 (963-TOUR)
(212) 963-4440 for reservations

Guided tours in many languages.

$7.50 for adults, less for children, seniors, and students

Calendar of Events

JANUARY

The New York National Boat Show (lasting 10 days), at the Javits Center, exhibits the latest in boats, related equipment, and sea-worthy toys (212-216-2000).

Leading dealers in the field of so-called visionary art—also sometimes called naive art or art of the self-taught— exhibit their wares at the Outsider Art Fair, at the Puck Building in SoHo (212-777-5218).

FEBRUARY

The New York Yankees Fan Festival celebrates both the team and the fans. Meet team players, past and present, test your swing, or participate in a memorabilia auction (718-293-4300).

Chinese New Year celebrations, which are spread over the course of two weeks, include lots of noisy fireworks, banquets, and the historical paper-dragon dance that winds through Chinatown (212-484-1222).

During the Westminster Kennel Club Dog Show, as many as 3,000 dogs strut their stuff at the annual event at Madison Square Garden (800-455-3647). It is the second-longest-running animal event in the country (after the Kentucky Derby).

The Annual Empire State Building Run-Up is an invitational event wherein 150 runners run, push, scramble, and wheeze up the 1,576 stairs to the 86th-floor observation deck.

February 14

The Empire State Building is the site of the Valentine's Day Marriage Marathon, when couples marry on the observation deck (212-736-3100).

MARCH

St. Patrick's Day Parade: One of the longest-running (and recently most controversial) events in NYC, the parade starts at 11:30 A.M. at 44th Street, goes up Fifth Avenue, and turns onto 86th Street for the finish.

The International Asian Art Fair, where dealers from around the world show articles from the Middle East, Southeast Asia, and the Far East (212-642-8572).

LATE MARCH–EARLY APRIL

The Ringling Bros. and Barnum & Bailey Circus arrives in New York each spring and, upon its arrival, the animals are walked (around midnight) from Penn Station to Madison Square Garden, where the circus takes place.

The Triple Pier Expo (Piers 88, 90, and 92) is a big antique event, but, if you miss it in the spring, there's a showing in November as well (212-255-0020).

APRIL

The Macy's Flower Show takes place each year in Rockefeller Center the week before Easter.

The Easter Parade goes up Fifth Avenue, ending at St. Patrick's Cathedral, at 51st and Fifth.

Antiquarian Book Fair at the Seventh Regiment Armory (featuring first editions, rare volumes, manuscripts, autographs, letters, atlases, drawings, prints, and maps, with prices ranging from low double digits well into five digits and beyond).

The Major League baseball season kicks off (running through September or October, if we're lucky).

New York Yankees in the Bronx (718-293-6000) and the New York Mets at Shea Stadium, in Queens (718-507-8499)

MAY

Cherry Blossom Festival at the Brooklyn Botanic Garden (718-622-4433)

Bike New York: The Great Five Borough Bike Tour. A forty-two-mile ride that begins in Battery Park and ends with a ride across the Verrazano-Narrows Bridge (212-932-0778).

The International Fine Art Fair. Renaissance to twentieth-century art.

Congregation Shearith Israel (the Spanish and Portuguese Synagogue, the oldest congregation in America) sponsors a Sephardic Fair (212-873-0300).

Tap Dance Extravaganza; events are held around Manhattan (718-597-4613).

Memorial Day Weekend (and following three weekends)

Washington Square Outdoor Art Exhibit, an arts-and-crafts fair with hundreds of exhibitors in and around the park (212-982-6255).

JUNE

The Belmont Stakes at Long Island's Belmont Park Racetrack (718-641-4700).

The Texaco New York Jazz Festival (212-219-3006), sponsoring 350 performances of classic, acid, Latin, and avant-garde jazz at clubs and public spaces around town.

Lesbian and Gay Pride Week features the world's biggest annual gay pride parade, a film festival, and countless other events.

National Puerto Rican Day Parade

JVC Jazz Festival New York is a huge jazz event featuring jazz greats and unknowns all around town.

LATE JUNE–EARLY JULY

The Washington Square Music Festival features free outdoor concerts on Tuesday evenings with classical, jazz, and big band sounds (212-431-1088).

JUNE–AUGUST

Midsummer Night Swing, a fabulous outdoor dance event at Lincoln Center's Fountain Plaza. Open dance and nightly lessons (212-875-5766).

Bryant Park Film Festival. Monday night movies in Bryant Park are a huge social scene and happening event—and there are free movies.

Central Park SummerStage features free events on weekday evenings and blues, Latin, pop, African, country, dance performances, opera, and readings on weekends (212-360-2777).

Shakespeare in the Park (212-539-8500; 212-539-8750 seasonal phone at the Delacorte), sponsored by the Joseph Papp Public Theater at Central Park's Delacorte Theater, tackles the Bard and other classics, often with a star performer or two from the big or small screen.

The New York Philharmonic. Free concerts around the City in area parks (212-875-5656).

Celebrate Brooklyn. Featuring pop, jazz, rock, classical, klezmer, African, Latin, and Caribbean music and theatrical performances, at the band shell in Prospect Park in Brooklyn (718-855-7882 ext. 52). And it's all free.

EARLY JULY–MID-AUGUST

The Museum of Modern Art. Classical music, performed by students of the Juilliard School, is presented in the Summergarden on Friday and Saturday evenings (212-708-9400).

JULY

Independence Day

Great 4th of July Festival. Downtown festivities include live entertainment, arts and crafts, and a parade from Bowling Green to City Hall.

South Street Seaport July 4 festival.

East River July 4 Fireworks. The best you're likely to see—ever! Vantage points are best from 14th to 41st streets along the FDR Drive (which is closed to cars for the event) and the Brooklyn Heights Promenade.

Lincoln Center Festival. Featuring classical and contemporary music concerts, dance, stage works, and non-Western arts.

AUGUST

Lincoln Center Out-of-Doors (212-875-5108) is a series of music, dance, and family-oriented events lasting almost the entire month.

Harlem Week. The world's largest African American and Hispanic festival. Events include concerts, gospel performances, the Black Film Festival, and Taste of Harlem Food Festival (212-862-7200).

Mostly Mozart. Music festival at Lincoln Center includes free afternoon concerts and evening concerts for a fee (212-875-5103).

Brooklyn County Fair, just like in the country (718-689-8600).

LATE AUGUST–EARLY SEPTEMBER

U.S. Open Tennis Tournament held at Flushing Meadows-Corona Park in Queens (800-524-8440).

SEPTEMBER

Labor Day Weekend

West Indian American Day Parade. New York's largest parade (held in Brooklyn) and only one of the many events that this festival features. Festivities begin Friday night with salsa, reggae, and calypso music at the Brooklyn Museum and end Monday afternoon with a huge parade—floats, costumed dancers, stilt walkers—nothing is missing. And don't forget about the West Indian food and music (212-484-1222).

Mid-September

Feast of San Gennaro, Little Italy on Mulberry Street. In honor of the patron saint of Naples, this fabulously colorful event is a great scene in New York's Little Italy.

Broadway on Broadway. A free two-hour outdoor concert in Times Square.

New York Is Book Country. Along Fifth Avenue, between 48th and 57th streets, publishers set up shop so you can see their upcoming wares, meet authors, play games, and sometimes even get free stuff (212-207-7242).

LATE SEPTEMBER–EARLY OCTOBER

The New York Film Festival. The city's most prestigious annual film event (212-875-5610).

OCTOBER

The International Fine Art and Antique Dealers Show. One of the world's finest shows (212-642-8572).

Greenwich Village Halloween Parade. A must-do event, at least once (914-758-5519).

OCTOBER–APRIL

New York Rangers hockey at home at Madison Square Garden.

New York Knicks basketball at home at Madison Square Garden.

NOVEMBER

The New York City Marathon. A citywide event for runners and spectators alike, participants run through all five boroughs before finishing up in Central Park.

Veteran's Day Parade. The parade heads down Fifth Avenue to the United War Veterans Council of New York County.

The Fall Antiques Show. Held at the Seventh Regiment Armory (212-777-5218).

Thanksgiving Day

The Macy's Thanksgiving Day Parade is a favorite New York event (as is now the "balloon stroll" the night before, where City folk gather to watch the balloons being inflated before the big event). Gigantic balloons coast down Central Park West, starting at 77th Street and finishing up at Macy's at Herald Square.

NOVEMBER–JANUARY

The Radio City Christmas Spectacular. Featuring the fabulous Rockettes at home at Radio City Music Hall (212-247-4777).

Thanksgiving Weekend through New Year's

Christmas windows are a New York City tradition. The best decorations are traditionally seen at:

Saks Fifth Avenue (611 Fifth Avenue at 49th Street)

Lord & Taylor (424 Fifth Avenue at 38th Street)

Bloomingdale's (Lexington Avenue at 59th Street)

F. A. O. Schwarz (767 Fifth Avenue at 58th Street)

Barney's (660 Madison Avenue between 60th and 61st Streets)

Macy's (Broadway at 34th Street)

> It's best to start at 58th Street and stroll down Fifth Avenue until you hit Saks (stopping at Rockefeller Center and St. Patrick's Cathedral), stroll up the other side of Fifth to 57th, and then walk over to Madison to see Barney's windows and the other shops along Madison Avenue (like the Polo stores at 72nd Street). Macy's requires a special detour farther downtown.

DECEMBER

Kwanzaa Fest. The world's largest celebration of African American culture includes entertainers, cultural exhibits and attractions for children. At the Javits Center, (718) 585-3530.

Handel's Messiah. At the Cathedral of St. John the Divine on Amsterdam Avenue (at 112th Street). (212) 316-7540. Usually begins at 7:30 P.M., call for details.

Greenwich Village pre-Christmas walking tour. Call Big Onion Walking Tours, (212) 439-1090 (also offers lots of other walking tours around the city).

Midnight Mass on Christmas Eve. Music for choir, brass, and organ, sermon, and candle lighting. At the Cathedral of St. John the Divine. The service usually begins at 10:30 P.M. (Call for details, 212-316-7540.)

Midnight Mass on Christmas Eve. At St. Patrick's Cathedral on Fifth Avenue and 50th Street, (212) 753-2261

Giant Chanukah Menorah is lighted at Grand Army Plaza (Fifth
Avenue and 59th Street)

The Rockefeller Center Christmas tree, one of the tallest in the
country, annually makes headlines when it is first lit—
it's an event that draws thousands of spectators each
year.

New Year's Eve

The ball drops in Times Square.

Midnight Run (five-mile fun run sponsored by the New York
Road Runners Club, 212-860-4455)

Fireworks

And at least one hundred other events.

Public Transportation

BUSES AND SUBWAYS

You'll be hard pressed to find better, more extensive, or more cost-
effective public transportation anywhere in the world. The public
transportation system in NYC is extensive; everything—buses and
subways—runs twenty-four hours a day, seven days a week. The per-
ride fare, whether you go one stop on the bus or subway, or ride from
one end of the Bronx to the other end of Queens, is $1.50. Transfers
between buses are free (have exact change and ask the driver for a
transfer), and the bus-to-subway transfer is free, too, if you have a
MetroCard. The Staten Island Ferry, departing from the southernmost
tip of Manhattan and running to Staten Island, is free of charge. All
five boroughs have extensive bus and subway routes, though the subway lines in Manhattan—which connect with the Bronx, Queens, and
Brooklyn—don't connect with Staten Island. The most direct way to
get to Staten Island from Manhattan via public transportation is on
the ferry.

Bus numbers, routes, and schedules are posted on poles at the bus
stops. Each borough has its own bus map, but they're not easy to come

by. Your best bet, if you must have a map, is to make a trip to the New York Convention and Visitors Bureau (NYCVB, 810 7th Avenue, at 53rd Street), and see if you can get one there. But they may not have the map you want, and for bus service in Manhattan, it's easiest to just ask around, study the "poles" where the routes are posted, and learn which buses are best for you. For the most part, you'll probably only use a few different routes, perhaps a crosstown and a downtown (many buses follow straightforward routes along the Manhattan grid up or down the north–south avenues and crosstown on the east–west streets). Subways are generally faster and more efficient, except when traffic is light. To cut your travel time during commuter hours, you can try a Limited Stops bus (they have fluorescent "Limited" signs on the dashboards). These buses make stops approximately every ten blocks at major intersections and cross-town connections.

Every subway station has a full size map, with the entire 714 miles of routes detailed. These maps are indispensable and are easy to obtain—just ask at the token booth and, if they're out, ask at the next one. If you're having difficulty figuring out your route or stop, just ask someone. Most New Yorkers are friendly and are more than happy to help if they can. You can also ask for help at the token booth.

For schedule and route information, call the New York City Transit Authority (MTA 718-330-1234).

Methods of Payment

There are currently three different ways to pay for bus transportation:

Cash: Have exact change (no free bus-to-subway transfer).

Token: Buy them at a subway station (an outdated, inefficient, and non–cost effective means of payment—if you're bothering to go to the subway to buy tokens, you're better off buying a MetroCard—and it'll save you money).

MetroCard: The MetroCard is a fairly new addition to the New York transit scene, but it is hugely popular and is overtaking all other methods of payment. Only about two and a half years old, the MetroCard has revolutionized the system. Whereas once the options were cash or tokens only, the MetroCard not only allows for a free bus–subway transfer (instituted only about a year and a half ago), but there are also discounts (when you buy ten rides, you get one free) and unlimited ride cards ($4 unlimited ride one-day fun pass, $17 unlimited ride week pass, $63 unlimited ride month pass).

For the subway, payment options include tokens (you already know how I feel about them) and MetroCards.

Reduced fares are available for seniors and disabled riders.

TAXIS AND CAR SERVICE

Taxis are widely available around Manhattan south of 96th Street (they're harder to come by north of 96th Street on the East Side and north of 118th Street—Columbia University—on the West Side). All you have to do is stick out your hand and hail one. Outside of Manhattan it's a bit trickier, but the general rule is that on the major thoroughfares in Queens and Brooklyn you can usually hail a cab. Otherwise, north of 96th Street in Manhattan, and around Queens, Brooklyn, and the Bronx, there are other certified taxi services besides the Yellow Cabs for transportation, and you can usually hail one that is circling about.

How do you tell if a taxi is available for a pickup? If the light on the roof is illuminated, the cab is available. If it's dark, the cab is full. If the "off duty" sign is illuminated, it's not available for service.

Taxi fares are regulated, and drivers stick to the meter (rates are posted on the doors and inside every cab). The fare is $2.00 for the first 1/5 mile and 30 cents each additional 1/5 of a mile. There is a 50-cent surcharge after 8 P.M. (until 6 A.M.), and a rate of 20 cents per minute if standing (though I don't remember ever experiencing the 20 cent increase). It is customary to tip 15–20 percent of the fare. If for some reason the driver doesn't start the meter, you can ask him to do so after he begins to drive.

Car Service is a comfortable way to travel around the city and to the airports (see following for listing and details). Rates are either by the trip, as with the airports, or by the hour. By the hour in Manhattan, usually with a two-hour minimum, prices start at $25 per hour for a sedan (through Carmel Car and Limousine Service, see car service listings below).

Airport Transportation

BY TAXI

La Guardia: Taxi fares will vary depending on your location within the City. To and from destinations within Manhattan, fares will run around $15–$29 plus tolls ($3.50) and tip, and can take fifteen to forty minutes (with no traffic). If you want to share a taxi, ask the dispatcher if he can match you up with someone else—you'll split tolls and share the fare.

JFK: From JFK there is a $30 flat rate to any destination within Manhattan (plus tolls—$3.50—and tip). From Manhattan the fare is $2.00 for the first ¹/₅ mile and 30 cents each additional ¹/₅ of a mile (plus tolls and tip). There is a 50-cent surcharge after 8 P.M. Expect the trip to be thirty to sixty minutes (with no traffic) depending upon your final destination. To share a cab, try to match up with someone on line or talk to the dispatcher.

Newark: The taxi fare to and from Newark airport is the most expensive, at about $34–$38 plus tolls ($10) and tip. Expect the trip to take anywhere from twenty-five to forty-five minutes (with light traffic). To share a cab, try to match up with someone on line or talk to the dispatcher.

BY BUS SHUTTLE

Olympia Trails, Airport Express
(212) 964-6233

Olympia offers round-trip bus service for Newark airport. It takes approximately thirty-five to fifty minutes (more during rush hours) to get into the City, depending on which drop-off destination you select (Grand Central Station, Penn Station, Port Authority, or World Trade Center). The cost is $11 each way.

Gray Line Air Shuttle

(212) 315-3006; (800) 451-0455

Gray Line offers service for La Guardia and JFK airports. It takes approximately thirty-five to forty-five minutes to get into Manhattan from La Guardia and forty-five to sixty minutes from JFK (more during rush hours and for travel below Midtown). The cost (one-way) from La Guardia is $13 and from JFK it's $14. The best thing about Gray Line is that they'll drop you off and pick you up anywhere within the City—door-to-door service in NYC without a full taxi fare is rare!

Super Shuttle

(212) 258-3826; (800) BLUE-VAN

Super Shuttle services La Guardia, JFK, and Newark airports. Service to and from La Guardia is $15, for JFK it's $16 and for Newark it's $19; if you're traveling in a pair, it's only an additional $9 for a second person. Once again, the driver will pick you up or drop you off anywhere within the City at no extra charge.

BY CAR SERVICE

There are dozens of car service companies in the city, and using one is a great way to get yourself a little peace of mind. The fare is predetermined (most companies charge $22 to La Guardia, $32 to JFK, and $29 to Newark, plus tolls and tip), so you don't have to worry about meters, directions, or hailing a cab. Call a day or more in advance for a reservation (though on occasion I've called only a few hours in advance, which works out some of the time), and a car will pick you up at home or meet you at the terminal. Note: If you're calling for an airport pickup and you have a lot of stuff, you can request to have your driver meet you near the luggage area—but usually you just meet outside so the driver doesn't have to park.

Accord Car & Limo Service

(212) 321-1212; (800) 801-3330

American Dream Car and Limo Service
(212) 426-1010;
(888) LIMO-4-VIP;
(888) 546-6484

Carmel Car and Limousine Service
(212) 666-6666
www.carmelcarservice.com

London Towncars
(212) 988-9700; (800) 221-4009

Sabra Travel, Inc.
(212) 777-7171;
(800) 722-7122;
(888) SABRA-NY
www.sabratravel.com

Skyline
(212) 741-3711; (800) 533-6325

Tel Aviv Car and Limousine Service
(212) 777-7777; (800) 222-9888
www.telavivlimo.com

MOVING TIP

"Don't be afraid to try something new just because you think you might not like it. Even if the Japanese sculpture garden doesn't exactly sound like your cup of tea, you'll never know for sure until you give it a whirl—and the story value alone could be worth the price of admission."

—Donelle Davis, actress

BY FERRY

Delta Water Shuttle
(800) 543-3779

The Delta Water Shuttle runs between the Marine Air Terminal (part of La Guardia) and 34th, 62nd (both on the East Side), and Wall Streets (Pier 11). The fare one-way is $15, and it takes approximately twenty-five to thirty-five minutes. Fun, if not entirely efficient for most people.

BY HELICOPTER

National Helicopter
(516) 756-9355

National Helicopter services all three airports to and from heliports within Manhattan. The fare is a flat rate of $389 per helicopter, and each helicopter carries up to five people.

BY PUBLIC TRANSPORTATION

There is no direct route from any of the airports into the City on public transportation, but it can be done if you're up for the challenge, and depending on which airport you're flying into, you can save quite a bit of money (especially compared to taxi fare).

From or to La Guardia

For the shockingly low fare of $1.50 (with a MetroCard, you get a free bus-to-subway transfer, but not with a token or bus transfer), from La Guardia you can take the M-60 bus to 116th Street and Broadway (Columbia University), and transfer to the 1 or 9 subway for locations on the West Side. You can also take the Q33 bus to the Roosevelt Avenue station (in Jackson Heights) and transfer to the E or F trains (subway) or take the Q33 to 74th Street Broadway station and transfer to the 7 train, which will bring you into Grand Central where you can transfer to the 4, 5, and 6 trains (East Side). To go to La Guardia, follow the directions in reverse. Expect ninety minutes of travel time for the trip.

From or to JFK

The Port Authority's free shuttle bus is somewhat of a "slow boat to China" method, but it will get you into Manhattan—eventually. The shuttle stops at all terminals in JFK before going to the Howard Beach subway station. From there, you catch the A train to Manhattan. You can also try the Q10 bus, getting off at the Union Turnpike Kew Gardens station, and catching the E or F trains into Midtown from there (free transfer with the MetroCard). The B15 goes to the New Lots station, where you can catch the 3 train (to the West Side). To go to JFK, follow the directions in reverse. Expect the trip to take two hours.

For further New York City bus and subway information contact:

New York City Transit (MTA)
(718) 330-1234

From or to Newark Airport
New Jersey Transit Airport Express buses depart for the Port Authority Bus Terminal every fifteen minutes on weekdays (every fifteen to thirty minutes on weekends). Purchase your ticket ($7) at the airport terminal (near the baggage claim). From Manhattan, purchase your tickets at Port Authority. Expect thirty-five to forty-five minutes in travel time, with light traffic.

You can also take New Jersey Transit's Airlink buses (departing every twenty minutes from 6:15 A.M. to 2 A.M.), to Penn Station *in Newark*. The ride takes about twenty minutes and the fare is $4. From there, you take the PATH train to Manhattan ($1) stopping at the World Trade Center, Christopher Street, 9th Street, 14th Street, 23rd Street, and 33rd Street. To go to Newark, follow the directions in reverse

For more information on New Jersey public transportation contact:

New Jersey Transit (NJT)
(973) 762-5100

CITY FACT

The first children's gardening program ever established at a botanical garden was begun at the Brooklyn Botanic Garden in 1914.

CHAPTER 7

What's Out of Town

New Yorkers travel far and wide for their weekend escapes. Some favorite destinations, like the Hamptons, the Jersey Shore, and most of the Hudson Valley, are less than 100 miles away. But others are far-flung, like the Vermont ski resorts of Mount Snow, Bromley, and Stratton. All of the following out-of-town destinations are accessible by public transportation, so don't fret if you don't have wheels—many New Yorkers don't own cars, yet they still manage to live well both in and out of the City.

Also, remember, one of the greatest places in the world to spend weekends, holidays, and vacation times is New York City itself. Don't get caught up in the get-out-of-town mentality common to so many young professionals. One of the reasons you're moving to New York is, presumably, to take advantage of all this town has to offer.

Often, instead of going out of town, my husband and I will "take a vacation" at home. We plan a solid weekend of activities, including arts performances, museum visits, restaurant meals, and even some touristy things we wouldn't ordinarily do. This is a particularly effective strategy on Memorial Day and Labor Day weekends, when Manhattan is deserted and reservations and tickets are easy to come by.

Long Island

Long Island is not only home to many of the most desirable New York suburbs, it's also a fabulous weekend and vacation destination all year round. With vineyards on the North Fork and the Hamptons on the South Fork, there is plenty to amuse the beachgoer, the nature lover, the socialite, and the anti-social. From Manhattan, you can get to the East End of Long Island on the Long Island Expressway. Or catch one of the many buses running from the City. This can be far more relaxing than driving—especially in heavy traffic—and the bus drivers know all the shortcuts and often get you there quicker than if you were driving yourself. Train service also runs between Penn Station and points east on Long Island. And some Long Island destinations, like Jones Beach, are only a few miles past the city limits.

CITY FACT

Built in 1904, the St. Regis Hotel (on 55th Street between Fifth and Madison Avenues) was designed and built with the intention of replacing, in elegance and distinction, the Waldorf-Astoria Hotel. Today, the St. Regis still ranks as one of New York's most expensive and distinguished hotels. Recent guests have included Michael Jordan and Elton John.

JONES BEACH

With enough parking for close to 25,000 cars, calling Jones Beach a popular destination would be an understatement, and it's easy to see why: Jones Beach is easily accessible to the City, and has six miles of beach and ocean. Despite the weekend crowds, the sand is clean, and it's a refreshing change and getaway from summer in the City. There are also dozens of concerts at the Jones Beach Boardwalk Bandshell all summer long (visit *www.jonesbeach.com* for details and listings).

Via public transportation from Manhattan, catch the LIRR out of Penn Station to Freeport and connect with buses to Jones Beach. From Queens and Nassau take the Metropolitan Suburban Authority buses. For information call (718) 217-5477 for Manhattan and (516) 766-6722 for Queens and Nassau.

If you're driving from Westchester, Manhattan, the Bronx, Brooklyn, or Queens, take the Long Island Expressway East or Grand Central Parkway East to Northern State Parkway East to Wantagh Parkway South to Jones Beach State Park. Or take the Belt Southern State Parkway East to Wantagh Parkway South to Jones Beach. If you're driving from Eastern Long Island take the Northern State Parkway West or Southern State Parkway West to Wantagh Parkway South to State Park.

THE HAMPTONS

Far more exclusive than any other beach community in the area (based on cost alone), the Hamptons, on the South Fork of Long Island, are the hot summer spot for Manhattan yuppies and West Coast movie moguls alike. Hitting the beach, shopping in town (East Hampton, oddly enough, has a host of outlet stores, such as Coach Leather), and simply soaking up the glitz is all part of a day in the life of the Hamptons summer scene. You can also have a look at the East Hampton Town Marine Museum (516-267-6544), the Parrish Art Museum (25 Job's Lane, 516-283-2118) in Southampton, or the Sag Harbor Whaling Museum (516-725-0770)—or grab a few holes at the Montauk Downs golf course. East Hampton is the heart of the Hampton scene, and worth a visit if you enjoy envying the lifestyles of the rich and famous. It also has some excellent restaurants, shopping, and nightspots. For further information contact the Southampton Chamber of Commerce (516-283-0402), the East Hampton Chamber of Commerce (516-324-0362), and the Montauk Chamber of Commerce (516-668-2428).

Via public transportation from Manhattan, head for LIRR for trains out of Penn Station (718-454-LIRR or 516-758-LIRR). Or if you prefer the bus, options include the Hampton Express (212-233-4403 or 516-874-2400) or the Hampton Jitney (212-936-0440 or 516-283-4600), which both make pickups around the City before heading east.

If you've got wheels, take the LIE to exit 70, right for three miles to Sunrise Highway East (also known as Route 27). Follow 27 to Southampton and beyond—it's the only route to the end of the island.

SHELTER ISLAND

Sheltered between the North and South Forks of eastern Long Island, this haven is ideal for those seeking refuge from the City, the Hamptons, and the see-and-be-seen scene prevalent in so many other summer resort areas. On the dossier are bike riding, fishing, golf, tennis, hiking, sunbathing, reading, or just plain relaxing. Most summer residents rent for the entire summer or own their houses, so the comings and goings aren't as pronounced as elsewhere. There's a selection of hotels, mostly B&B accommodations, which are pleasant and fit in perfectly with the spirit and atmosphere of the island. For more information contact the Shelter Island Chamber of Commerce at (516) 749-0399.

Via public transportation from Manhattan, try the Sunrise Express Bus Service (516-477-1200) or the LIRR to Greenport.

By car from Manhattan take the Midtown Tunnel to I-495, LIE to exit 73 (Riverhead). Turn right onto Route 58 (Old Country Road) east to the traffic circle (about two miles). Continue heading east on 58 for approximately two more miles (until 58 turns into Route 25). Continue until you reach Greenport and see the Shelter Island Ferry sign. Turn off of Front Street (Route 25) and onto Fifth Street headed south. Take a left onto Wiggins Street (Route 114) to the ferry landing.

Fire Island

One of the most interesting beach communities in America, with a heavy gay population, Fire Island offers a remarkable, wide beach and quaint, diverse, walkable towns (cars are forbidden on most of the island) only an hour from the City. A narrow barrier island, with the Atlantic Ocean on one side and the Great South Bay on the other, Fire Island is a summer playground as well as a nature lover's paradise. Ocean-washed beaches, dunes, and maritime forests round out the thirty-two-mile-long Fire Island National Seashore, which contains natural features such as the Otis Pike Wilderness Area (the only federal wilderness in New York) and the Sunken Forest (a 300-year-old holly forest).

Ferries to the various Fire Island communities (operated by Fire Island Ferries, Inc., 516-665-3600) depart from the town of Bay Shore, on the South Shore of Long Island. Frequent LIRR trains to Bay Shore, plus a cheap, shared cab ride to the ferry, provide the simplest means of getting to Fire Island. It's also possible to drive (about an hour from midtown Manhattan) and park at the ferry terminals.

The Hudson Valley

Just north of New York City, the Hudson Valley is ripe with charming towns. The area is especially beautiful (and popular) in the autumn months, when many New Yorkers journey north to see the leaves change hue. If you're up for a scenic drive (as opposed to heading for a particular destination) take Route 9 along the eastern side of the river, or, if you're on a schedule, take the Taconic State Parkway. Trains run up the Valley from Grand Central Station, or you can take a boat tour of the Hudson River. The Hudson Valley is also a favorite destination of devoted cyclists.

MOVING TIP

"Take a vacation at home. While most New Yorkers are fleeing the City on summer weekends and holidays, smart city slickers stay at home and take advantage of all the town has to offer while the hordes are competing for beach space in the Hamptons."

—Mazi Schonfeld, art dealer

Harriman State Park, to the west of the Hudson River, is a great place for hiking or a summer swim in one of the park's three lakes. Bear Mountain State Park is popular with nature lovers from all around, with hiking trails, swimming, fishing, cross-country skiing, sledding, and ice skating. The park's Trailside Museum & Zoo has exhibits on the area and acts as a refuge for rescued animals.

North of Bear Mountain is West Point (where Grant, MacArthur, and Eisenhower did their training). The campus is made up of red brick and graystone Gothic and Federal buildings.

Via public transportation, contact the Shortline bus for service to Bear Mountain and West Point (718-389-8611). For information on Hudson River cruises, try Hudson Highlands Cruises (914-446-7171) or Rip Van Winkle Cruises (914-255-6515). Another option for those without wheels is to sign yourself up for a tour, especially during the fall foliage season. One of the best is through the 92nd Street Y (212-996-1100, *www.92ndsty.org*), but the buses fill up early, so plan ahead.

With wheels: Drive across the George Washington Bridge to the Palisades Parkway to Bear Mountain. Pick up Route 9W north to Highland Falls and West Point.

For information, contact the Palisades Interstate Park Commission (914-786-2701).

The Jersey Shore

If your only knowledge of New Jersey comes from the movies, where the much-maligned state is portrayed as New York's garbage dump, you'll be completely floored by the majestic New Jersey coastline.

CITY FACT

Central Park, in the middle of Manhattan, covers an area larger than the principality of Monaco.

More than 125 miles long, the Jersey Shore runs from Sandy Hook in the north to Cape May in the south. By far the most touristed area of New Jersey, the Shore's commerce centers around the beaches and, of course, the casinos of Atlantic City (which account for most of the 178 million annual tourists). The New Jersey Transit North Jersey Coast train service provides frequent train service, from May through Labor Day, to beaches from Long Branch to Bay Head. Trains run from Penn Station, Hoboken, and Newark.

By car, take the Lincoln Tunnel or the George Washington Bridge out of the city to the Garden State Parkway, which goes to all major Jersey Shore destinations.

BELMAR, SPRING LAKE, BAY HEAD, AND LONG BRANCH

Belmar's long-standing reputation as a party town has eroded over the past few years, and it's now far less wild than it used to be. Still, even though the bars now close at midnight and the police are cracking down on loud parties and public drinking, it's a young, vibrant, beach-party scene. Very popular with those who want to let off a little steam without traveling too far from the City, and with fishing aficionados. Nearby Long Branch (fifteen miles north) is the destination of choice for surfing.

Spring Lake, traditionally called the Irish Riviera because of its heavy population of Irish Catholic vacationers, offers beautiful Victorian inns, B&Bs, and hotels. It is probably the most expensive and exclusive town on the Jersey Shore.

Bay Head is the last stop on the North Jersey Coast line. Known as a quiet, peaceful hamlet, Bay Head offers public access to the beach, although there's no boardwalk. Instead, the beach is lined with Cape Cod homes. Swimming conditions are excellent.

ATLANTIC CITY

Since 1977, when casinos (and gambling) came to town, Atlantic City has become one of the most popular tourist destinations in the country. Though there's little beyond gambling and boxing (there is a boardwalk, but it's a bit seedy, even by traditional boardwalk standards), if you're into gaming, it's a fun place to visit. Avoid the town and head right for your casino hotel of choice (Trump, Caesar's, whichever). It's best to make an overnight trip of it if you're coming from the City, though die-hard gamblers utilize the many bus companies (like Academy) that have departure points from all over the City and will do the whirlwind bus-gamble-buffet-gamble-buffet-gamble-bus round-trip in a day. You can also score some great off-season and midweek hotel deals and turn your trip to Atlantic City into a real extravaganza. On a personal note, one of my great life casino moments was when I was at Merv Griffin's Beverly Hills Buffet at the Resorts International casino, and I saw none other than Merv Griffin—with Eva Gabor on his arm. Just try to beat that action!

The Poconos

Formerly identified with tacky honeymoon resorts, the Poconos has undergone a renaissance of late and is now dotted with tasteful, secluded country inns and offers incredible scenery and a variety of outdoor activities.

Towns include East Stroudsburg (and the famous Inn at Meadowbrook), Canadensis (the Overlook Inn and the Old Village Inn), and South Sterling (the Sterling Inn). Shopping centers around Route 390 between Cresco and Mountainhome, with crafts, country stores, Portuguese linens, and antiques. Three classic old Poconos resorts are the Manor (3,000 acres of grounds), Buck Hill (6,000 acres of grounds), and Sky Top Lodge (newly renovated with 5,500 unspoiled acres).

Contact Pocono Mountains Vacation Bureau (717-421-5791) for further information.

By car, GWB to I-80W to Pennsylvania exit 52, follow Route 447N toward Canadensis.

The Catskills

Lying north of the City and west of the Hudson River, New York's Catskill Mountains are associated the world over with great comedy and entertainment. Milton Berle, Danny Kaye, Jackie Mason, Eddie Fisher, Neil Sedaka, Buddy Hackett, Red Buttons, Alan King, Joan Rivers, Woody Allen, Mel Brooks, Jerry Lewis, Freddie Roman, and Sid Caesar all got their starts at the "Borscht Belt" resorts of the Catskills. People still come in droves to the famed resort hotels of the region, such as Kutsher's, the Raleigh, and the Villa Roma, but the Catskills now also boast a more epicurean side, with country inns and bed & breakfast retreats popping up all over the beautiful landscape. Nature lovers will find plenty to do around the high peaks of the majestic Catskill mountaintops, in the crystal clear mountain lakes, and on the rapids of the Delaware River.

Automobile access to the Catskill region is via Route 17, also known as the Quickway. The Quickway begins at Harriman, exit 16 off the New York State Thruway (I-87). The Quickway heads west toward

Lake Erie and intersects several north–south highways: I-81 at Binghamton; Route 15 at Painted Post; and I-84 at Middletown.

Shortline Buses (212-736-4700 or 800-631-8405) run often from the Port Authority Bus Terminal.

Vermont

Primarily a winter ski destination for New Yorkers (most aren't willing to travel this far for outdoor activities at other times of the year, because we have equally great attractions much closer by), southern Vermont ski resorts are the closest thing to big mountain skiing that the East Coast has to offer. Mount Snow Resort is the closest, and boasts 135 trails (800-245-7669 for general information and reservations, *www.mountsnow.com*). A little farther north is the Stratton Mountain Resort with ninety trails and southern Vermont's highest peak (802-297-2200 for general information, 800-787-2886 for reservations, *www.stratton.com*). And rounding out the trio is Bromley Mountain Resort with forty-two trails (802-824-5522 for general information, 800-865-4786 for reservations, *www.bromley.com*). In 1999, *SKI* magazine picked Bromley as one of the Top 12 family ski resorts in the country. By car, take the Taconic Parkway all the way north to the border, then follow directions for the individual resorts. There is some bus service and limited train service available, but it's slow and intermittent.

The Connecticut Shore

Just minutes beyond New Haven, you'll discover the charming coastal towns of Connecticut. Starting with Stony Creek, Guilford, and Madison, these coastal towns dot the shoreline eastward to the border with Rhode Island. This is New England at its best: old saltbox homes, 300-year old churches, quaint town greens (planned during colonial times as the center of every town—a meeting place for people and grazing spot for animals), and village stores. Antiquing here is serious business—you're likely to find plenty of antique furnishings to accompany all those colonial homes. Many people living here are year-round residents, so you're less likely to find the shifting population common in beach towns during summer months—here, you're likely to see the same people in town, at the neighborhood grocer, or the ice cream parlor as you would at the movie theater and the beach, though you will notice a slight swell during the summer months.

Farther east along the shoreline, in towns like Niantic, Old Lyme, and Mystic, there is a dramatic population change (it gets larger) during summer months, with tourists traveling the coast and stopping at many of the towns for a real taste of coastal Connecticut and New England. B&Bs line the coast, and many are the quintessence of what a B&B is all about: Victorian homes, antique furnishings, home-baked scones for breakfast, and perhaps even a refreshing glass of iced tea on arrival, sitting in your rocking chair on the wraparound porch.

By car take I-95 past New Haven. Follow I-95, watching for signs to each and all of the towns you wish to visit. For a more scenic route, beyond Branford, exit at the first town of interest and, after visiting the town, continue along on Route 1 instead of the interstate. For views of the coast and the communities, look for other route numbers, like Route 146 near Guilford (all of which will eventually hook you back up with Route 1) and Route 156 near Niantic and Old Lyme.

It's very difficult to access the Connecticut shore via public transportation. You can get as far as New Haven on the Metro North trains out of Grand Central, and then it's possible to rent a car or catch a cab. But, realistically, to visit this region, you're best off with a car.

CHAPTER 8

Volunteer and Community Involvement

When people first move to New York City, they're usually so busy and overwhelmed that the last thing they want to think about is volunteering their time to help others. Big mistake.

Volunteering in New York City is not only a great opportunity to do some good in the community, it's also one of the best ways to meet like-minded people and make new friends. And making friends is what makes life in the big city livable. I know people who have found jobs, lifelong friends, apartments, and even spouses through the incredible social network of New York's volunteer organizations. So find a couple of extra hours in your week to help the community— you'll be doing everybody a favor.

In addition to the organizations listed, the following are ways to unearth some of the best philanthropic prospects:

- Contact your block, neighborhood, or community association. Most residential areas of New York City have several active, overlapping, local organizations that do everything from run soup kitchens to plant trees.

- Consult with your church, synagogue, mosque, or temple. Religious organizations are some of the foremost providers of charitable services in the area.

- Check with your college or graduate school alumni association. Most major institutions of higher learning have thriving New York–area alumni chapters, which often host annual or semiannual volunteer projects.

- Inquire with any professional or political organizations to which you belong. Most have long-standing relationships with reputable charities.

- Ask at your office about employee volunteer days and weekend or evening projects organized by your employer.

- Call the local chapters of major national philanthropic organizations, like the American Lung Association. All the big players on the national charity scene have New York chapters, and most welcome volunteers.

- Visit Master Planner Online (*www.masterplanneronline.com*) for a comprehensive listing of thousands of major benefits, openings, and special events for the upcoming year. Many of these events tie into organizations that need volunteers.

- As with all things in New York City, talk to *everybody*. You never know—your next-door neighbor could be the world's number one authority on charitable organizations. And there's no substitute for a firsthand account when you're trying to learn which group is for you.

Volunteer Opportunities

Bronx Zoo
Friends of Wildlife Conservation
The Wildlife Conservation Society
2300 Southern Boulevard
Bronx, NY 10460
(718) 220-5142

www.wcs.org.action

Volunteering at the Bronx Zoo is a highly desirable endeavor, but it isn't for everyone. You can't just walk in and volunteer for an hour a month. Volunteering requires an extended commitment (two years or more) and a devoted personality. But the rewards are tremendous, and volunteers (or docents, as they call them) do everything from giving zoo tours to schoolchildren to participating in outreach programs that bring zoo animals to those physically incapable of visiting the zoo. To become a Friend of Wildlife Conservation, candidates need to complete an application form, pass an interview, and successfully complete a twelve-week training course. To volunteer at the other city zoos, check out the wcs.org Web site for additional details.

Central Park Conservancy

14 East 60th Street
New York, NY 10022
(212) 310-6600

www.centralparknyc.org

To volunteer call (212) 360-2752 or e-mail to *volunteer@centralparknyc.org*

Volunteer opportunities abound at the CPC. You can be a Horticulture and Maintenance volunteer, a Conservancy Greeter, you can volunteer in Visitor Services or as an Office Assistant, or perhaps you'd prefer to spend your time working as a Conservancy Guide or a Special Events Assistant. Perfect for those who love the outdoors.

MOVING TIP

"Even though New Yorkers can be abrasive, we don't mean any harm by the sarcasm and directness. It's just our way. You'll get used to it."

—Hank Vergona, artist

City Harvest

(212) 463-0456

www.cityharvest.org

City Harvest aims to feed the City's hungry and goes a long way toward doing so by collecting food daily from restaurants, cafeterias, and individuals. CH collects forty tons of food per week and distributes it to emergency food programs operated by 150 CH-approved agencies throughout New York City. To get involved, CH encourages people to sponsor canned food drives, Thanksgiving turkey drives, or baby food infant formula drives (runs from Mothers' Day through Fathers' Day each year) from home or office. Other volunteer opportunities range from driver's assistant (truck driver) to office assistant. "Food In-kind Support," such as office equipment and supplies, is also welcome.

CITY FACT

Lincoln Center for the Performing Arts (known locally as Lincoln Center) is the largest performing arts complex in the United States. The center consists of Avery Fisher Hall, the New York State Theatre (home to the New York City Ballet and New York City Opera), the Metropolitan Opera House, the Juilliard School, Alice Tully Hall, and the Vivian Beaumont and Mitzi E. Newhouse Theaters.

Green Guerillas

625 Broadway, 9th Floor
New York, NY 10012
(212) 674-8124

www.greenguerillas.org

In 1973, Liz Christy, a Lower East Side artist, collected friends and neighbors to clean out a vacant lot on the corner of Bowery and Houston Streets. Calling themselves the Green Guerillas, they created a vibrant community garden and established the modern community gardening movement. Each year, hundreds of Green Guerillas volunteer thousands of hours in community gardens citywide. "Workdays are festivals of planting, weeding, watering, and mulching."

The International Center in New York

50 West 23rd Street, 7th Floor
New York, NY 10010
(212) 255-9555

www.intlcenter.org

mholman@intlcenter.org.

The Center works toward helping newcomers to the country adjust with ease (English conversation and American culture for newcomers to the United States). There are a number of different areas in which volunteers can get involved, ranging from one-on-one program tutorials (writing tutor, professional mentor), workshop instructors, or consultants, administrative, fundraising, and marketing assistants. To volunteer you must submit a completed application form and interview with a staff member.

New York Aquarium

Volunteer Coordinator
Education Department
Boardwalk at West 8th Street
Brooklyn, NY 11224

www.wcs.org action

Interested parties are required to apply, interview, and attend training sessions in order to become aquarium volunteers (docents, as they call them), and therefore must be committed individuals. Volunteers might assist in hands-on exhibits, showing visitors how to handle animals in the Rocky Coast Touch-It-Tank and the Ray Pool, or teach visitors about marine habitats and animals, answer questions, give directions, and assist the Education Staff.

NY Cares

116 East 16th Street, 6th Floor
New York, NY 10003
(212) 228-5000

www.nycares.org

NY_Cares@nycares.org

New York Cares is ideal for the newcomer to New York, because the organization coordinates volunteer projects to fit in with busy lifestyles, while making the activities social at the same time. Projects are scheduled on weekdays and weekend mornings, afternoons, and evenings, and a volunteer can give a few hours per week or a few hours per year. There is no intensive training or screening process and volunteers can participate on a short- or long-term basis. All projects are team-based, so you get to bond as a team and meet new people. You can also arrange to volunteer with or as a group, such as an alumni association, a group from work, a club, or a religious group.

Partnership for Parks

The Arsenal
Central Park
(212) 360-1310

www.partnershipsforparks.org

An initiative of the City Parks Foundation and the City of New York Parks & Recreation. Anyone can volunteer with Partnership for Parks, be it for a few hours or on a more regular basis. Volunteers work in the City parks doing everything from leaf cleaning in the fall to helping with the crowds and handing out leaflets and maps on New Year's Eve.

Police Athletic League

34¹/₂ East 12th Street
New York, NY 10003
(800) PAL-4KIDS

www.palnyc.org

The Police Athletic League is the largest youth agency in New York City, serving 65,000 youngsters each year with a wide range of educational and recreational programs. PAL is always looking for volunteer athletic coaches and part-time teachers of dance, drama, ceramics, arts and crafts, and more.

Recording for the Blind

545 Fifth Avenue
New York, NY 10017
(212) 557-5720

www.rfbd.org

Recording for the Blind is in
need of devoted volunteers who
have science or professional
backgrounds and a minimum of
two hours a week to share on an
ongoing basis. Volunteers will be
involved with all aspects of
recording.

Share Our Strength

733 15th Street NW, Suite 640
Washington, DC 20005
(800) 969-4767
(202) 393-2925

www.strength.org

SOS is one of the nation's leading anti-hunger and anti-
poverty organizations. Founded
in 1984, Share Our Strength has
distributed more than $50 mil-

MOVING
TIP

"Find a place where you enjoy hanging
out—a restaurant, bar, coffee shop—
and become a regular there. Surprisingly,
even in this huge town, it's not difficult to
become a regular after only a few visits—and it's nice to have a place where
you can comfortably hang out alone, or
impress your friends when you share your
haunt."

—Mary Lesser, artist

lion to more than 1,000 anti-hunger and anti-poverty efforts worldwide. In New York City, SOS is primarily linked to the Taste of the
Nation event, which is held annually in the spring in more than
eighty cities. People in the restaurant industry—waiters, chefs, prep
cooks, bussers—mostly volunteer through work. But if you aren't in
the field and want to get involved, call SOS because they can always
use volunteers in different areas and will welcome your assistance.

Finding the Essentials

CHAPTER 9

Important Places to Know

One of the most disorienting things about moving to a new town is the disruption of your daily routine. You need a new dry cleaner, a new pharmacist, and a new place of worship. New York is doubly confusing, though, because New Yorkers do everything differently than most of the rest of the country. We don't have cars, we shop in tiny urban grocery stores, and we're used to having every conceivable service at our beck and call twenty-four hours a day. In this chapter you'll learn how New Yorkers get their essential services—including some things you didn't even know were essential until you decided to become a New Yorker!

Medical Emergencies

A medical emergency is perhaps the most terrifying occurrence for a newcomer to any city, and most people have no idea what to do in an emergency beyond a vague notion that they should dial 911. But a call to 911 is just the beginning of effective management of a health emergency, and smart New Yorkers have to be aware of some information that's unique to this city.

Dr. Stephen Lynn, director of the emergency department at St. Luke's-Roosevelt Hospital (one of the best in the City), offers the following advice that may save your life:

- As soon as you move to New York, learn the name and address of the best hospital within a reasonable distance of your home. When you are picked up by an ambulance, demand to be taken to that hospital. You have the right to be taken to any hospital you request as long as it is within ten minutes' drive and provided the ambulance staff does not believe your condition is critical (if you're critical, your request will be overruled and you'll be taken to the closest available hospital).

- When deciding whether to call for an ambulance, try to determine whether moving the patient will present a hazard. If there is any uncertainty, of course you should call for an ambulance. But if the person can be moved without damage, the fastest way to get somebody to an emergency room may be in a taxi.

- When you speak to the ambulance operator, give as much specific information as you can. Be sure to indicate your cross-streets (not just your numerical address), your apartment number and floor, and any special instructions for locating and entering your building. Give your phone number and make sure the line stays open in case the operator needs to reach you again.

- Contact your personal physician after you've summoned an ambulance. Your physician should be able to streamline the hospital admission and treatment processes.

- Don't be surprised if additional vehicles, such as police cars, arrive at the scene.

- In most cases, an ambulance will allow one person to accompany the patient in the ambulance, but this is not always the case. If you need to travel separately to the hospital, be sure to get the exact name and address of the hospital where the patient is being taken (many of the hospitals in New York have similar-sounding names).

- When you call 911 and report a medical emergency, an Emergency Medical Service (EMS) ambulance will be dispatched to your location. Most people aren't aware, however, that there are several private ambulance companies that compete with

EMS. An ambulance from EMS is not free—you or your insurance will have to pay for it—and a private ambulance should cost the same and be eligible for the same insurance coverage as an EMS ambulance. In addition, private ambulance services are often (but not always) quicker than EMS, and they give you more control over where you'll be taken and what type of ambulance will be dispatched (an EMS ambulance with limited capabilities versus a full-fledged paramedic ambulance with more extensive equipment). The best strategy, according to many doctors, is to call both 911 and one of the private ambulance services and take whichever ambulance arrives first.

• For private ambulance service, Dr. Lynn recommends: Metropolitan Ambulance Co., (212) 251-8888.

OTHER EMERGENCY NUMBERS

Police and Fire Departments:
 Dial 911 (Note: For non-emergency police calls, dial 212-374-5000 to learn the number of your local precinct.)

Animal Bites: (212) 566-2068

Bureau of Alcohol, Tobacco, and Firearms: (212) 466-5149

Child Abuse and Maltreatment Reporting Center: (800) 342-3720

Crime Victims Hotline: (212) 577-7777

Doctors on Call: (718) 745-5900

Domestic Violence Hotline: (800) 621-4673

Electric or Steam Emergency: (212) 683-0862

MOVING TIP

"A private school may be of the highest quality and the best reputation, but if it isn't a good match for your child, or doesn't mesh with your personal outlook and philosophy, then look elsewhere. A great school that's a bad match equals a bad school for your child's needs."

—Elayne Landis, educational consultant

FBI: (212) 384-1000

Gas Emergency: (212) 683-8830

Poison Control Center: (212) 764-7667

Sex Crimes Report Line: (212) 267-7273

Suicide Prevention: (212) 673-3000

U.S. Coast Guard: (212) 668-7936

U.S. Customs Investigations: (212) 637-3900

U.S. Secret Service: (212) 637-4500

HOSPITALS AND EMERGENCY ROOMS

New York has some of the world's finest hospitals, and virtually all of them (save for the specialty centers) have twenty-four-hour emergency rooms. But while the City's hospitals are excellent, they are also large and intimidating. Julie and Paul Lerner, authors of the *Lerner Survey of Health Care in New York*, advise you to be a "defensive patient." In particular, make certain all hospital staff members who touch you have washed their hands, and double-check all medications to be certain you've been given the correct prescription.

CITY FACT

More than 16 million immigrants passed through the Ellis Island immigration station in New York Harbor between 1892 and 1924.

For the most part, if you require surgery or other hospital services, you won't choose your hospital—you'll just go to the hospital with which your physician or surgeon is affiliated. For specialized care and emergency room purposes, however, you should be aware of the most important New York hospitals and their areas of expertise. The lists of specialties following some of these listings are meant to highlight a hospital's strongest practice areas, but each hospital has many areas of competence that are not listed here. In the end, you'll want to choose a hospital in consultation with a qualified doctor.

Important Hospitals in Manhattan

Beth Israel Medical Center
16th Street & First Avenue
New York, NY 10003
(212) 420-2881

www.wehealnewyork.org

Specialties: Cardiology, orthopedics

Hospital for Joint Diseases
301 East 17th Street
New York, NY 10003
(212) 260-1203

www.hjd.edu

Specialties: Orthopedics, rheumatology

Hospital for Special Surgery
535 East 70th Street
New York, NY 10021
(212) 606-1930

www.hss.edu

Specialties: Orthopedics, rheumatology

Lenox Hill Hospital
100 East 77th Street
New York, NY 10021
(212) 434-2000

www.lenoxhillhospital.org

Specialties: Cardiology, obstetrics, orthopedics

Memorial Sloan-Kettering Cancer Center
1275 York Avenue
New York, NY 10021
(212) 639-2000

www.mskcc.org

Specialties: Cancer treatment (by most accounts, the best in the country), gynecology, urology

Mount Sinai Hospital
1 Gustave L. Levy Place (99th Street)
New York, NY 10029
(212) 241-6500

www.mountsinai.org

One of the best overall hospitals in America. Specialties: Geriatrics; gastroenterology; ear nose, and throat; psychiatry; neurology; cardiology; obstetrics; urology

New York Eye and Ear Infirmary
310 East 14th Street
New York, NY 10003
(212) 979-4000
www.nyee.edu
Specialties: Ophthalmology

Columbia Presbyterian Center, New York Presbyterian Hospital
161 Fort Washington Avenue
New York, NY
(212) 305-2500
www.nyp.org
Specialties: Neurology, psychiatry, pediatrics, urology, cardiology, orthopedics, gastroenterology

New York Weill Cornell Center, New York Presbyterian Hospital (commonly known as New York Hospital)
525 East 68th Street
New York, NY 10021
(212) 746-5454
www.nyp.org
Specialties: Psychiatry, neurology, urology, gynecology, gastroenterology, rheumatology

NYU Downtown Hospital
170 William Street
New York, NY 10038
(212) 312-5000
www.nyudh.med.nyu.edu
Specialties: Cardiology

NYU Hospitals Center, Rusk Institute
400 East 34th Street
New York, NY 10016
(212) 273-7300
www.med.nyu.edu
Specialties: Rehabilitation

NYU Hospitals Center, Tisch Hospital
550 First Avenue
New York, NY 10016
(212) 263-7300
www.med.nyu.edu
Specialties: Rehabilitation, rheumatology, orthopedics, cardiology

Roosevelt Hospital Division, St. Luke's-Roosevelt Hospital Center
1000 Tenth Avenue
New York, NY 10019
(212) 523-4000
www.wehealnewyork.org

St. Luke's Hospital Division, St. Luke's-Roosevelt Hospital Center
1111 Amsterdam Avenue
New York, NY 10025
(212) 523-4000
www.wehealnewyork.org

Important Metro-Area Hospitals Outside Manhattan

Brooklyn Hospital Center
Downtown Campus
121 DeKalb Avenue
Brooklyn, NY 11201

Caledonian Campus
100 Parkside Avenue
Brooklyn, NY 11226
(718) 250-8000
www.tbh.org

Long Island Jewish Medical Center
270-05 76th Avenue
New Hyde Park, NY 11040
(718) 470-7000
www.lij.edu
Specialties: Geriatrics, cardiology

Maimonides Medical Center
4802 10th Avenue
Brooklyn, NY 11219
(718) 283-8533
www.maimonidesmed.org
Specialties: Cardiology

Montefiore Medical Center
111 East 210th Street
Bronx, NY 10467
(718) 920-4321
www.montefiore.org
Specialties: Geriatrics, rheumatology, cardiology

North Shore University Hospital
300 Community Drive
Manhasset, NY 11030
www.nsuh.edu

Staten Island University Hospital
North Site
475 Seaview Avenue
Staten Island, NY 10305
(718) 226-9000

South Site
375 Seguine Avenue
Staten Island, NY 10309
www.siuh.edu

Westchester Medical Center
Valhalla Campus
Valhalla, NY 10595
(914) 493-7000
www.wcmc.com

HHC Hospitals

In addition to the hospitals mentioned previously (and many others), the New York City Health and Hospitals Corporation (HHC) operates eleven public hospitals that contain one-third of the City's hospital beds. At these hospitals, everybody, whether insured or not, has the right to medical care based on a sliding scale of fees. For more information about HHC hospitals, contact:

New York City Health and Hospitals Corporation

125 Worth Street, Room 510
New York, NY 10013
(212) 788-3339

www.ci.nyc.ny.us/html/hhc/home.html

Cleaners and Laundries

With more than 2,200 dry cleaners and laundries in New York City, you're likely to find a half-dozen dry cleaning shops within a two-minute walk of your apartment. Or, if you live in a full-service high-rise building, you'll have access to in-building cleaning services (just drop your clothes with the doorman, pick them up the next day, and pay the bill each month). Sometimes, however, your cleaning needs will go beyond the ordinary—and that's when you'll be glad you live in New York City.

Cleantex

235 12th Avenue (133rd Street)
(212) 283-1200

Hours: Mon–Fri, 8 A.M.–4 P.M.

Furniture, draperies, shades, blinds, rugs

Glove Masters

808 East 139th Street (Bronx)
(718) 585-3615

Gloves (will accept mail orders—call for information)

Hallak Cleaners

1232 Second Avenue (65th Street)
(212) 879-4694

Hours: Mon–Fri, 7 A.M.–6:30 P.M.; Sat, 8 A.M.–3 P.M. (closed Sat during July and August)

Wedding gowns and other especially delicate garments

Jeeves

39 East 65th Street (between Madison & Park Avenues)
(212) 570-9130

Ultra-premium dry cleaning

Leathercraft Process of America

several area locations
(212) 564-8980 for info

Leather, suede, and sheepskins

Meurice Garment Care

31 University Place (between 8th & 9th Streets)
(212) 475-2778

Hours: Mon–Sat, 7:30 A.M.–7 P.M.; Sat, 7:30 A.M.–5 P.M.

245 East 57th Street (between. 2nd & 3rd Avenues)
(212) 759-9057

Hours: Mon–Fri, 8 A.M.–6 P.M.; Sat, 7:30 A.M.–5 P.M.

Cleaning and restoration of especially fine garments

Midnight Express Cleaners

(212) 921-0111

Hours: Mon–Fri, 9 A.M.–11 P.M.; Sat, 9 A.M.–3 P.M.

Offers late-night pickup and delivery

Mme Paulette Dry Cleaners

1255 Second Avenue (between 65th & 66th Streets)
(877) COUTURE

Hours: Mon–Fri, 7:30 A.M.–6:30 P.M.; Sat, 8 A.M.–5 P.M.

160 Columbus Avenue (in the Reebok Club)
(212) 501-1408

Hours: Mon–Fri, 5 A.M.–11 P.M.; Sat, 8 A.M.–9 P.M.

Ultra-premium dry cleaning

Perry Process

1315 Third Avenue (between 75th & 76th Streets)
(212) 628-8300

Knits

Peter & Irving

36 West 38th Street (between 5th & 6th Avenues)
(212) 730-4369

Hats

Tiecrafters

252 West 29th Street
(212) 629-5800

Hours: Mon–Fri, 9 A.M.–5 P.M.

Neckties (service also available through several local outlets)

Zotta, Alice
2 West 45th Street (between Fifth & Sixth Avenues)
(212) 840-7657

Stain Removal

As a last resort, if money is no object, contact the New York School of Dry Cleaners at (212) 684-0945. The school does work for museums and restoration projects and, for a hefty fee, the school's experts can perform an analysis of your stain. If they can't get the stain out, nobody can.

Markets and Grocery Stores

There are no wide-aisle mega-supermarkets in the City, so New Yorkers tend to be very European in their shopping habits. We often visit three or four specialty stores (perhaps a butcher, a fish market, a fruit and vegetable stand, and a general grocery store) rather than buy everything in one place. And, because storage space is limited and station wagons are few, we tend to shop more often than suburbanites. For an excellent overview of neighborhood specialty stores, see the book *New York Eats*, by Ed Levine.

At the same time, New York's major gourmet markets are some of the largest and best in the world. They are truly a sight to behold if you're used to suburban chain supermarkets. If you're lucky enough to live near one of these markets, you'll have the best of both worlds: the quality of a dozen specialists, but all under one roof. Some of the best New York gourmet markets are:

Agata & Valentina

1505 First Avenue (corner of 79th Street)
(212) 452-0690

Hours: 8 A.M.–9 P.M., 7 days

A relative newcomer with a bright future

Balducci's

424 Avenue of the Americas (corner of 9th Street)
(212) 673-2600

www.balducci.com

Hours: 7 A.M.–8:30 P.M., 7 days

Far and away the best gourmet store in New York

Chelsea Market

75 Ninth Avenue (between 15th and 16th Streets)
(212) 243-6005

Hours: Mon–Fri, 7 A.M.–8 P.M.;
Sun, 10 A.M.–6 P.M.

Top-notch multi-vendor marketplace in Chelsea

Citarella

2135 Broadway (corner of 75th Street)
(212) 874-0383

1313 Third Avenue (corner of 75th Street)
(212) 874-0383

www.citarella.com

Hours: Mon–Sat, 7 A.M.–9 P.M.;
Sun, 9 A.M.–7 P.M.

Originally one of New York's premier fish markets, now offering first-rate meat, produce and everything else

MOVING TIP

"New York City is full of excellent public schools, some of which rank among the top schools in America. To make public school work for your child, though, you need to do your homework. Start planning far, far in advance—at least a full year ahead of time—especially if you want your child to attend a public school other than the one for which your residence is zoned."

—Jessica Wolff, public school parent and director of Program Outreach at the Public Education Association

Dean & DeLuca
560 Broadway (corner of Prince Street)
(212) 431-1691
www.dean-deluca.com

Hours: Mon–Sat, 10 A.M.–8 P.M.; Sun, 10 A.M.–7 P.M.

Tony, overpriced, gorgeous

Eli's
1411 Third Avenue (between 80th & 81st Streets)
(212) 717-7664

Hours: 7 A.M.–9 P.M., 7 days

Similar inventory to Vinegar Factory (same owner), but in more luxurious surroundings

Fairway Downtown
2127 Broadway (corner of 74th Street)
(212) 595-1888

Hours: 24 hours, 7 days

The king of the price/quality equation

Fairway Uptown
2328 Twelfth Avenue
(212) 234-3883

Hours: 8 A.M.–11 P.M., 7 days

Like Fairway downtown, but larger, better, less crowded, and free parking (a *really* big deal for New Yorkers)

Foodmart International (New Jersey)
100 Boyle Plaza
Jersey City, NJ 07310
(201) 656-6950

Hours: 7 A.M.–2 A.M., 7 days

Perhaps the world's largest multi-ethnic mega-market

Gourmet Garage
453 Broome Street (corner of Mercer Street)
(212) 941-5850

Hours: 7 A.M.–9 P.M., 7 days

301 East 64th Street (between First & Second Avenues)
(212) 535-6271

Hours: 7:30 A.M.–8:30 P.M., 7 days

2567 Broadway (between 96th & 97th Streets)
(212) 663-0656

Hours: 7:30 A.M.–9 P.M., 7 days

A mini-chain of warehouse-style gourmet stores. Some great stuff, but hit-or-miss overall.

Grace's Marketplace
1237 Third Avenue (corner of 71st Street)
(212) 737-0600

Hours: Mon–Sat, 7 A.M.–8:30 P.M.; Sun, 8 A.M.–7 P.M.

Lovely Upper East Side store owned by a Balducci family faction

Grand Central Marketplace
On the Grand Central Station Main Concourse

Each purveyor/stall has its own telephone number

Hours: Mon–Fri, 7 A.M.–9 P.M.; Sat, 9 A.M.–7 P.M.; Sun, 9 A.M.–5 P.M.

Elegant new marketplace with dozens of gourmet food stalls

Union Square Greenmarket
Union Square Park (along Broadway & East 17th Street)

Hours: Early morning–mid-afternoon, Mon, Wed, Fri, and Sat

New York's premier farmers market. Go very early for the best selection. For other area greenmarkets, see the Council

on the Environment of NYC's Web site *www.users. interport.net/~conyc/*

Vinegar Factory
431 East 91st Street (between First & York Avenues)
(212) 987-0885
Hours: 7 A.M.–9 P.M., 7 days

Warehouse-style gourmet store, expensive with beautiful produce

Zabar's
2245 Broadway (corner of 80th Street)
(212) 787-2000
www.zabars.com

Hours: Mon–Sat, 8 A.M.–7:30 P.M.; Sun, 9 A.M.–7 P.M.

A classic (a temple to some, a homecoming to others, or just a really good place to shop to the rest), and still one of the best

New York also has an ample supply of chain supermarkets (although they tend to be miniature versions of their suburban cousins), such as Food Emporium, Gristedes, and Pioneer.

Twenty-Four-Hour Pharmacies

You'll no doubt have several competing pharmacies within a few blocks of your home, some of which will be open twenty-four-hours a day for over-the-counter pharmaceutical sales (you can also get a limited selection of pharmaceuticals at twenty-four-hour supermarkets, bodegas, and newsstands). In addition, the following pharmacies can fill prescriptions twenty-four-hours a day:

Duane Reade

224 West 57th Street (at Broadway)
(212) 541-9708

2465 Broadway (at 91st street)
(212) 799-3172

1279 Third Avenue (at East 74th Street)
(212) 744-2668

For a complete listing of locations and store hours go to *www.duanereade.com*.

Rite-Aid

303 West 50th Street (at Eighth Avenue)
(212) 247-8384; (212) 247-8736

542 Second Avenue (at 30th Street)
(212) 213-5284 (main number)
(212) 213-9887 (pharmacy number)

For a complete listing of locations and store hours go to *www.riteaid.com*.

CITY **FACT**

The New York Police Department (NYPD) traces its roots back to 1845, when the City established a municipal police force with 900 officers. Today, the NYPD is one of the largest police departments in the world, with 38,000 uniformed officers and 9,000 civilian employees. The NYPD patrols 320 square miles and has a budget of $2.4 billion.

Places of Worship

Whatever your religious beliefs, an astounding number of options await you in New York. Choosing a place of worship is a very personal (and sometimes political) decision, but the following tips from noted religion scholar Professor Richard I. Sugarman can help get you started:

- If you're already an observer, discuss your move to New York with your current clergyperson. Using this approach, you may be able to get in touch with like-minded clergy here in New York.

- Visit several places of worship before deciding on one. Talk to members of the congregation and make sure you feel comfortable with the group's beliefs.

- The best listing of places of worship and times of services can be found in the first ("National") section of each Saturday's *New York Times.*

- If you have a strong affiliation to a specific branch of a particular religion (for example, Lutheran Church of America, Reform Judaism), use the New York Yellow Pages to contact the headquarters of that group. This is the surest way to get a list of all the appropriate places of worship for you.

- Many people are prone to forget their religious observances when they move to a new community, especially if that community is a huge, anonymous-seeming city like New York. But your religion can be a great source of strength and comfort during this difficult transitional period, and participation in organized religion is a great way to meet local people who share your values. A relationship with a specific religious organization also gives you access to familiar clergy during emergencies, and can help you access school, child-care, counseling, and community information.

- Remember, you're more likely to go to services if you choose a place of worship in your neighborhood.

The Mail

POST OFFICES

There are 183 United States Post Office locations in New York City. Most are open at least from 9 A.M. to 5 P.M. on weekdays, from 9 A.M. to 1:00 P.M. on Saturdays, and are closed on Sundays and national holidays. Some of the larger post offices have longer hours, and the General Post Office (zip code 10001), located on 33rd Street and Eighth Avenue, is open twenty-four hours a day, seven days a week. See *www.usps.gov* for information about post offices in a given zip code.

POST OFFICE BOXES

There is often a waiting list for post office boxes at the U.S. Post Offices, so many New Yorkers have turned to private vendors. There are thirty-three Mail Boxes, Etc., franchises in New York, which tend to offer longer hours (many are open on Sunday) and better availability of private boxes than the post office. See *www.mbe.com* for specific neighborhood locations.

CITY FACT

More than 200 major studio films are shot on location in New York City each year— and that only accounts for a quarter of the filming done on the city streets. Combined with television shows and commercials, the City grants permits for more than 20,000 "production days" of filming per year.

PACKAGES AND EXPRESS SHIPPING

FedEx has offices throughout New York (800-Go-FedEx or 800-463-3339, *www.fedex.com*) as do UPS (800-PICK-UPS or 800-742-5877, *www.ups.com*) and DHL (800-CALL-DHL or 800-225-5345, *www.dhl.com*).

MESSENGERS

For local messenger service, try the very reliable Thunderball, (212) 675-1700. Also, most of the car services listed in chapter 6 will deliver packages twenty-four hours a day (for a hefty fee).

CHAPTER 10

Local Schools and Colleges

Picking the right school for your child from among the more than 1,300 choices in New York City (and thousands more in the metro area) can be a daunting and overwhelming task. Just tackling the categories of schools—public and private, single-sex and coeducational, religious and secular, English language, bilingual and ESL—can give you a headache. This chapter will arm you with the tools you need to begin the process of finding the best school for your child. In addition to listing contact information for each of the thirty-two public school districts in the City, there's also a list of what are generally considered to be the most noteworthy private schools, plus lists of private education consultants and organizations that can aid you in decoding the system.

Choosing a college for yourself is a little easier (there are merely hundreds, not thousands, of colleges in New York), but it's still a challenge. The second part of this chapter lists higher education resources in several relevant categories.

Public Schools

The New York City public school system is the largest in the country, with thirty-two school districts, 1,100 public schools, and 75,000 teachers serving more than 1 million students. It's a massive bureaucracy—due to the decentralized nature of the system (each district has its own superintendent, policies, outlook, and philosophy), it can take dozens of surreal phone calls to learn the smallest tidbit of information and months of research to figure out whether your child is best off in your neighborhood school or in one of the alternative, magnet, or gifted-and-talented schools. But if you start your research early (at least one full year in advance) and you follow the advice in this chapter (I spoke to dozens of education experts and made my own fair share of surreal phone calls, to obtain the information following), your child can receive an excellent and free education within the City's multicultural (New York City is the original melting pot, and it continues to grow), multiracial, multilingual (Spanish, Arabic, Urdu, Korean, Chinese, Hindi, Hebrew, and Russian are spoken) public school system.

Before you do anything else, call the Board of Education Zoning Unit (see following) to learn which zone your residence falls into, unless of course you selected your residence based on this criterion, in which case you probably already know.

Board of Education (BOE) Headquarters
110 Livingston Street
Brooklyn, NY 11201
(718) 935-3555

To find out what zone a school is in, call:

BOE Zoning Unit
(718) 935-3566

You can also walk into the nearest school in your neighborhood and inquire about your local school district and board.

In most of America, your child will attend the school in the district in which you live. The New York suburbs work the same way—in New Jersey, Westchester, Long Island, and Connecticut, where you decide to live ultimately determines if and where your child goes to public school, which is why residences in certain suburban school districts are more desirable and therefore more expensive than others. But in the five boroughs of New York City, it's a different world. There are dozens of public schools in each district, and there are so-called gifted-and-talented schools, for which your child must be tested and admitted, sprinkled throughout the boroughs. Thus, though you may decide to live in Cobble Hill in Brooklyn, your child may commute to Hunter College Elementary School in Manhattan every day.

On the elementary and middle school levels, students are generally registered for the school within their zone or catchment area (districts are broken down into zones based on geography) during the spring preceding the September they will begin school. But the specialized schools (see following), for which your child must apply (and often be tested), begin the admissions process well in advance.

For kindergartners, preregistration is normally held in the beginning of May for the following academic year. And although kindergarten isn't mandatory in New York City schools, in order to be enrolled in a kindergarten class your child must be five years old by December 31 of the year for which you are requesting enrollment.

As for the nitty-gritty of registering your child, one parent (or guardian) must go to the designated

CITY FACT

The Empire State Building, which was the tallest building in New York until the construction of the World Trade Center in 1973, has its own zip code and eleven dedicated mail carriers. In July 1945, a B-25 army cargo plane crashed into the building between the 79th and 80th floors, killing fourteen people and sending one elevator plummeting to the bottom of its shaft. The structure at the top of the building was designed as a mooring mast for dirigibles, although it was only used once.

school in your zone with proof of address (a copy of your lease or utility bill is sufficient); proof of immunization; either a birth certificate, baptismal certificate, or passport; and, of course, the child. For children entering kindergarten, proof of the countless (and painful) immunizations that your child has received is required (ask in your child's school or call the Board of Education for the excruciating details).

But this straightforward registration process is only the beginning, and only applies if you are sending your child to the district school for which your residence is zoned. There are, however, zones within every district, and many districts have "free choice," "school choice," or "parent choice" policies (they're all synonymous), which allow you to choose from among the many schools within the entire district rather than being limited to the school within your zone. So if you would like to pursue public schools that are located outside of your designated zone, you should begin the process of learning about the schools, educating yourself, and obtaining the necessary variances *a full year ahead* of the school year for which you are registering your child.

Children within the zone have first priority for entrance, children within the district but outside of the zone come second, and children outside of the district are given third priority. Only children within the zone absolutely must be accommodated by that school (assuming it is not a specialized school for which all children must be tested and where admission is based on performance). All others are accepted on a space-available basis.

For high school zoning and admission, there is yet another, entirely different, set of rules and standards. There is zoning for high schools within the districts; however, there are so many specialized and alternative schools spread throughout each of the five boroughs that many students test to gain admission to their school of choice. Students take the high school admissions test in eighth grade in the hope of gaining admission to one of their selected (top eight choices) specialized or gifted-and-talented schools. So not only might your child be coming from a different zone and district, but possibly even from an entirely different borough than where the school is located. All high schools within the City accept students from throughout the entire City, and the more restrictive rules that apply to elementary and middle schools do not apply to the high schools.

You may have gathered that the process of getting your child into a public school other than the one for which your residence is zoned is slightly more complicated than finding a taxi in the rain during rush hour in Midtown. But take heart—thousands of parents each year take the initiative to secure the best educations for their children (a parent with a child especially gifted in music may be in a perfectly desirable school zone but opt instead to jump through hoops in order to get the child into the Clinton School for Writers and Artists). If they can do it, so can you.

Schools that make it a policy of accepting students from different zones, and even districts, go by many names: *magnet schools, open zoned schools, choice, gifted-and-talented schools,* and *alternative schools..* For more information on these options, put a call into your designated district at the Board of Education. Within each district, there is a healthy and continual evolution of the school programs that are offered.

GLOSSARY OF TERMS FOR ELEMENTARY AND MIDDLE SCHOOLS

Magnet School: The term "magnet school" is based on the concept of schools that attract students from other places, like a magnet. In most cities the term is used to describe schools that are for especially gifted children. It will not surprise you to learn, however, that in New York City the term has a different meaning—several meanings, in fact. Many magnet schools at the elementary and middle school levels are geared toward attracting a stronger or more diverse student body. For example, an underutilized school within a zone—one that has enrollment of 300 students but has the capacity for 1,000— may introduce a special program like a computer lab, in which each child is promised two hours of computer time each day, in order to attract students from other schools. Or a school within a certain district may be heavily populated by a certain racial group and, in order to introduce more diversity into that school, the district may institute a special program, like an arts program, and give priority of entrance to children of the racial groups that are underrepresented within the school. Gone are the days of forced zoning or busing. If a school wants to attract children from other places to improve its program and create a stronger student body, it must do it by instituting programs that will make parents and children *want* to attend that school, not by forcing them to do so.

Open Zoned School: Open zoned schools are not required to accept children within the school's zone before accepting students from other zones. And because each district has its own determination, contact your district for details on how your zone is broken down, what the specifications are, and who, if anyone, gets priority.

Choice: Rather than being limited to schools within your zone or district only, you can ask for a variance from the Board of Education and apply to a school anywhere within the City (the child would be admitted to your school of choice based upon space availability).

Gifted-and-Talented School: G&T programs are for children who are especially gifted or talented in a specific area: intellectually, artistically, or physically. These schools, or special programs within a school, require a testing process for admission. Different districts have different requirements for admission as determined by the superintendent of that zone. For example, District Three G&T schools base admission on IQ tests, whereas District Two has an interview process.

Alternative School: The term "alternative school" is primarily applicable to the high school level (though there are a handful of alternative schools on the elementary and middle school levels). A specific set of high schools are part of the *alternative* grouping, which is run by a separate superintendent and offers a range of programs from one school to the next for children with special needs—from those who need special attention to the especially gifted who flourish in an alternative education environment.

USEFUL CONTACTS

Office of Access and Compliance
Division of High Schools
110 Livingston Street
(718) 935-3415

The BOE offers a free, annually updated publication, *The Directory of Public High Schools*, which is comprehensive and informative.

Division of Assessment and Accountability
110 Livingston Street
(718) 935-3767

To get a copy of the annual report listing the statistics on a school's performance, ethnic makeup, test scores from the previous year (known as a "report card"), call the DAA.

Office of Parent Advocacy and Engagement
110 Livingston Street, Room 108
(718) 935-5202; (718) 935-3040

To receive helpful pamphlets, like the *Elementary & Intermediate School Parent Guide* or the *High School Parent Guide*, contact this office.

MOVING TIP

"Get to know the wonders of New York by renting some of the most important movies about the City: *Breakfast at Tiffany's, Midnight Cowboy, When Harry Met Sally, A Thousand Clowns, The Apartment, Barefoot in the Park, King Kong, Metropolitan, On the Town, The Freshman*, plus *Annie Hall* and anything else by Woody Allen."

—Irving Metzman, actor

SCHOOL DISTRICTS

Following is a list of the thirty-two New York City school districts and the contact information for each.

Manhattan

Community School District 1
Superintendent: Dr. Sonia Diaz-
Salcedo
80 Montgomery Street
New York, NY 10002
(212) 602-9701

Community School District 2
Superintendent: Ms. Elaine Fink
333 7th Avenue
New York, NY 10001
(212) 330-9400

Community School District 3
Superintendent: Ms. Patricia
Romandetto
154 West 93rd Street
New York, NY 10025
(212) 678-2880

Community School District 4
Superintendent: Ms. Evelyn
Castro
319 East 117th Street
New York, NY 10035
(212) 828-3500

Community School District 5
Superintendent: Ms. Thelma
Baxter
433 West 123rd Street
New York, NY 10027
(212) 769-7500

Community School District 6
Superintendent: Mr. Brian
Morrow
4360 Broadway, 4th Floor
New York, NY 10033
(212) 795-4111

The Bronx

Community School District 7
Superintendent: Dr. Edna Vega
501 Courtlandt Avenue
Bronx, NY 10451
(718) 292-0481

Community School District 8
Superintendent: Dr. Betty A. Rosa
650 White Plains Road
Bronx, NY 10473
(718) 409-8100

Community School District 9
Superintendent: Ms. Maria
Guasp
1377 Jerome Avenue
Bronx, NY 10452
(718) 681-6160

Community School District 10
Superintendent: Ms. Irma
Zardoya
1 Fordham Plaza
Bronx, NY 10458
(718) 584-7070

Community School District 11
Superintendent: Mr. Joseph Kovaly
1250 Arnow Avenue
Bronx, NY 10469
(718) 519-2614

Community School District 12
Superintendent: Ms. Althea Serrant
1000 Jennings Street
Bronx, NY 10460
(718) 328-2310

Brooklyn

Community School District 13
Superintendent: Dr. Lester Young
355 Park Place
Brooklyn, NY 11238
(718) 636-3204

Community School District 14
Superintendent: Mr. Robert Sheedy
215 Heyward Street
Brooklyn, NY 11206
(718) 963-4800

Community School District 15
Superintendent: Mr. Frank DeStefano
360 Smith Street
Brooklyn, NY 11231
(718) 330-9300

Community School District 16
Superintendent: Dr. Marcia Lyles
1010 Lafayette Avenue
Brooklyn, NY 11221
(718) 574-2800

CITY FACT

Manhattan's rectilinear street grid was designed in 1811, long before most of it was actually built. John Randel, Jr., an engineer, headed up a commission that mapped out all the streets from Houston Street to 155th Street. With minor modifications (like the addition of Central Park) this is the grid we see in New York today. Below Houston Street, the streets still run on the old meandering Dutch plan— which is why it's so hard to find your way around down there!

Community School District 17
Superintendent: Dr. Evelyn W. Castro
19 Duryea Place
Brooklyn, NY 11226
(718) 826-7800

Community School District 18
Superintendent: Ms. Paula LeCompte Speed
755 East 100th Street
Brooklyn, NY 11236
(718) 927-5100

Community School District 19
Superintendent: Ms. Joan East Mahon-Powell
557 Pennsylvania Avenue
Brooklyn, NY 11207
(718) 257-6900

Community School District 20
Superintendent: Mr. Vincent Grippo
1031 59th Street
Brooklyn, NY 11219
(718) 692-5200

Community School District 21
Superintendent: Mr. Donald Weber
521 West Avenue
Brooklyn, NY 11224
(718) 714-2500

Community School District 22
Superintendent: Mr. John Comer
2525 Haring Street
Brooklyn, NY 11235
(718) 368-8000

MOVING TIP

"Take advantage of all the free events and performances in New York City. There are many, many offerings, especially in the summer: The New York Philharmonic, Metropolitan Opera, and Shakespeare performances in Central Park, free outdoor movies in Bryant Park, lunchtime concerts at the World Trade Center. And, come November, don't forget to cheer the almost 30,000 runners in the NYC Marathon!"

—Aaron Laiserin, Web designer

Community School District 23
Superintendent: Dr. Kathleen Cashin
2240 Dean Street
Brooklyn, NY 11233
(718) 270-8600

Community School District 32
Superintendent: Mr. Felix Vazquez
797 Bushwick Avenue
Brooklyn, NY 11221
(718) 574-1125

Queens

Community School District 24
Superintendent: Mr. Joseph Quinn
8000 Cooper Avenue
Queens, NY 11385
(718) 417-2600

Community School District 25
Superintendent: Ms. Michele Fratti
30-48 Linden Place
Queens, NY 11354
(718) 281-7600

Community School District 26
Superintendent: Ms. Claire McIntee
61-15 Oceania Street
Queens, NY 11364
(718) 631-6900

Community School District 27
Superintendent: Mr. Matthew Bromme
82-01 Rockaway Boulevard
Queens, NY 11416
(718) 642-5700

Community School District 28
Superintendent: Mr. Neil Kreinik
108-55 69th Avenue
Queens, NY 11375
(718) 830-8800

Community School District 29
Superintendent: Mr. Michael Cinquemani
1 Cross Island Plaza
Queens, NY 11422
(718) 978-5900

Community School District 30
Superintendent: Dr. Angelo Gimondo
49-05 20th Avenue
Queens, NY 11370
(718) 777-4600

Staten Island

Community School District 31
Superintendent: Mr. Christy Cugini
715 Ocean Terrace, Building A
Staten Island, NY 10301
(718) 390-1600

TOP PUBLIC SCHOOLS

These are commonly regarded as the most competitive public high schools (all of which are specialized), for which testing is (and auditions may be) required.

MOVING TIP

"Despite rising admission prices, some of the best museums in New York offer free or 'pay-what-you-wish' admission on one night each week: The Cooper Hewitt and the Jewish Museum on Tuesday; the Museum of Modern Art and the Whitney on Thursday; and the Guggenheim on Friday. Plus, watch for the 'Museum Mile' celebration each summer, where all the Fifth Avenue museums open their doors for free."

—Maria Tucci, accountant

Bronx High School of Science ("Bronx Science")
75 West 205th Street
Bronx, NY 10468
(718) 817-7700
www.bxscience.edu

Brooklyn Technical High School ("Brooklyn Tech")
DeKalb Avenue & South Elliott Place
Brooklyn, NY 11217
(718) 858-5150
www.bths.edu

Fiorello H. La Guardia High School of Music & Art and Performing Arts ("Music & Art")
100 Amsterdam Avenue
New York, NY 10023
(212) 496-0700
www.laguardiahs.com

Stuyvesant High School
345 Chambers Street
New York, NY 10282
(212) 312-4800
www.stuy.edu

OTHER USEFUL CONTACTS

The Public Education Association

28 West 44th Street, Suite 914
New York, NY 10036
(212) 868-1640

www.pea-online.org

The PEA (since 1895) is a public advocacy group that works to help parents learn about and navigate the public school system. It offers a vast storehouse of helpful information, including personal advisory sessions and files of helpful information on the City's public schools. Don't forget to ask for useful and free publications like *New York City Public Middle Schools at a Glance, A Consumers Guide; New York City Public High Schools at a Glance, A Consumer's Guide;* and *A PEA Alert.* You can stop by for copies of these publications (it's always best to call ahead) or have them mailed (you pay the postage). The PEA also runs a very useful hotline (same number as listed) to answer parent queries about the public school system, ranging from "How can I get my child into a gifted program?" to "What is the best school in my district?"

Early Childhood Resource and Information Center

Division of New York Public Libraries
66 Leroy Street (corner of 7th Avenue)
New York, NY 10014
(212) 929-0815

Primarily a research center for adults with information pertaining to early childhood education. A family room with picture books (appropriate for children up to age eight) is also available.

92nd Street Y

1395 Lexington Avenue
New York, NY 10128
(212) 996-1100

The 92nd Street Y offers a school series each fall ("Public School Options Fair") at which parents can learn more about different

CITY FACT

The Great Fire of 1835 lasted three days and destroyed most of lower Manhattan. The blaze engulfed seventeen city blocks and ruined 700 buildings, including many important commercial buildings (such as the original Merchant's Exchange) and beautiful churches from the Dutch period.

school options (public and private), meet teachers, and ask questions. Advanced registration is required and the programs do fill up.

Manhattan Borough President's Office
1 Centre Street, 19th Floor
New York, NY 10007
(212) 669-3951

The MBPO offers a free guide, *Parent's Guide to Choosing a Public Elementary School in New York City.*

The Toussaint Institute
(212) 422-5338

The TI annually offers a seminar on public schools for African American and Hispanic parents.

HELPFUL WEB SITES ABOUT NYC PUBLIC SCHOOLS

New York City Board of Education
www.nycenet.edu

New York City Board of Education Web site contains volumes of information and extensive links to other helpful sites.

New York State Education Department
www.nysed.gov

Also check out *www.nysed.gov/nycscs/* (New York City Schools and Community Service) from the NYSED page.

New York State School Boards Association
www.nyssba.org/home6.html

New Visions for Public Schools

www.newvisions.org/home.html

Gotham Gazette

www.gothamgazette.com

"New York City news, politics, and policy"

HELPFUL REFERENCE GUIDES

The Parents' Guide to New York City's Best Public Elementary Schools, Clara Hemphill

Public Middle Schools: New York City's Best, Clara Hemphill

New York Independent Schools Directory, Hendin and Schulman, eds. (published by ISAAGNY and available at the Corner Bookstore (93rd & Madison) and from the Parents League of New York (see following for details)

The Grownup's Guide to Living with Kids in Manhattan, Diane Chernoff-Rosen & Lisa Levinson

The Hunter College Campus Schools for the Gifted, Elizabeth Stone

---

Independent and Private Schools

There are well over 100 private schools in and around New York City, ranging from religious to college preparatory in nature.

If you decide to pursue a private school for your child, you will likely hear the term "independent school" tossed around. An Independent School is a private, nonprofit organization that has membership in the Independent Schools Admissions Association of Greater New York (ISAAGNY). All participating ISAAGNY schools have agreed to accept the test administered by the Educational Records Bureau (ERB), which your child will have to take in order to gain admission to any of the independent schools.

Private schools are also privately owned and run, but unlike the independent schools, the schools must answer to someone other than the board of trustees (such as a religious official, if the private school has a religious affiliation and receives monies as a result of that affiliation).

The example of "questionable" literature illustrates the difference: If a teacher at the Trinity School (which is an independent school) puts a "questionable" title, such as *Catcher in the Rye*, on the curriculum, and the Episcopal Church decides that it does not approve, it is still ultimately the school's rather than the church's decision how to proceed because the school is an independent, self-governed entity. If, however, Trinity had been organized as a private school, with specific church affiliation and funding, that decision would be made by the church.

When narrowing the scope of independent and private schools, there are a number of issues to consider. Cost is clearly one factor. When the specifics of New York area tuition are discussed (often upward of $15,000–$20,000 per student per year), involuntary reactions like drop-jawed fathers and fainting mothers are common occurrences. But if it's any consolation, private school tuition doesn't really vary that greatly from one state to another. Private schools in and around other cities, like the Hawken School in the suburbs of Cleveland, have tuition in the same ballpark (upward of $15,000 per year for a high school education, slightly less for grades K–8, on a scaled grade-level basis, not including transportation) as New York City and area schools. If cost is an issue, ask about scholarships and financial aid.

If you are in need of financial assistance, researching the options within the parochial school set is a good bet. Religiously affiliated schools, if they have the means available, are often the most accommodating of families in need of financial assistance. Remember though, that your child will spend part of the day learning about religious subject matter and may be taught by nuns, priests, rabbis, ministers. Personally, I have no problem with this (I attended a religious school from nursery school through eighth grade and received what I believe to be a good secular education), but some people are opposed to mixing a secular education with a religious one, and these schools most definitely do.

Other considerations are proximity to your home (Horace Mann, for instance, is in Riverdale, as are the Fieldston and Riverdale Country schools), grade span (K–6, K–8 or 9, K–12), school philosophy and outlook, the number of children per class and overall size of the school, religious affiliation, and whether you want your child to attend a single-sex or coeducational program. Obviously there are other factors to consider and, as you sift, you may find that your child would be best served by a small religious school, an all-girls program, or by a neighborhood public school (where perhaps your child can be a big fish in a small pond and really shine).

IMPORTANT PRIVATE SCHOOLS

The Brearley School
610 East 83rd Street
New York, NY 10028
(212) 744-8582

www.brearley.org

All girls, K–12

Collegiate School
260 West 78th Street
New York, NY 10024
(212) 721-2300

All boys, K–12

The Dalton School
108 East 89th Street
New York, NY 10128
(212) 423-5200

www.dalton.org

Coeducational, K–12

Dwight-Englewood School
315 East Palisade Avenue
Englewood, NJ 07631
(201) 569-9500

Coeducational, N–12

MOVING TIP

"If you hear of a good apartment building that has a long waiting list, and you're even so much as thinking about living in that building, you should get on the list no matter how long it is. The months and years pass by with unanticipated speed, you'll probably end up staying in New York longer than you planned (perhaps forever!), and good deals are worth the wait."

—Rachel Laiserin, technology project manager

Fieldston
*Fieldston Road & Manhattan
College Parkway
Bronx, NY 10471*

Fieldston Lower
(718) 329-7313

Coeducational, N–6

Fieldston Upper
(718) 329-7306

Coeducational, 7–12

Hackley School
*293 Benedict Avenue
Tarrytown, NY 10591
(914) 366-2642*

Coeducational, K–12 day and boarding

Horace Mann School (upper and lower schools)
*231 West 246 Street
Riverdale, NY 10471
(718) 432-4100*

www.horacemann.org

Coeducational, N–12

The Nightingale-Bamford School
*20 East 92nd Street
New York, NY 10128
(212) 289-5020
(212) 289-8844*

All girls, K–12

Poly Prep Country Day School (upper and lower schools)
*9216 Seventh Avenue
Brooklyn, NY 11228
(718) 836-9800*

Coeducational, 5–12

*50 Prospect Park West
Brooklyn, NY 11215
(718) 768-1103*

Coeducational, N–4

The Riverdale Country School (upper and lower schools)
*5250 Fieldston Road
Riverdale, NY 10471*

*Lower School
River Campus (249th & Hudson
River)
(718) 549-7780*

Coeducational, N–6

*Upper School
(718) 549-8810*

Coeducational, 7–12

Rye Country Day School
*Cedar Street
Rye, NY 10580
(914) 967-1417*

webserver.rcds.rye.ny.us/

Coeducational, K–12

St. Bernard's School
4 East 98th Street
New York, NY 10029
(212) 289-2878

All boys, K–9

The Spence School
22 East 91st Street
New York, NY 10128
(212) 289-5940

All girls, K–12

The Town School
540 East 76th Street
New York, NY 10021
(212) 288-4383

www.townschool.org

Coeducational, N–8

Trinity School
139 West 91st Street
New York, NY 10024
(212) 873-1650

Coeducational, K–12

CITY FACT

The five boroughs of New York—Brooklyn, Queens, Staten Island, the Bronx, and Manhattan—were separate cities and counties until 1898, when they were consolidated into one municipal entity. In 1993, in a show of voter anger at the municipal government, the residents of Staten Island voted 2-to-1 to secede from the City, but the referendum was never approved by the state legislature.

For additional nursery school and pre-K programs, inquire at places of worship. Synagogues and churches are excellent sources of information, and many offer their own programs. If you work in the medical field, some of the more forward-thinking organizations (especially hospitals) offer early childhood education centers, usually giving preference to employees and affiliated faculty and doctors. Also check in at your neighborhood YMCA/YWCA. Many offer early childhood programs, as does the 92nd Street Y (the famous YMHA/YWHA on the Upper East Side of Manhattan).

RESOURCES FOR INDEPENDENT AND PRIVATE SCHOOLS

American School Directory

www.asd.com

Internet directory of schools, public and private

MOVING TIP

"One of most effective ways to learn all about New York is to spend a ton of time walking around the City. Treat it as a formal course of study—make a schedule and say, 'Today I'm going to explore SoHo; next weekend, TriBeCa!' In addition to providing unlimited free entertainment, the act of exploring by foot makes you more of a New Yorker with every step you take."

—Andrea Hendler, global volunteer

programs coordinator

Advocates for Children

151 West 30th Street, 5th Floor
New York, NY 10001
(212) 947-9779

www.advocatesforchildren.org

Special Needs

Board of Jewish Educators, New York

www.bjeny.org/

Superintendent of Catholic Schools

1011 First Avenue
New York, NY 10022
(212) 371-1000;
(800) SCHOOLFOR

www.nycatholicschools.org

The Catholic Center will provide you with a list of Catholic schools within a specified region.

Catholic Education Network

www.catholic.org/cen/

Links to Catholic schools on the Internet

The Educational Register
Vincent-Curtis
224 Clarendon Street
Boston, MA 02116
(617) 536-0100

A directory of private schools

The Guild of Independent Schools of New York
(212) 289-5020

The GISNY is an unstaffed group chaired by the head of Nightingale-Bamford School, Dorothy Hutcheson.

Handbook of Private Schools
Porter Sargent Publishers
11 Beacon Street, Suite 1400
Boston, MA 02108
(617) 523-1670

Independent Educational Consultants Association
4085 Chain Bridge Road
Fairfax, VA 22030
(703) 591-4850

IECA offers a free consultant directory to families seeking professional advice in school selection.

International Coalition of Boys' Schools
c/o Dr. Richard Hawley
2785 S.O.M. Center Road
Hunting Valley, OH 44022
(216) 831-2200

ICBS offers a free brochure and personalized assistance.

Islamic Foundation of North America
www.islamicedfoundation.com

Jesuit Secondary Education Association
www.jsea.org

Information and links to Jesuit schools around the country

The Learning Disabilities Association of New York City Telephone Referral Service
(212) 645-6730

Information and referral agency and family support groups

National Association of Independent Schools (NAIS)
1620 L Street NW
Washington, DC 20036
(202) 973-9700

www.nais-schools.org

The National Center for Learning Disabilities
381 Park Avenue South, Suite 1041
New York, NY 10016
(212) 545-7510

National Coalition of Girls' Schools
228 Main Street
Concord, MA 01742
(508) 287-4485

www.ncgs.org

Free directory and a list of publications

Network of Sacred Heart Schools
860 Beacon Street
Newton Centre, MA 02459
(617) 244-9260

The New York Branch of the International Dyslexia Association
71 West 23rd Street, Suite 514
New York, NY 10010
(212) 691-1930

www.interdys.org/3-ny.stm

New York State Association of Independent Schools (NYSAIS)
287 Pawling Avenue
Troy, NY 12180
(518) 274-0184

www.nysais.org

Choosing a School—A Guide for Parents
The Parents League of New York
115 East 82nd Street
New York, NY 10028
(212) 737-7385

www.parentsleague.org

An excellent source for learning all about the private, nonparochial, and special schools in the New York area is the Parents League of New York, which has been helping parents navigate the private school system of the City and surrounding areas since 1913. For a modest membership fee of $60 (it usually goes up a couple of dollars every year), members receive copies of five different books published independently by the Parent's League (*Parents League Guide to NY, Summer in New York, Parents League Review, Toddler Book,* and *Parents League News*). Also included in the membership fee is an educational counseling session (one hour with a counselor and follow-up on the phone or on an as-needed basis over the telephone) to further aid parents in aptly placing their children. A one-hour advising session for summer camp placements (and other summer programs like summer abroad and summer school) is also available on an annual basis.

In addition to the educational resources, the Parents League keeps extensive, annually updated files on baby-sitters, tutors (categorized by test preparation, learning disabilities, ESL, English, history, science, math, French, and other common school subjects), birthday parties (two entire file cabinets), summer programs, and parenting resources (advice, articles, referrals). Programs and workshops covering a wide range of topics ("Applying to Independent Schools" is always the biggest draw and is offered in a number of different locations) are also offered with membership. The Parents League also accepts volunteers. See chapter 8 for further volunteer information.

Peterson's Annual Guide to Independent Secondary Schools

P.O. Box 2123
Princeton, NJ 08543-2123
(609) 243-9111

A directory of private secondary schools

City Fact

New York's unusual and massive underground steam delivery system, built by Consolidated Edison in the 1890s, is by far the largest in the world. In winter, the system carries more than 10 million pounds of 400-degree steam per hour to heat thousands of large office and apartment buildings.

Private Independent Schools
Bunting and Lyon
238 North Main Street
Wallingford, CT 06492
(203) 269-3333

A directory of private schools

Resources for Children with Special Needs
200 Park Avenue South, Suite 816
New York, NY 10003
(212) 677-4650

www.resourcesnyc.org

New York State Education Department
Non-public School Services Team
Room 471 Education Building Annex
Washington Avenue
Albany, NY 12234
(518) 474-3879

www.nysed.gov/rscs

For statistics and other useful information on private schools in NYC

EDUCATIONAL CONSULTANTS

Given the incredible range of school options in New York, it's no surprise that a cottage industry has arisen in the area of education consulting. Because they charge a fee, however, educational consultants are utilized primarily by parents looking to place their children into private schools. The following list includes only consultants who charge a fee to the family rather than to the school into which the child is placed (as with a headhunter, some schools pay a fee to the consultant, who, working with a family, places a child at their school). There is a range of fees for educational consultants, but the common practice is to charge a retainer fee (approximately $1,000) and 10 percent of the first year's tuition, which in total usually works out to be approximately $3,000.

Virginia Bush
444 East 86th Street
New York, NY 10028
(212) 772-3244

Howard Greene Associates
39 East 72nd Street
New York, NY 10021
(212) 737-8866

Dr. Frank Leana is the director.
Advisory service offering counseling on private schools, camps,
college, graduate school, and
professional school. With offices
in New York City, Westport, and
London.

Jane Hewes
1326 Madison Avenue
New York, NY 10128
(212) 289-5679

Leonard Krivy
888 8th Avenue
New York, NY 10019
(212) 777-2443

Elayne Landis
40 East 88th Street
New York, NY 10128
(212) 831-6198

Previously was the admissions
director of the Allen-Stevenson
School

Brinton Taylor Parson
17 East 84th Street, Apt. 4A
New York, NY 10028
(212) 744-6192

Francis Spataro
80-46 234th Street
Queens, NY 11427
(718) 740-4134

Colleges and Universities

The number of options for higher education in New York is, as you've
by now come to expect with everything in New York, simply mind-
boggling. The City alone has twenty of its own public institutions,
and that doesn't include all of the private universities and colleges, the
adult education programs, and the institutions that offer the non-
credit-bound student a selection of courses just for the sake of learning. The lists that follow should help you get started on your path to
discovery.

CITY COLLEGES AND UNIVERSITIES

There are twenty City Universities and Colleges of New York (CUNY, 212-817-7700; ten senior colleges; six community colleges; one technical college; a graduate school; a law school; and a medical school, which are all located within the five boroughs of New York City), many of which are highly reputable schools. In the "old days," especially following the big waves of immigration to the United States, ambitious people seeking a university education but lacking the necessary funds for private university pursued degrees at the city-subsidized schools, which were hotbeds of debate, discovery, and intellectual pursuits.

Baruch College
17 Lexington Avenue
New York, NY 10010
(212) 802-2222
www.baruch.cuny.edu

Borough of Manhattan Community College
199 Chambers Street
New York, NY 10007
(212) 346-8000
www.cuny.edu

Bronx Community College
West 181st Street & University Avenue
Bronx, NY 10453
(718) 220-5100
www.cuny.edu

Brooklyn College
Bedford Avenue (at Avenue H)
Brooklyn, NY 11210
(718) 951-5000
www.brooklyn.cuny.edu

City College
138th Street (at Convent Avenue)
New York, NY 10031
(212) 650-6977
www.ccny.cuny.edu

City University of New York Law School
65-21 Main Street
Flushing, NY 11367
(718) 575-4200
www.cuny.edu

City University of New York Medical School

138 Street (at Convent Avenue),
Room 5609
New York, NY 10031
(212) 650-5276

www.cuny.edu

College of Staten Island

2800 Victory Boulevard
Staten Island, NY 10314
(718) 982-2010

www.csi.cuny.edu

Eugenio Maria de Hostos Community College

475 Grand Concourse
Bronx, NY 10451
(718) 518-4444

www.cuny.edu

Hunter College

695 Park Avenue
New York, NY 10021
(212) 772-4490

www.hunter.cuny.edu

John Jay College of Criminal Justice

899 Tenth Avenue
New York, NY 10019
(212) 237-8000

www.cuny.edu

MOVING TIP

"Find the local thrift store, Salvation Army office (212-663-2258), Goodwill Industries (212-447-7270), or another charity that accepts clothing and furniture donations. With apartment space at a premium, when you buy new items you usually have to give away some of the old to make room. If you give to charity, you'll help the needy—and get a tax deduction to boot! Some good organizations: Cancer Care Thrift Shop (212-879-9868, free pickups for some items), Memorial Sloan-Kettering Thrift Shop (212-535-1250, free pickups for furniture), Grand Street Settlement (212-831-1830, 212-674-1740 ext. 257 for free pickup), City Opera Thrift Shop (212-684-5344)."

—Toby Kovacs, client services manager

Kingsborough Community College

2001 Oriental Boulevard
Brooklyn, NY 11235
(718) 368-5000

www.cuny.edu

MOVING TIP

"A savvy New Yorker is an off-season traveler in her own town. The top attractions, restaurants, and stores in New York are often brutally crowded—so don't go when they're busy. The same restaurant that was packed on Saturday night may be nearly empty at lunchtime on Tuesday. Even the most popular stores tend to be empty first thing in the morning, when they've just opened. Learn what everybody else is doing, and then don't follow the herd."

—Emily Fries, health care consultant

La Guardia Community College

31-10 Thomson Avenue
Long Island City, NY 11101
(718) 482-5000

Lehman College

230 Bedford Park Boulevard West
Bronx, NY 10468
(718) 960-8000

www.lehman.cuny.edu

Medgar Evers College

1650 Bedford Avenue
Brooklyn, NY 11225
(212) 947-4800

www.cuny.edu

Mount Sinai School of Medicine (affiliated)

4 East 102nd Street
New York, NY 10029
(212) 241-6500

www.cuny.edu

New York City Technical College

300 Jay Street
Brooklyn, NY 11201
(718) 260-5006

www.cuny.edu

Queens College

65-30 Kissena Boulevard
Flushing, NY 11367
(718) 997-5000

www.qc.edu

Queensborough Community College
222-05 56th Avenue
Bayside, NY 11354
(718) 631-6262
www.cuny.edu

York College
94-20 Guy R. Brewer Boulevard
Jamaica, NY 11451
(718) 262-2000
www.cuny.edu

PRIVATE COLLEGES AND UNIVERSITIES

Adelphi University
South Avenue
Garden City, NY 11530
(516) 877-3052; (800) ADELPHI
www.adelphi.edu

Audrey Cohen College
75 Varick Street
New York, NY 10013
(212) 343-1234;
(800) 33-THINK
www.audrey-cohen.edu

Barnard College
3009 Broadway
New York, NY 10027
(212) 854-5262
www.barnard.edu

Columbia University
2960 Broadway (at 116th Street)
New York, NY 10027
(212) 854-1754; (212) 854-5609
(career services)
www.columbia.edu

Concordia College
171 White Plains Road
Bronxville, NY 10708
(914) 337-9300
www.concordia-ny.edu

Cooper Union
30 Cooper Square
New York, NY 10003
(212) 353-4120
www.cooper.edu

Cornell University (Medical College)
1300 York Avenue
New York, NY 10021
(212) 746-1036

Eugene Lang College
65 West 11th Street
New York, NY 10011
(212) 229-5665
www.newschool.edu

Five Towns College
305 North Service Road
Dix Hills, NY 11746
(516) 424-7000
www.fivetowns.edu

Fordham University
441 East Fordham Road
Thebaud Hall
New York, NY 10458
(800) FORDHAM
www.fordham.edu

Hofstra University
Bernon Hall
Hempstead, NY 11549
(516) 463-6700
www.hofstra.edu

Iona College
715 North Avenue
New Rochelle, NY 10801
(914) 633-2502
www.iona.edu

Julliard School
60 Lincoln Center Plaza
New York, NY 10023
(212) 799-5000
www.julliard.edu

Long Island University, Brooklyn
University Plaza
Brooklyn, NY 11201
(800) 548-7526
www.liunet.edu

Long Island University, C. W. Post
720 Northern Boulevard
Brookville, NY 11548
(516) 299-2900

Long Island University, Southampton
239 Montauk Highway
Southampton, NY 11968
(800) 548-7526
www.southampton.liunet.edu

Manhattan College
Manhattan College Parkway
Riverdale, NY 10471
(718) 862-7200
www.manhattan.edu

Manhattan School of Music
120 Claremont Avenue
New York, NY 10027
(212) 749-2802
www.msmnyc.edu

New School University
66 West 12th Street
New York, NY 10011
(212) 229-5600
www.newschool.edu

New York University
22 Washington Square North
New York, NY 10011
(212) 998-4500
www.nyu.edu

Pace University
1 Pace Plaza
New York, NY 10038
(212) 346-1323
www.pace.edu

Parsons School of Design
66 Fifth Avenue
New York, NY 10011
(212) 229-8910; (800) 252-0852
www.parsons.edu

Polytechnic University, Brooklyn
6 Metrotech Center
Brooklyn, NY 11201
(718) 260-3100
www.poly.edu

Pratt Institute
200 Willoughby Avenue
Brooklyn, NY 11205
(718) 636-3670
www.pratt.edu

Sarah Lawrence College
One Mead Way
Bronxville, NY 10708
(914) 395-2510
www.slc.edu

School of Visual Arts
209 East 23rd Street
New York, NY 10010
(212) 592-2100
www.schoolofvisualarts.edu

State University of New York (SUNY)
(800) 342-3811
www.suny.edu

Sixty-four campuses located throughout the state. SUNY is the largest university system in the country.

CITY FACT

Central Park was designed by Frederick Law Olmstead and Calvert Vaux in 1858. The entire 843-acre park was carefully landscaped—very few of the original topographic features remain. Five million trees were planted and 10 million cartloads of dirt and rocks were moved by thousands of workers. The park took twenty years to complete.

Adult Education

Many of the colleges and universities mentioned offer continuing education classes that can be taken as night courses toward a degree. But for those looking to simply expand their horizons, there are a few New York classics that should not go unnoticed.

Actors Studio and School of Dramatic Arts

New School University
66 West 12th Street, Room 616
New York, NY 10011
(212) 229-5859

www.newschool.edu/academic/drama/index.html

Gotham Writers' Workshop

1841 Broadway, Suite 809
New York, NY 10023
(212) WRITERS

www.writingclasses.com

Offering ten-week and one-day courses for adults (eight-week courses for teens) on all aspects of writing from adult and children's books to sitcom, poetry, and memoir writing.

The Learning Annex

16 East 53rd Street, 4th Floor
New York, NY 10022
(212) 371-0280

www.learningannex.com

Offering courses ranging from CPR training and Zen Meditation & Everyday Life to How to Break into Stand-Up Comedy and Country-Western Line Dancing

New School for Social Research

New School University
66 West 12th Street
New York, NY 10011
(212) 229-5859

92nd Street Y

1395 Lexington Avenue
New York, NY 10128
(212) 996-1100

A broad range of courses from painting and photography to modern dance and financial planning

Parsons School of Design

Registration Office
New School for Social Research
66 West 12th Street
New York, NY 10011
(212) 229-5690

www.parsons.edu

MOVING TIP

"Statistically, New York City is now safer than most other cities in America, but you still have to be careful. In particular, always be aware of your surroundings, know exactly where you are, keep a close eye on your property at all times, and, if you feel you're being followed or harassed, step into a shop or restaurant, hop in a taxi, or call the police. When walking alone at night, walk briskly and with confidence. Have your keys ready when entering your building—never stand around fumbling for your keys in the vestibule."

—Jonathan Shapiro, criminal prosecutor

Finding a Job

CHAPTER 11

Working in the City

New York City is the economic capital of the world, and there are more Fortune 1000 companies headquartered in New York than anyplace else. Combined with the businesses that service them, these mega-corporations are the City's most significant employers, responsible for a third of New York's economy.

New York is the national center of the arts, banking, publishing, finance, accounting, advertising, fashion, and law. It is home to the United Nations, and many major overseas corporations choose New York as their base of U.S. operations. New York is also the world's number one tourism destination, and its hospitality industry is a major—and growing—employer. Other significant industries include wholesale and retail, construction, real estate, health care, education, law enforcement, security, recruiting, graphic design, and nonprofit organizations. In addition, a substantial percentage of the workforce devotes itself just to making the City function, which translates into hundreds of thousands of jobs in public administration, transportation, and related services.

And that's only a partial list. Talk to ten different New Yorkers and they'll have ten (or more) different jobs, half of which you've probably never even considered or knew existed. The number of job descriptions in New York is infinite, limited only by your imagination. As with many things in New York (not just the job market), if you can't find it here, it probably doesn't exist (though a professional surfer might be better off in Hawaii than Long Island).

Many dreamers come to New York and live off their savings (or work as temps, part-timers, or seasonal employees) while waiting for a break in the arts or in entrepreneurial ventures. Others, seeking an escape from the nine-to-five lifestyle, have carved out niches that could only exist in such a large city (you can make a nice living walking dogs or delivering doughnuts in New York—if you have enough clients). Unconventional employment arrangements are the norm in this most unconventional of cities.

For example, I have one friend who worked the night shift as a typist at a law firm to put herself through social work school. That's right, in the city that never sleeps, the major law firms—and many other businesses—have twenty-four-hour secretarial pools. A more daring friend, trying to survive while starting his Internet business, supplemented his income by (among other things) participating in medical studies at Columbia University, each of which put an extra $500 in his pocket (today, he spends that much on dinner any time he wants). And another friend, an assistant chef suffering from burnout after five years at a three-star restaurant, took a job working at one of the farmstands at the Union Square Greenmarket, which enabled him to be outside all day and act as the "Dear Abby" of the greenmarket, advising people on how best to use the herbs they just bought to spice up their cooking. One day, he sold some carrots to a rich investor— and now he's the head chef at his own restaurant. As E. B. White writes, "No one should come to New York to live unless he is willing to be lucky. . . . In New York, the chances are endless."

Basic Economic Statistics

New York is a city of extremes, with precious few statistically average residents. It's the richest and the poorest city in the country, with a huge immigrant population (more than half of New York's residents were born overseas) and a large, unofficial cash economy. Facts and figures can only tell us so much. New York is about opportunity and dreams, for which there are no statistics. And remember, you only need one job—although many New Yorkers have two or three!

WAGES AND COST OF LIVING

In most of the professions, New York salaries are the highest in the nation. Correspondingly, it is often said that New York has the highest cost of living of any American city—and this can be true if you don't adapt to the local way of life. Still, the three major items in the federal cost-of-living calculation are mortgage payments, property taxes, and the cost of maintaining two automobiles (these three items constitute 36.7 percent of the cost-of-living picture). Many New Yorkers, however, rent their homes and live happily without cars (the City's walkability, combined with excellent public transportation, makes them unnecessary). Just switching from two cars to two MetroCards can free up nearly $14,000 for other purposes.

Many people perceive New York as expensive because it presents so many opportunities to spend money. But if you adhere to a strict household budget and avoid impulse buying, you can live very well on a moderate income. The rewards of living in New York are infinite, and cannot be measured in square feet or traffic flow. So, while New York consistently ranks low in the "Places Rated Almanac" and other national surveys of livability, it still remains the destination of choice for anybody with a dream.

MOVING TIP

"When furnishing and decorating your apartment, carry a tape measure and floor plan with you at all times—you never know when you're going to stumble across that perfect end table you've been searching for. Measure not only your apartment but also the dimensions of all doorways, staircases, and elevators through which you'll have to transport your purchases. If possible, take these measurements before you even move in."

—Tim Shepard, design consultant

Salary and Income Examples

First-year associate at a top New York law firm: $110,000 (national average: $70,000)

Waiter at one of New York's premier restaurants: up to $105,000 (mostly from tips)

Special education teacher: $56,940

Makeup artist with a Broadway show: $55,000

Dog walker: $13 per day per dog

Average household income for New York City residents: $94,800

Average household income in surrounding suburbs: Long Island: $117,000; Southern Connecticut: $114,200; Northern New Jersey: $112,200 (the three highest figures in the country)

CITY FACT

New York City boasts more than 100 ethnic newspapers, including twenty-five catering to the Russian community alone. A typical neighborhood newsstand in Queens stocks newspapers in a dozen languages.

Cost-of-Living Examples

NY Consumer Price Index: 178.9 (versus 168.2 nationally)

Average home price: $278,000

Average citywide rent: $900

Average food bill: $10,982

Average state income taxes: $4,088

UNEMPLOYMENT AND DEMAND FOR WORKERS

New York has a relatively high rate of unemployment, yet most employers complain of a shortage of qualified workers. People with advanced degrees, good communication abilities (especially in Asian languages), and specific technical skills are in extremely high demand.

Unemployment: 6.5% at the end of 1999 (down from 8% the previous year)

Job growth: 1.5% annually. New York's labor force grows slowly, but with an employment base of millions, a 1.5% increase can represent quite a few jobs.

KEY AREAS OF FUTURE ECONOMIC EXPANSION

As New York continues to grow as a post-industrial city, blue-collar jobs will continue to dwindle (with the noteworthy exception of the construction industry). With the rise of technology in every business, formal education and training will become more and more important. Demand for computer skills will be the highest as "Silicon Alley" (New York's technology community) expands and companies of all kinds hire more computer support staff. Other key skills are written communication ability and foreign languages.

Best Bets for the Future

Technology (systems analysts, computer scientists, programmers)

Health care (nursing, dental, mental health)

Management and administration (especially in the technology and health care fields)

Environmental careers (lawyers, accountants, educators, engineers)

Hospitality/tourism (hotel, restaurant, travel, and tourism careers)

Business and professional services (financial services, human resources, law, media, communications, public relations, advertising sales, marketing, support services)

Public service (social services, education, state and local government)

Shrinking Employment Prospects

Most manufacturing, agricultural, and blue-collar jobs (except construction)

Typists and secretaries (except legal and medical)

Banking (hurt by consolidation)

Employment Resources

The employment options in New York are virtually endless, and you might find yourself overwhelmed by the selection. Take steps to narrow the field and focus on the industries that interest you most. Use Web sites and placement agencies that specialize in your field. Talk to people at professional organizations—they might be able help you with your search or direct you to someone else who can. Most important, talk to as many people as you can. Casually tell everyone you meet that you're hunting for a job. It's amazing how many people find jobs that way.

The listings that follow are meant to be suggestions and aids to help you tackle your job search with ease, but this list is only a starting point. Some of these resources, especially the Web sites, will lead you to many others. And don't forget about the handy and *free* yellow pages. Last I checked, there were seventeen pages of "Employment Agencies" alone.

RECRUITING CENTERS AND PERSONNEL AGENCIES

There are hundreds of recruiting centers, personnel agencies, and executive search firms in the City. These companies all perform essentially the same service: They match qualified employees with appropriate employers—and they get a handsome commission from the employer for the service.

Tips for Selecting a Recruiting Center or Personnel Agency

1. Never pay a fee. Reputable agencies make their money exclusively through commissions paid by employers. If an agency asks you for money, find another one. There are plenty of fish in the sea, and you don't want to work with a company that can't even cover its own costs (or is trying to rip you off).

2. Find out how long the agency has been around. It's a dog-eat-dog world out there and, generally speaking, if the agency isn't a good one, it won't last long enough to make its mark.

3. Check an agency's Web site before you call. If you do a little homework, you might learn something you especially like about a particular agency—or something you don't. And you'll know

from the Web site whether or not the agency even makes placements within your industry of choice. Ask about the number of placements the agency makes each year. Obviously, the higher the number, the more successful the agency (and the better for you, of course).

4. Don't be afraid to ask a lot of questions. If for some reason you don't like the agency you've found, try another—there are plenty to choose from, and it's important to find a comfortable fit.

Absolutely Professional Staffing (APS)

7 Dey Street, 14th Floor
New York, NY 10007
(212) 608-1444

www.aps-botal.com

Full-range placement agency with positions from part-time to permanent. Incentives include benefits, free training, and vacation pay (with restrictions, of course).

Adam Personnel, Inc.

11 East 44th Street
New York, NY 10017
(212) 557-9510

Specializing in placements for accounting, auditing, banking, fashion industry, legal, non-profit, and secretarial

MOVING TIP

"New York is expensive, but it's also the discount and bargain capital of the world. Be sure to seek out discount dining plans (like the Transmedia card) and theater tickets (through the official Theater Development Fund half-price ticket booths). And if you see something that's too expensive, ask when it goes on sale—or try to negotiate. Real New Yorkers never pay retail!"

—Jane Smith, paralegal

Atrium

420 Lexington Avenue, 14th Floor
New York, NY 10170
(212) 292-0550

www.atriumstaff.com

Full-range placement agency for part-time and full-time positions. Also offers benefits (medical benefits, 401k plan, paid vacations, with restrictions) to registered staff.

MOVING TIP

"Don't put anything in your apartment unless you absolutely love it. If you've lived in a house all your life, get ready to pare down to the bare essentials in preparation for apartment life. Most New York apartments offer limited closet space, no storage space, and little room for expansion. Better to have a few nice things than a lot of junk and clutter."

—Steve Mohr, antiques dealer

Career Blazers Personnel Service

590 Fifth Avenue
New York, NY 10036
(212) 719 -3232

www.cblazers.com

National job placement in every arena

Cross Staffing

150 Broadway, Suite 902
New York, NY 10038
(212) 374-1980

Specializing in financial staffing—banking, brokerage, and clerical. Placements range from accountants and auditors to data entry, secretarial, bookkeeping, and word processing.

Diversity Services

295 Madison Avenue
New York, NY 10017
(212) 685-9338

www.diversity-services.com

Full-service recruitment firm, from temporary placements to full-time, covering the wide spectrum of industries in New York

Eden Staffing Services

280 Madison Avenue
New York, NY 10016
(212) 685-8600

www.edenstaffing.com

Full- and part-time placements from clerical to Fortune 500

E. E. Brooke, Inc.

420 Lexington Avenue, Suite 2560
New York, NY 10170
(212) 687-8400

Making placements throughout the kaleidoscopic options of New York careers from personnel and publishing to hotel management, secretarial, and travel agents

Friedman Employment Agency, Inc.

45 West 34th Street
New York, NY 10001
(212) 695-4750

Specializing in placements for legal and secretarial positions

Headway Corporate Staffing

317 Madison Avenue, 3rd Floor
New York, NY 10017

Headway specializes in accounting, administration, finance, legal, personnel, secretarial, and publishing placements.

In Search Of

58 West 40th Street
New York, NY 10018
(212) 354-8787
www.lloydstaffing.com

The new bilingual staffing division of Lloyd, including Japanese language placement. Also look to Lloyd for nursing and health care placements and computing and technology jobs.

Peak

25 West 31st Street, Penthouse
New York, NY 10001
(212) 947-6600

www.peakorg.com

General placements from part-time to full-time including investment banking, computer related, graphics, and legal

Placement Plus, Inc.

228 East 45th Street, 9th Floor
New York, NY 10017
(212) 849-2239

Placements throughout the multitudinous New York industries

Spider Staffing

58 West 40th Street
New York, NY 10018
(212) 354-8787
www.lloydstaffing.com

New media and Web specialists

Tiger

130 William Street, 10th Floor
New York, NY 10038
(212) 412-0660
www.tigerinfo.com

Full-service placement agency
from training to part-time and
full-time placements

The Tuttle Agency New York
295 Madison Avenue
New York, NY 10017
(212) 499-0759

www.tuttleagency.com

Making temporary, "temp to
perm" and permanent placements

EXECUTIVE RECRUITERS

Executive recruiters generally make placements for people who have
been in an industry a minimum of two years—but this is not a hard-
and-fast rule. Recruiters sometimes make placements for people who
are new to an industry if they see a good match. Remember, it never
hurts to ask!

Tips for Dealing with Executive Recruiters

1. Ask for references. How many people a year does the recruiter
   place in your field and at what salaries? How well established is
   the recruiter? Are the recruiter's clients happy, and do they stay
   at their jobs?

2. Does the recruiter demand an exclusive arrangement? If you're
   required to commit to just one recruiter, what do you get in
   exchange for that commitment? Ideally, a recruiter that demands
   an exclusive should guarantee you time, effort, and industry
   contacts above and beyond what any other recruiter can offer.

3. Don't be pressured into signing anything. If you're asked to sign
   an agreement, be sure you take the time to read and fully understand its provisions. A good, ethical recruiter will give you the
   time you need to make an intelligent choice.

Advice Personnel
230 Park Avenue, Suite 903
New York, NY 10169
(212) 682-4400

Making accounting, auditing,
electronic media, financial, and
secretarial placements

Alfus Group

353 Lexington Avenue
New York, NY 10016
(212) 599-1000

Specializing in the hospitality and leisure industries and making placements such as general managers and sales executives. Additional offices in San Francisco and Rome.

Alpha Health Services Corporation

200 East 82nd Street
New York, NY 10028
(212) 517-8110

Placements for nurses and other health care professionals in registered nursing, physical therapists, medical records technicians, systems analysts, dietitians, nutritionists, and medical equipment technicians (like EKG) positions

Bartle & Evins

Fidelity Investment Services
333 North Broadway
Jericho, NY 11753
(516) 433-3333

Accounting and auditing, administrative, and financial placements

CITY FACT

The Brooklyn Bridge opened on May 24, 1883, and was for many years the world's longest suspension bridge. It was the brainchild of John Augustus Roebling, who died during its construction, and was completed by his son, Washington Roebling. A week after its opening, a dozen pedestrians were trampled to death in a stampede when somebody shouted (falsely) that the bridge was collapsing. A year later, P. T. Barnum crossed the bridge with a herd of twenty-one circus elephants to demonstrate its architectural soundness.

Bert Davis Publishing Placement Consultants

425 Madison Avenue, Suite 14A
New York, NY 10017
(212) 838-4000

Publishing, communications, electronic media, advertising, public relations, and software

Bornholdt, Shivas & Friends

400 East 87th Street, Basement Suite
New York, NY 10128

www.members.aol.com bsandf

Advertising, art, design, general management, publishing, and retail sales

D & L Associates, Inc.

505 Madison Avenue, Suite 302
New York, NY 10017
(212) 687-7111

www.dlassociates.com

Placements for Fortune 500 companies in accounting and auditing, the financial sector, and information services

Executive Link

8 West 38th Street, Suite 1208
New York, NY 10018
(212) 840-7270

Servicing the hotel and restaurant industries

Fifth Avenue Executive Staffing

507 Fifth Avenue, 3rd Floor
New York, NY 10017
(212) 692-0800

www.executive-staffing.com

Placements in the computer sciences, software, Internet development, and MIS EDP industries

First Choice

40 Rector Street, Suite 1620
New York, NY 10006
(212) 406-1866

Specializing in the financial and legal sectors

Kris Edwards Agency, Inc.

405 Lexington Avenue
New York, NY 10174
(212) 986-9400

Placements for Fortune 500 companies including graphic design, advertising, and publishing

KPA Staffing Group, Inc.

150 Broadway, Suite 1900
New York, NY 10038
(212) 964-3640
(800) 226-5TEMP

www.kpastaff.com

Accounting, banking, finance, marketing, MIS, PR, sales, and administrative placements. KPA also does temp placements.

The G. A. Park Group, Inc.

230 Park Avenue, Suite 450
New York, NY 10169
(212) 286-0777

www.gaparks.com

Specializing in computer and technology firms

S. W. Management

170 Broadway, Suite 608
New York, NY 10038
(212) 962-6310

Placements for banking, finance, economics, legal, and insurance industries, including administrative positions throughout

Seth Diamond Associates, Inc.

45 West 45th Street, Suite 801
New York, NY 10036

Full-range placements including accounting, auditing, advertising, architecture, banking, computer science, construction, fashion, finance, health care and medicine, legal, management, MIS, personnel, publishing, retail, sales, secretarial, and software

Spring Associates, Inc.

10 East 23rd Street
New York, NY 10010
(212) 473-0013

www.springassociates.com

Public relations, corporate marketing communications, public affairs, and investor relations

MOVING TIP

"New York is so big, it can be a lonely place, especially for new people. But if you find a group of folks with similar interests to your own, you've found an instant community—and New York has an organization for everything. If you're in a profession, join a professional association. If you're a ball player, get involved in a league. Or just volunteer for a charity you admire."

—Kevin Hayden, civil engineer

JOB FAIRS

Job fairs, where dozens (and sometimes hundreds) of employers get together under one roof, are one of the most efficient ways to learn about a wide variety of jobs and to streamline the application and interview processes.

In addition to the job fair resources listed, check these sources for the latest information:

Newpapers: Scour the local papers (including the free ones like *New York Press* and the *Village Voice*) for information on upcoming career-related events. For example, the *New York Times* sponsors Systems Information Technology (SIT) career fairs on a semi-annual to quarterly basis. And don't forget to check the Help Wanted sections for listings of upcoming job fairs sponsored by corporations (to maximize recruiting at their company career drives) and search firms.

Hotels and Convention Centers: Stay on top of the goings on at area hotels and convention centers (such as the Javits Center, 212-216-2000—call for a brochure of upcoming events or go online at *www.javitscenter.com*). These are the largest spaces available in the City and are regularly used for job fairs and recruiting. Many fairs are also held just over the river in New Jersey (because space is cheaper and more plentiful). Check out the schedules for the job fairs listed with the organizations mentioned to get an idea of where fairs are held, and call the hotels and convention centers periodically to stay informed.

Online: See the Internet section following. Many of the Web sites listed there include calendars of events (which often include listings of job fairs) and calendars of national career fairs. Search around; though they may be a bit tricky to find, most of the Web sites *do* include regional job and career fair information.

American Recruitment

23461 South Pointe Drive, Suite 200
Laguna Hills, CA 92653
(949) 470-2000; (800) 969-6881;
(800) 44-FAIRS

www.americanrecruitment.com

Sales, marketing, and retail career fairs. Call the toll-free number to learn more about upcoming career fairs.

Diversity Expo

(212) 655-4505

www.diversityexpo.com

A career fair geared toward the hiring of culturally diverse individuals within the technical and sales industries. For a complete listing of dates and sites, call or check out the Web site.

Job Expo International

(212) 655-4505

www.job-expo.com

Job fairs specializing primarily in technical careers

JobsAmerica

4701 Patrick Henry Drive,
Suite 1801
Santa Clara, CA 95054
(408) 748-7600

www.jobsamerica.com

"The career fair professionals." Check out the Web site for the calendar of upcoming fairs. A list of corporate participants is posted two weeks before each event.

CITY FACT

The City has more than 20,000 restaurants, representing nearly every one of the world's cuisines. The largest is the Bryant Park Grill, which seats 1,420 people, followed by Tavern on the Green, which seats 800. Chinatown's largest restaurant, Jing Fong, is the size of a professional football field.

Jonathan Ladd Co.

(800) 752-6343

Organizing job fairs throughout the country. Call for a schedule of events and look for their Web site, which is currently under construction.

MOVING TIP

"New Yorkers move fast, and they don't usually smile at one another on the streets. But beneath these gruff exteriors lie the nicest people in the world. Don't be afraid to ask for directions, or advice, from that New Yorker on line ahead of you. Every New Yorker has an opinion about everything—and you may even make a new friend!"

—Robert Woods, bookseller

NAACP Diversity & Hi-Tech Career Fair

(800) 562-7469

www.naacpjobfair.com

Offering job fairs throughout the country, often making appearances in the same city multiple times over the course of a year

NACE JobWeb

National Association of Colleges and Employers
62 Highland Avenue
Bethlehem, PA 18017-9085
(610) 868-1421; (800) 544-5272

www.jobweb.org

Search for job fairs by location, date, and keyword. More than 1,200 career fairs listed.

Personnel Strategies, Inc.

350 Norwest Building
1809 South Plymouth Road
Minnetonka, MN 55305-1977
(800) 390-5561

www.psijobfair.com

A recruitment agency, sponsoring job fairs nationwide

SUNEXPO
(212) 655-4505

www.sunexpo99.com

A new hiring event sponsored by Sun Microsystems. This job fair is geared toward the recruitment of sales and technical professionals with UNIX experience.

TechExpo
(212) 655-4505

www.tech-expo.com

One of the leading technical career fairs in the nation, TechExpo offers multiple dates throughout the northeastern United States. Check out the Web site for details on dates and locations.

Tech Fest
(800) 445-3600

www.professional-exchange.com

Tech Fest, hosted by Professional Exchange, offers what has become one of the most prestigious technical job fairs in the country, featuring many Fortune 1000 companies.

T-Rex Productions
(888) 550-TREX

www.trexproductions.com

More than 2,000 companies participating in T-Rex job fairs, which are hosted nationwide. Check the Web site for local calendar of events. Also check out *americasbestjobfairs.com.*

UNIVERSITY JOBS AND JOB PLACEMENT

Many universities and colleges have Career Services Centers or Career Development Offices where alumni (and sometimes referrals from other universities) can get free access to career counseling, job listings (job banks), and the multitudes of reference materials for which university career offices are famous. If you are neither an alumnus of the school nor a referral, sometimes you can still gain access to the resources. Some private universities charge a fee for this service, but many of the public universities don't. Plus, here's a secret born of the computer age: Many universities (even the ones that charge a fee for walk-in career services) have their career resources online for free.

In addition, you may want to work *for* a university or college as administrative staff in one of the offices or departments. Check in regularly at each university's employment office, because jobs go quickly. If you are seeking a faculty position at a local university, contact that discipline's department directly, but be advised—the market is extremely competitive.

For a complete listing of New York area universities and colleges, see chapter 10, "Local Schools and Colleges."

INTERNET RESOURCES

The Internet is an invaluable tool for finding jobs, and you don't have to be in New York to use it. As Jim Brown of the New York Department of Labor explains, "We always advise people to start their job search *before* they relocate." And the Department of Labor's Web site (*www.labor.state.ny.us*) is a great place to start. In addition to having perhaps the most extensive job bank on the Internet, it lists fifty international links, as well as links by region within the state. Be sure to check out Facts & Figures and CareerZone.

There are also dozens of Web sites with huge job banks that are designed specifically to help you find your dream job, be it as a teacher, a pastry chef, or the manager of a hotel. Navigating the Internet takes some getting used to, and it will take some time to figure out which site is best suited to you, but it's an excellent way to stay on top of things. And the Internet is fast—many Web sites have jobs listed a day or two before the ink ever hits the paper at conventional newspapers.

About Work

www.aboutwork.com

AW offers tips on networking, advises which jobs are the good jobs, offers a free self-assessment test and advice groups, and lists other top job sites online.

Academic Employment Network

www.academploy.com

AEN lists teaching jobs and other academic positions. Searches by job or state. AEN also has a relocation services page that includes information on property rental rates in the area in question and demographics.

Academic Position Network

www.umn.edu apn

APN posts jobs in higher education including faculty, professorships, staff, administrative positions, graduate fellowships, assistant fellowships, and post-doctoral positions. Searches can be done by availability in field of interest, position, country, and state.

American Jobs

www.americanjobs.com

AJ concentrates on computing and engineering jobs.

America's Employers

www.americasemployers.com

In addition to the ever important listings of available jobs, AE also includes a résumé bank, information on recruiters, a chat forum, and networking.

America's Job Bank

www.ajb.dni.us index.html

Listing over 90,000 available jobs (nationwide) in the government and private sector. Also an excellent source of links to other job banks.

Best Jobs USA

www.bestjobsusa.com

BJ USA features a job bank search, résumé services, listings of job fairs, career links, health care careers, relocation guide, salary survey, trade shows, best places to live and work, Best Jobs University, recruiting services, HR publications, and the list goes on.

CITY FACT

The New York City public bus system consists of 300 routes and carries 600 million people a year (by far the most in the nation) on 4,200 buses. By tradition, New York's bus and subway fares have always been identical, but they strayed apart for two years (between 1948 and 1950), when the bus fare was 7 cents and the subway fare was 10.

Career Builder

www.careerbuilder.com

A full-service Web site with a job bank searchable by location, description, and keyword; offers advice on interviewing, résumés, and salary negotiations and a host of other helpful insights.

MOVING TIP

"In New York City, anything can be delivered—and often at any time of the day or night. A lot of newcomers don't realize this, because they come from towns where everyone has a car. So just remember that, here, you don't have to carry anything—not even your groceries (most markets will deliver for free or for a nominal charge, although you're expected to tip the delivery person)."

—Nancy Kessler, attorney

Career Magazine

www.careermag.com careermag

CM features a job bank, advice, résumé board, and articles pertinent to every aspect of work and your job search.

Career Mosaic

www.careermosaic.com

Running the career gambit, CM daily lists 23,000 jobs in North America collected from various newsgroups around the world.

CareerPath.com

www.careerpath.com

Featuring the Help Wanted sections (which offer approximately 150,000 job listings) from newspapers in six U.S. cities (including New York)

Career Resource Center

www.careers.org

A very comprehensive Web site with thousands of links. CRC claims to be "the most complete and extensive index of career related Web sites."

CareerWeb

www.cweb.com

Extensive job bank (one of the days that I checked the site, CareerWeb claimed to have 39,700 jobs in the bank), advice, resources, and useful links to other career search sites like Healthcare Web for people in the medical profession, and Corporate Gray, for military personnel transitioning into civilian life

E-Span's Interactive Employment Network

www.espan.com

All searchable by key words, E-Span lists current job openings, résumé tips, and salary guidelines.

eXploring Careers

www.explore.cornell.edu

A Web site sponsored by Cornell University and the New York Department of Labor, to help you "think about yourself and the world of work." Options include Career Resources (which breaks down to education, job search, and planning categories) and Career Zone, which details available jobs, searchable by location, salary, education, and title.

Federal Jobs Digest

www.jobsfed.com fedjob4.html

If working for the federal government is your dream, FJD is a good place to start your search. With opportunities in postal, clerical, management, legal, law enforcement, secretarial, engineering, science, computers, medical, math, accounting, auditing, and a host of others, FJD lists over 2,500 available jobs around the country.

4 Work.com

www.4work.com

National job listings, broken down by location and job. Also features information on and listings of volunteer positions and internships.

Government Jobs

www.ci.nyc.ny.us

A helpful and extensive Web site about New York City, including a job bank of NYC government jobs

Headhunter.net

www.headhunter.net

Professional job listings, searchable by location, salary, and industry, résumé posting, and invitations to employers and recruiters to access candidate résumés

Hoover's Online

www.hoovers.com

Hoover's details the best and the brightest with a "top 2,500 employers" listing. Also an excellent resource for links—Hoover's lists more than 4,000 company Web sites to which you can connect with the click of your mouse.

Incpad (formerly Westech's Virtual Job Fair)

www.incpad.com

A technology-related site with job listings, résumé posting, events calendar (including career fairs), expos, and industry-related articles.

JobTrak

www.jobtrak.com

More than 300 university career counseling centers across the country act in partnership with JobTrak to place college students and recent college graduates in appealing jobs. JobTrak's database lists more than 500 new jobs daily from employers specifically seeking these college candidates.

Law Employment Center

www.lawjobs.com

LEC includes posts of current openings, a roster of the 250 largest law firms in the country, salary survey, links, Q & A, and a law employment library.

MedSearch America

www.medsearch.com

Extensive national listing of health-related jobs

Monster.com

www.monster.com

Listing more than 400,000 jobs, Monster.com also provides numerous resources, from company profiles and career advice to résumé posting and a personal career account.

MOVING TIP

"Learn your way around New York City as soon as you can. Study the maps, find the best subway stations and bus routes near your home and office, and memorize which major streets run north, south, east, and west. Make this a priority, because it'll save you a whole lot of time."

—Johnny Moore, actor

New York Government Jobs

ftp.fedworld.gov pub jobs ny.txt

National listing of government jobs

Online Career Center

www.occ.com

OCC is one of the greatest (in terms of sheer volume) tools for your online job search. The job bank database enables you to search by job type and region. It also features career counseling, résumé posting, college recruiting, job fairs, and other events.

MOVING TIP

"I grew up in rural California, where we took space, peace, and quiet for granted. But in New York, with so many people packed into such a small area, you have to make time to find private places. They're out there—parks, museums, atriums, gardens, libraries, grand old hotel lobbies, and out-of-the-way cafés—so discover a few favorites and visit them often. That's how I stay sane."

—Sarah Bleasdale, opera singer

USAJobs

www.usajobs.opm.gov

The U.S. Government's official Web site, provided by the United States Office of Personnel Management. Offerings include listing of current job openings, openings that give preference to veterans, and online application.

Women's Wire

www.women.com work

This site is a good reference point for women in the workplace. It includes a listing of WW's top 100 companies, hot career trends, resources, career reviews, profiles, articles, and helpful links.

The World Wide Web Employment Office

www.employmentoffice.net

Jobs listed with direct links to participating company Web sites, résumés posted in five different languages

In addition to the sites listed here, each of the Internet search engines (Yahoo, Excite, and others) has job postings and resources, and many corporations have job banks and bulletin boards on their own Web sites.

TEMPORARY JOB PLACEMENT AGENCIES

Temp agencies are an ideal starting point for those who are unsure about their future career paths, need some cash in a hurry, or want to ease their way into the New York workforce. I have many friends, in various stages of life—just out of college, in-between jobs, pursuing new careers, recently relocated to the City—who have taken advantage of the lifestyle that temp work affords. And the universal opinion is that temp work is a great way to get a taste for a job without being committed.

Questions for Temp Agencies

1. Does the agency offer benefits? Many agencies, in response to the growing demand for temps, are now offering health benefits, 401k plans, bonuses, vacation time, and training in order to attract and keep a dependable and trustworthy bank of people in their employ. But be sure to read the fine print and ask lots of questions—many of these plans have strings attached or require substantial contributions from you.

2. Do the agency's temps get permanent jobs? Temporary placements sometimes lead to full-time positions, and it can only be a good sign if an agency has a strong track record of its temps being hired permanently.

3. Who are the agency's clients? An agency is only as good as the companies that use its temps.

4. How long will the initial appointment take? You may need to set aside half a day or more to register with a temp agency. You'll fill out many forms and possibly take some tests before you meet with a counselor.

Some of the agencies listed make not only temporary placements but also permanent ones. Be sure to call first—virtually all of the agencies require appointments.

Bon Temps

170 Broadway, 18th floor
New York, NY 10038
(212) 732-3921

Specializing in placement of legal word processing and proofreading temps

CITY FACT

The City is home to thirty-eight farmers' markets (known locally as greenmarkets) administered by the Council on the Environment of NYC (*www.usersinterport.net/~conyc/*). The greenmarkets represent 260 local farmers—the most extensive program in America—serving 100,000 customers weekly. Best known is the Union Square Greenmarket (open year-round Monday, Wednesday, Friday, and Saturday). Despite its urban image, New York state is a major agricultural producer, ranking third in dairy production, and second in apples, grapes, cabbage, and maple syrup.

Core Staffing Services, Inc.
295 Madison Avenue, Suite 715
New York, NY 10017
(212) 557-6252

jsung@coretemps.com

Covering the whole range of employment opportunities in the City, from the entertainment industry to music, cosmetics, publishing, Internet, legal, financial, and investment banking. Positions from executive assistants to accountants and sales assistants available on a temporary and temporary-to-permanent basis.

Forum Temporary Services
342 Madison Avenue
New York, NY 10017
(212) 687-7200

www.forumpersonnel.com

Secretarial, data entry, customer service, proofreading, and reception placements

Lloyd Staffing
58 West 40th Street
New York, NY 10018
(212) 354-8787

www.lloydstaffing.com

Lloyd staffing covers the temporary placement market like a blanket. Chances are, if you're interested in a specific career, they can place you there on a temporary basis. Includes customer service–oriented work and special events staffing for trade shows.

Madison Avenue Temporary Service for Communications

275 Madison Avenue, Suite 1314
New York, NY 10016
(212) 922-9040

www.matsforcommunications.com

Daily, weekly, long-term, temp, and permanent assignments for secretaries, administrative assistants, receptionists, and data entry in advertising, publishing, public relations, broadcasting, and Fortune 500 companies.

Merlin Temps

261 Madison, 27th floor
New York, NY 10016
(212) 972-0090

Office support staff, primarily reception, word processing, bookkeeping, and secretarial

Rand Legal

271 Madison Avenue, 5th Floor
New York, NY 10016
(212) 557-8411

Legal support (for example, legal secretaries, word processors, and proofreaders—with law firm experience), entertainment, fash-ion, new media, advertising, public relations, finance, music, medical, and publishing

RAS

6 East 39th Street
New York, NY 10016
(212) 686-0123

Primarily office support staff

Sloan Personnel

317 Madison Avenue
New York, NY 10017
(212) 882-0200

Office support staff, mainly word processing, reception, and clerical

StaffMark

420 Lexington Avenue
New York, NY 10170
(212) 271-3900

www.progressiveinfo.com

Office support staff

Taylor Grey, Inc.

330 Madison Avenue
New York, NY 10017
(212) 687-8100

www.taylorgrey.com

Offices in New York and San Francisco. Makes placements for temporary and full-time employment and specializes in, among other things, accounting, advertising, entertainment, finance, legal, nonprofit, and publishing.

CITY FACT

New York City's subway system is the world's largest, with 714 miles of track, 469 stations, and 6,089 subway cars. The subways run twenty-four hours a day and carry 1.2 billion passengers a year.

Temporarily Yours
505 Fifth Avenue
New York, NY 10017
(212) 661-4850

staffing@tempyours.com

Office support staff. Benefits available (health care, 401k, and others) with some restrictions.

Todays Office Staffing
15 East 40th Street, Suite 100
New York, NY 10016
(212) 889-3232

www.todays.com

Primarily placement for support staff, administrative assistants, secretaries, and customer service. Benefits available with restrictions.

Vanguard Temporaries, Inc.
633 Third Avenue
New York, NY 10017
(212) 682-6060

Placing temps in the music, fashion, television, cosmetics, publishing, legal, public relations, and finance industries

Winston
535 Fifth Avenue
New York, NY 10017
(212) 687-7890

www.winston.com

Office support staff, Internet, financial banking, entertainment, advertising, legal, publishing, and medical placements. Benefits available with restrictions.

SOCIAL SERVICE AGENCIES

Social service agencies, an excellent and underutilized job hunting resource, offer career placement and sometimes career counseling. Because these organizations are nonprofit, they may charge you a nominal fee (the placement agencies do not because they receive a finder's fee or bonus from the hiring company on placing a candidate), but many of them counsel free of charge.

Federation Employment and Guidance Service (FEGS)
114 Fifth Avenue
New York, NY 10011
(212) 488-0100

Goodwill Industries of Greater New York
4-21 27th Avenue
Astoria, NY 11102
718 728-5400

www.ocgoodwill.org

Job placement and training for the disabled

New York Urban League
204 West 136th Street
New York, NY 10030
(212) 926-8000

NYUL has a job book that lists available positions and offers a three-week job readiness training program (STRIVE), which includes basic computer training.

New York Women's Employment Center
45 John Street, Suite 605
New York, NY 10038
(212) 964-8934

Workshops, career counseling and "coaching," résumé assistance, training referrals, job placements

Selfhelp Community Services

440 9th Avenue
New York, NY 10001
(212) 971-7600

SCS offers a three-week training program in home health aid and places trainees into jobs usually within two days of completion.

PROFESSIONAL ORGANIZATIONS

Professional organizations are often excellent reference points for newcomers to New York because many organizations have branch chapters in other cities. Members from near and far who move to New York can have an immediate support network on arrival and more often than not even have access to the organization's resources before they move, thereby making an easier and smoother transition. Those who are not yet members of a professional organization within their field may want to consider joining one (or many), because these organizations are not only excellent networking arenas but many also offer job-hunting resources (job banks, reference material, advice), educational seminars, lectures, luncheons, information centers, and a great place to make some new friends. And for those who are not yet set on a career path, many professional organizations also offer career fairs and conferences to educate and direct those just entering the field (primarily recent college graduates).

Advertising Club of New York

235 Park Avenue South, 6th Floor
New York, NY 10003
(212) 533-8080

www.adclubny.org

Advertising Women of New York

153 East 57th Street
New York, NY 10022
(212) 593-1950

Web site planned for Spring 2000

AWNY is an organization of women (primarily executives) involved in all aspects of the advertising industry—advertising, media, marketing, promotion, PR, and research. AWNY sponsors an annual career conference for both professionals and students, offers scholarships and public service programs, hosts seminars, luncheons (no ladies' lunching here, this is power lunching), and keeps a job bank.

American Association of Advertising Agencies

405 Lexington Avenue
New York, NY 10174
(212) 682-2500

www.aaaa.org

The AAAA is an association of advertising agencies. It gathers statistics, conducts surveys, and operates a research library (which is a storehouse of information on the advertising industry).

American Association of Exporters and Importers

11 West 42nd Street
New York, NY 10036
(212) 944-2230

www.aaei.org

American Institute of Aeronautics and Astronautics

85 John Street
New York, NY 10038
(212) 349-1120

www.aiaa.org

American Institute of Architects

200 Lexington Avenue, Suite 600
New York, NY 10016
(212) 683-0023

www.aiaonline.com

American Institute of Certified Public Accountants

1211 Avenue of the Americas
New York, NY 10036
(212) 596-6200

www.aicpa.org

MOVING TIP

"Finding the right doctor takes time and effort, so do it when you're healthy. As soon as you move to New York, schedule a physical exam. That way, if you have medical problems in the future, you'll already have a relationship with a physician and you won't get stuck being treated by a stranger—or in an emergency room."

—Penny Shaw, physical therapist

American Institute of Chemical Engineers
3 Park Avenue
New York, NY 10016
(212) 591-7338
www.aiche.org

American Institute of Graphic Arts
545 West 45th Street
New York, NY 10036
(212) 246-7060
www.aigany.org

American Insurance Association
85 John Street
New York, NY 10038
(212) 669-0400
www.web@iso.com

American Marketing Association
60 East 42nd Street, Suite 1765
New York, NY 10165
(212) 687-3280
www.nyama.org

Offers a mentoring program run by the career advisory board, online job listings, and seminars on marketing-related issues, including how to get a job and selling yourself through your résumé.

American Society of Composers, Authors and Publishers (ASCAP)
1 Lincoln Plaza
New York, NY 10023
(212) 595-3050
www.ascap.com

American Society of Interior Designers (ASID)
200 Lexington Avenue
New York, NY 10016
(877) ASK-ASID (877-275-2743)

Primarily a networking organization; local chapters offer placement services and job bank.

American Society of Magazine Editors
919 Third Avenue
New York, NY 10022
(212) 872-3700
www.asme.magazine.org

Must be a senior editor to be a member. Hosts approximately twenty-four networking luncheons and guest speaker seminars per year.

American Society of Mechanical Engineers
345 East 47th Street
New York, NY 10017
(212) 591-7000

Offers employment counseling and bimonthly regional job postings. ASME also offers seminars and conferences.

American Society of Travel Agents

18 West Marie Street
Hicksville, NY 11801
(516) 822-4602

www.astanet.com

Asian Women in Business

1 West 34th Street, Suite 1202
New York, NY 10001
(212) 868-1368

Association of Real Estate Women

15 West 72nd Street, Suite 31G
New York, NY 10023
(212) 787-7124

Provides information on real estate trends and issues. Membership is open to men and women.

Association for Women in Computing, NYC

P.O. Box 1503
Grand Central Station
New York, NY 10163

www.serve.com awcnyc

Cosmetic Executive Women

217 East 85th Street, Suite 214
New York, NY 10028
(212) 759-3283

A not-for-profit organization open to women in the beauty industry. A minimum of two years' experience in a given field is required to join, though sponsorships, referrals, and mentoring are available to young women interested in pursuing a career in the industry.

MOVING TIP

"Open bank accounts in New York City at the earliest possible time. Many landlords and other important service providers won't accept out-of-state checks, or they'll make you wait ten days for an out-of-state check to clear. Having a local bank account can save you a lot of headaches."

—Kenneth Matthews, landlord

CITY FACT

The Dakota, completed in 1884 on the corner of Central Park West and 72nd Street, was New York's first luxury apartment building. It has been featured prominently in literature (Jack Finney's *Time and Again*) and film (*Rosemary's Baby*) and has been home to many celebrities (such as Leonard Bernstein, Lauren Bacall, and Judy Garland). Perhaps the Dakota's most famous occupant, John Lennon, was murdered in front of the building in the early morning hours of December 8, 1980.

Environmental Action Coalition
625 Broadway, 9th Floor
New York, NY 10012
(212) 677-1601

Job listings, internships, and volunteer opportunities

Institute of Electrical and Electronics Engineers
345 East 47th Street
New York, NY 10017
(212) 705-7900

www.ieee.org

Large membership, with approximately 50,000 student members

International Academy of Healthcare Professionals
70 Glen Cove Road, Suite 209
Roslyn Heights, NY 11577
(516) 621-0620

Psychologists, social workers, and health care professionals

League of Professional Theatre Women, New York
300 East 56th Street
New York, NY 10022
(212) 583-0177

Members can fall within any area of theater production, including production staff, playwrights, administrators, lawyers, and critics. Must be sponsored by two members.

National Association of Black Social Workers
1969 Madison Avenue
New York, NY 10035
(212) 348-0035

National Association of Social Workers, New York chapter
15 Park Row, 20th Floor
New York, NY 10038
(212) 577-5000

Mentoring, job listings, and employment seminars

National League for Nursing
350 Hudson Street
New York, NY 10014
(212) 989-9393

New York County Lawyers' Association
14 Vesey Street
New York, NY 10007
(212) 267-6646

www.nycla.org

More than 9,000 attorneys belong to the NYCLA. Benefits include a Legal Referral Service (referring more than 40,000 cases a year), forums, lectures and special events, Courtlink, financial services, Lexis-Nexis access, continuing legal education courses, and an extensive legal library housing more than 200,000 volumes.

New York State Bar Association
One Elk Street
Albany, NY 12207
(518) 463-3200

www.nysba.org

More than 64,000 members (all lawyers, of course), representing every corner of the state.

The NYSBA is the oldest and largest voluntary state bar association in the country. Be sure to check out the LawMatch Career Services link on the NYSBA Web site. It will lead you to a host of other helpful sites and possibly even help you find your dream law job.

New York Women in Communications
355 Lexington Avenue, 17th Floor
New York, NY 10016
(212) 679-0870

Sponsors mentoring programs and career counseling

New York Women's Bar Association
234 Fifth Avenue, Suite 403
New York, NY 10016
(212) 889-7873

Job listings, mentoring, classes, and workshops

NY New Media Association
55 Broad Street
New York, NY 10004
(212) 785-7898

www.nynma.org

Hosts "cybersuds" networking events for its more than 3,000

members and publishes a semi-annual membership directory. Members' careers include a wide spectrum of new media occupations.

Public Relations Society of America

33 Irving Place, 3rd Floor
New York, NY 10003
(212) 995-2230

Job referral service, research center, and development programs

Women's Sports Foundation

Eisenhower Park
East Meadow, NY 11554
(516) 542-4700

Sponsors an internship program, offers training grants, and maintains a large information bank on women's sports and fitness

Young Menswear Association

1328 Broadway
New York, NY 10001
(212) 594-6422

To young individuals wishing to enter the industry, YMA offers scholarships and helps with job placement (résumé bank).

INDEX

About

Because moving affects almost *every aspect* of a person's life, Monstermoving.com is committed to improving the way people move. Focusing on an individual's needs, timing, and dreams, the site provides everything for the entire lifestyle transition and every stage of the move. Free service provider content, interactive products, and resources give consumers more control, saving them time and money, and reducing stress. Site features include cost-of-living comparisons, home and apartment searches, mortgage calculators and services, an interactive move-planning application, an address change service, relocation tax advice, and virtual city tours. Monstermoving.com is committed to remaining the most effective, comprehensive, and lifestyle-centric point of service for everyone involved in moving.

Monstermoving.com is part of the Interactive Division of TMP Worldwide (NASDAQ: "TMPW;" ASX: "TMP"). For information, visit *www.monstermoving.com* or call (800) 567-7952.

Bekins is pleased to offer you the following extra value services and cost savings on your next out of state move.

You will receive:

- A minimum discount of 52% off a move between 5,000–7,999 lbs., or a minimum discount of 55% off a move 8,000 lbs. and over.
- Free First Day Service – Bekins will unpack up to 5 cartons of essential items that you will need upon arriving at your new home.
- The FAS-Hotline – Instant access to a powerful collection of relocation assistance services such as a preferred mortgage program, cost of living reports and much more.
- Firm Pick-Up and Delivery Dates on shipments greater than 5,000 lbs.

To find the participating agent nearest you, please use our agent locator at www.bekinsagent.com, or look in the yellow pages under the "movers" heading.

Terms & Conditions

You must have a minimum weight of 5,000 lbs. within the continental U.S. to qualify for the discounts. The rules and restrictions of all programs are described in and governed by HGB 400-M tariff and section 13 of the HGB 104-F tariff, or as amended or reissued.

Coupon must be presented at the time of the estimate, must accompany your moving documents, has no cash value, is void where prohibited, may not be combined with any other discount and is subject to service availability. Coupon sets forth minimum discount level; final discount offer may be affected by prevailing market conditions. Offer is valid at participating Bekins agents only and cannot be used if estimate has already been performed. Offer is not valid for local or intrastate moves. DOT52793. Shipment must be registered using corporate code number 31402.

$10 Off an Avis Weekend Rental

Rent an Avis car for a minimum of two consecutive weekend days and you can save $10 off your rental.
For reservations and information, call your travel consultant or Avis toll free at: 1-800-831-8000.

- Rental must begin by December 31, 2001.
- Valid on an Intermediate through Full Size four-door car.
  - Valid at participating locations in the contiguous U.S.
  - Subject to complete Terms and Conditions on reverse side.
  - An advance reservation is required
  - Visit Avis Online at www.avis.com

Coupon # **MUWA014**